# DIVE DORSET

## A DIVER GUIDE

John and Vicki Hinchcliffe

Underwater World Publications

*Above:* The maker's plate from the Aparima (Site **271**) was
discovered on the sea bed near the wreck. Photo: Authors
*Title page:* The gently sloping, wide slipway at Ferrybridge. There is
also plenty of space for car and trailer parking. Photo: Roy Smallpage
*Front cover:* Triggerfish *(Balistes carolinesis)* on the *Royal Adelaide*
– now a regular summer visitor to this wreck. Photo: Peter Glanvill

Editorial production by Martyn Yeo

Map artwork by Design IT, Liphook, Hampshire

Produced by Diver Magazine

Published by Underwater World Publications Ltd,
55 High Street, Teddington, Middlesex, TW11 8HA

First published 1984
Second edition 1987
Reprinted 1990, 1993, 1995
Third edition 1999

Printed in the United Arab Emirates by Emirates Printing Press,
PO Box 5106, Airport Road, Dubai

ii

# Contents

*A diver explores the wreck of the Countess of Erne in Portland Harbour (Site 141).* Photo: Peter Glanvill

# Preface

As if preparing for the age of the aqualung there has been – slowly evolving for hundreds of years, but greatly accelerated by the two World Wars – a remarkable infrastructure of shipwreck in the shallow seas around the British Isles. Today for the diver, nowhere in the world is there the possibility of such exciting exploration and discovery than in British waters, and nowhere in British waters is there such an abundance of wrecks than off the Dorset coast. Many are totally or virtually unexplored.

The almost unbelievable list of recent finds in Dorset waters includes gold watches and silver purses from the holds of the *Kyarra*, gold guineas, silver coins and diamonds from the *Halsewell* site, a gold pointer recovered from waist deep water at Bowleaze, Spanish silver coin from the privateer *Hope*, almost £30,000 worth of lead ingots near Swanage, and the remarkable discovery from within the inky blackness of the interior of the great liner *Salsette* of the second gentleman's Victorian watch chain, perfect in every detail, hallmarked on each link.

But perhaps only a minute fraction of such lost artefacts, hidden on the Dorset sea bed, have so far been discovered. For instance, where is the wreck of the *Miniota*, a 422ft long, 6,422 gross ton Canadian steamship? She was disabled by a German torpedo and reported to have sunk off Portland in 1917 while under tow into the safety of Weymouth Bay. A lot of money has already been spent by professional salvors attempting to seek out her whereabouts, for in her holds, among other metals and "general cargo" is more then 3 tons of silver. Is she one of the many unidentified wrecks already being visited by divers who are unaware what fortune lies deep within her? Since the summer of 1996 there have been continual whispers that she had at last been located.

# Acknowledgements

This guide to diving the Dorset coast is intended to be the most comprehensive, detailed and accurate ever written. It would not have been possible to compile it without the enthusiastic help and advice freely given by so many people. The authors wish especially to thank the following:

- Nick Chipchase – wrecks off Lyme Bay
- John Walker – reef dives in Lyme Bay
- Dave Saywell allowed us access to his personal archive on the wrecks off Poole Bay and the Purbeck Coast
- Pat Carlin and Chris Caines – wrecks off Portland and Lyme Bay
- Steve Liscoe – the *Himalaya* in Portland Harbour
- Douglas Lawson and Janine Gould for enthusiastic and accurate descriptions of wreck and reef dives
- Steve Jones – for his research on the Abbotsbury bomber
- Roger Wagstaff for his help with up to date information about the *Kyarra*
- Dave Dillingham for his help with position fixing information
- Brian King
- Ted Nicklen
- Bob Campbell for information for the area he knows so well around Swanage
- Alan Tennent
- John Ayling
- Jim Scott – the wrecks off Poole Bay
- Chris Collins
- Mike Cooper
- Ian Parry – local wrecks and diving around Chesil and Portland
- Steve Marley
- Maureen Attwooll, Weymouth Librarian
- Chris Hovard – Portland Harbour
- Richard Greenaway – for his thorough account of the *Heroine*
- John, Steve and Mike Ballett
- Peter Knight – for his information on virtually undived wrecks off the Bill of Portland
- Brian Charles – for his help with details of the inshore wrecks of Portland Bill
- Mike Markey – for help with archaeological information

- Steve Shovlar
- Eddie Bennett
- Adrian Ponchaud – for allowing use of ship photographs from his extensive collection

Andy Smith, who died just before this book went to press, provided much detail from his extensive knowledge and personal records of Dorset wrecks.

The authors are grateful to all these people, together with many other individuals too numerous to mention individually. It is hoped they will all find a lasting satisfaction in the fact that their assistance will ensure that those who use this guide will find greater enjoyment from their underwater expeditions diving off Dorset.

The Diver's Code of Conduct (pages 219–21) has been included with the kind permission of the BSAC.

*John and Vicki Hinchcliffe, January 1999*

*RIB off Durdle Door.*
Photo: John Bantin

# How to use
# this Guide

This guide covers a total of 110 miles of coastline. It accurately describes all possible shore dives and launching sites and features most known wreck sites out as far as 50° 20'N, which is virtually 25 miles offshore. Besides wrecks, the Dorset coastline provides the diver with perhaps the most varied arena in Britain. Along the coast of the English Channel the scene varies from the massive landslips and fossil-bearing shales of Black Ven at Lyme Regis in the west to the wide, sandy bays of Poole and Christchurch.

Between these two extremities lie several interesting coastal features – the 18 mile Chesil pebble bank, the harsh yet strangely beautiful Isle of Portland, the secret cliffs of Purbeck, and Poole Harbour, one of the largest natural harbours in the world. Underwater, the scene is equally varied. This guide will take you to places of scenic delight, and to places where large and small fish of many varieties live. You are guided to reefs of unbelievable beauty, some with strange underwater caverns, never recorded or described previously. This guide points you straight to places that only expert local knowledge and years of diving would otherwise reveal.

If you know the name of the wreck or dive site for which information is required, you can use the index at the back of the guide. If you want information on a general area, a glance at the contents page will send you to it. The coastline is broken down into four areas, defined mainly by natural features such as bays and headlands. At the start of each area is a short introduction that gives any relevant safety information together with current and tidal details. We then go on to give details of shore diving and boat diving locations, site by site. Appendix 1 gives much additional information useful to the diver.

Statute miles (or yards) are used on land, but nautical miles are used over water. Depths are given in metres; dimensions of wrecks in feet. Positions offshore are given in latitude and longitude in degrees, minutes and decimal points of a minute.

The information contained in this guide was correct at the time of going to press, but changes will have occurred since and the authors would be most grateful for any new information that divers can send them (c/o the publishers) for inclusion in future editions.

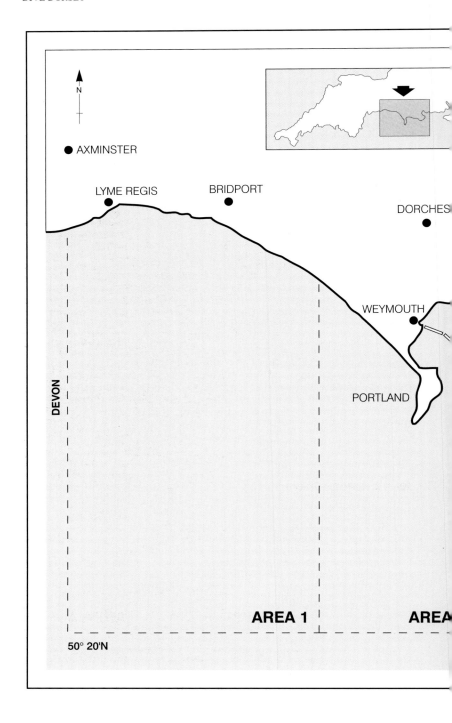

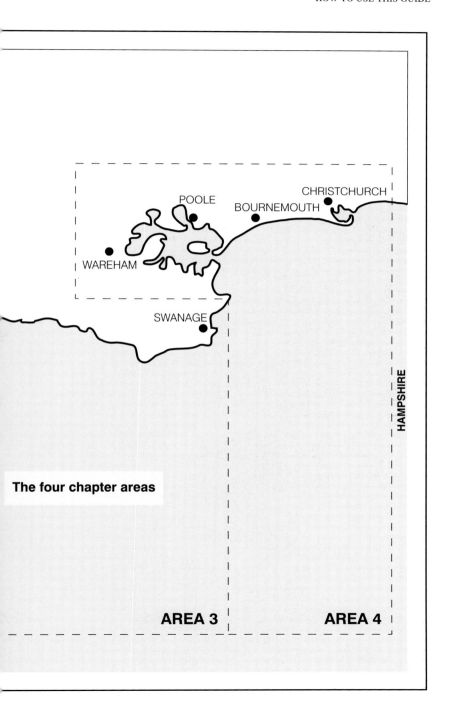

CHRISTCHURCH

POOLE

BOURNEMOUTH

WAREHAM

SWANAGE

HAMPSHIRE

**The four chapter areas**

**AREA 3**

**AREA 4**

*The wreck of the 18th century ship Halsewell lies right here in the foreground at the foot of the cliff near Winspit, not at the mouth of the cave near Seacombe, as was previously thought.*

*Photo: Authors*

# About Dorset

Dorset is a truly empty county. Apart from Poole and Bournemouth in the east and a few other holiday resorts along the coast, it is a land of small market towns and villages spread sparingly in the countryside. Much of Dorset's heathland remains substantially as it was centuries ago.

The geology creates the beautiful and rapidly changing scenery typical of the Dorset coast. In places, the sea has made a slow advance against the land. In others, it has been stalled by bulwarks of iron-hard rock cliffs. In yet others, it has chosen to throw up vast pebble beaches. Almost central to the area is Portland Island, sitting in the sea like a giant slug with its head forever facing the mainland and its bastions of hard rock receiving an eternal pounding from the Atlantic storms that sweep across Lyme Bay.

West of Portland is the amazing Chesil Beach behind which lies the Fleet, where both birds and fish breed in profusion. East of Portland is the Isle of Purbeck shoreline. Here there are cliffs of the hardest and softest rocks and many quiet – almost secret – places to explore. East of Purbeck, the sea has advanced into vast areas of sandy heathlands to form Poole Harbour, Poole Bay and Christchurch Bay.

## Access by road

Divers travelling from London will find that the M3 leads them to the M27, A31 and A35, giving a direct east–west route across the county, conveniently close to the coastline. Drivers coming from Wales, the Midlands and northern parts of the UK have a slightly more difficult journey: from the M5, a careful choice of route has to be made depending on the exact area of coast being visited. One choice is to take the M4 to Junction 18, then go through Bath, Warminster and Shaftesbury to Blandford Forum, where there are then a number of routes available. Another good approach is the A34, which, coming from north of Oxford, crosses the M4 and links into the M3.

If you approach Dorset from the south-west, follow the A30 to Honiton and then join the A35. Visitors from Continental Europe can use the Channel Tunnel or ferries into Portsmouth and then the M27 coastal motorway, or take a ferry direct to Poole.

Road congestion in Dorset is not a particular problem, except at one consistent bottleneck. When vehicles leave Swanage at the end of the afternoon and early evening during the summer (particularly at weekends), slow moving queues of traffic build up around Wareham near where the A351 from Swanage joins the A352, which is also busy at these times bringing traffic from the west back to the urban areas of Poole and Bournemouth. One consolation is that such hold-ups rarely occur in the opposite direction in the mornings.

# Dive Planning

This new edition of *Dive Dorset* contains the most complete listing and description of shipwrecks ever attempted off the Dorset coast. Almost a hundred extra wrecks, some only recently discovered and identified, have been included. There is a thorough description and short history of most of the more shallow wrecks, but with the advent of much deeper exploration by amateur divers, we have also included a large number of ships lying farther offshore in deeper water. In the past these sites were regarded as the exclusive domain of the professional salvor or military diver.

The information, with accurate fixes given for distant offshore sites, must not be taken as a suggestion that diving there is possible from anything less than a well equipped charter boat with a suitable DoT licence and a very experienced professional skipper in charge of the vessel. The skipper's experience must not only cover the operation of the boat, but must also encompass intimate awareness of the tides and other hazards of the proposed diving area. This experience will probably also include a thorough knowledge of the diving techniques to be employed.

Throughout the day, the skipper will not only be in radio contact with the rescue services through the local marine rescue sub-centre, but will probably also be in constant radio contact with other charter vessels (diving or angling) operating throughout the general area, who can be called up should assistance be required.

Except as a tender to a charter vessel, the club or privately owned rigid inflatable craft – no matter how well equipped – has no safe part to play in diving remote, offshore wrecks. No sharp dividing line can be drawn at which the RIB should be discarded for the services of a charter boat, but bearing in mind the possibility of unexpected bad weather, accident, illness or injury, all complicated by long decompression schedules, there is a good argument for the amateur-crewed small boat not venturing more than two miles or so from the shore.

# Snorkel, shore and boat dive sites

In each area the snorkel, shore dive and launching sites are listed in order from west to east. These are sites that can be reached easily from the shore without excessive distances to swim. But of course one diver's easy swim may well exhaust a less fit diver. And what on a calm day may be an easily attained shore dive site might well demand boat cover or transport in less favourable conditions.

Following the shore dive sites, all the sites that require a boat to transport the diver to his point of entry are listed. No differentiation is made between those sites easily reached by a small, basically equipped inflatable and those sites where the distance from the shore may demand a larger boat, but please be very heedful of the warnings given above.

# Position finding

Each shore site has its position given by a six-figure Ordnance Survey reference number, easily seen on the 1:25,000 series map. Considerable care has been taken with the accuracy of these positions, and, where appropriate, gives the entry point to the water. It should be noted that the OS six-figure reference represents a square on the earth's surface with each side measuring 100 metres. Where there are good, easily seen transit marks for sites near the shore, these are also illustrated.

Wrecks and other features away from the shore are given a latitude and longitude grid reference. These are calibrated in degrees, minutes and *decimal points of a minute* – for instance the position of the wreck of the *Kyarra* is shown as 50 34.90N: 01 56.59W. Because the position is given only to an accuracy of two decimal points, there is a possible maximum error of 18m on the north–south line and, in the general latitude of southern England, a possible error on the east–west line of up to 12m.

Decimal references are suitable and intended to be programmed (without conversion) straight into the many types of electronic navigators now available and increasingly being used by diving groups. The positions given are to the OSGB 36 datum, which is that used on British Admiralty charts. Some GPS navigational sets use the WSG 84 system. In this case, the positions will need adjusting 0.04 minutes southwards and 0.08 minutes eastwards.

In the past some confusion has arisen when positions quoted in their non-decimal form (degrees, minutes and seconds) have been fed, without conversion, into electronic navigators. Given this mistake, the resultant error in the position located can be as much as 729m from the required point! This magnitude of error would almost certainly ruin any chance of locating a target wreck. To decimalise any position, convert only the seconds (dividing them by 6 and multiplying by 10).

If the Decca system is used, positions will vary very slightly in accuracy from place to place and day to day, and can be affected by atmospheric influences, particularly around sunrise and sunset. Finding wrecks still needs a lot of skill!

# Maps and charts

The relevant Admiralty chart number is given for each coastal area, together with that of the recommended ordnance survey map covering the adjacent coastline. Most of the sites in this guide are covered by more than one Admiralty chart. The chart numbers given against the general map at the start of each chapter are those of the largest scale chart available.

Admiralty charts can be obtained from local chart agents W.L. Bussell & Company, Weymouth (tel. 01305 785633), H. Pipler & Sons Ltd, Poole (tel. 01202 673056) and Rossiter Yacht Builders, Christchurch (tel. 01202 483250). W.F. Price & Company of Bristol (tel. 0117 929 2229) offer a mail order service. Local tide tables can be obtained at most diving equipment stores and air stations.

Large sections of the Dorset coastline are now covered by two Ordnance Survey Outdoor Leisure Maps at a scale of 1:25,000 (2½ inches to the mile). These maps show much special information, such as local camping and caravan sites. Sheet 15 covers Bridport to Poole and includes Portland, while Sheet 22 covers Bournemouth eastwards, including the New Forest. Sections of the coast not covered by these two maps are covered by sheets of the Pathfinder Series, again at a scale of 1:25,000. The maps to this scale clearly show coastal features, footpaths and public rights of way.

# Weather

The worst winds for diving along this coast are southerly gales. But even then, good diving conditions may be found in Poole Harbour and Portland Harbour. Advice is given within the text of the shore dive sites as to their suitability with various wind strengths and directions. Visibility underwater varies enormously.

---

### WEATHER INFORMATION

Local weather forecasts are available from these sources:

*Coastguard Portland Marine Rescue sub centre* (tel. 01305 760439).

*Marine Call* For the area from Lyme Regis to Selsey Bill and 12 miles offshore (tel. 0891 505357 for taped forecast). For onshore Dorset and Hampshire (tel. 0891 505303 for taped forecast).

*Fax Marine Call* Two day local inshore forecast and chart (fax 0336 400457).

*Radio* Wessex FM (97.2MHz) broadcasts a coastal weather report and forecast, together with local tide times, at 6.30, 7.30 and 8.30am and 1.25pm every day, also at 4.30 and 5.30pm on weekdays.

*Coast Watch* Peveril Point Look Out Post, Swanage – not continuously staffed (tel. 01929 422596).

---

Generally, the visibility west of Swanage is excellent, with anything up to 15m offshore in summer. In the east, the sandier bays reduce visibility, particularly in windy weather. Up to 4m can be expected in this area.

The sun along the southern coastline can be surprisingly powerful, especially on the south facing beaches and out at sea where the sun's power is multiplied by reflection off the water. The application of a high factor sun block to exposed areas of skin is strongly advised at the start of a day's expedition. The sun does not always shine though, and you should be aware of the latest weather forecasts for the area. In some locations, only just offshore, a rising wind against the tidal current can change a slight slop into vertical-faced short waves capable of swamping small boats.

For weather reports and forecasting, the sea areas to listen out for are Portland in the west and Wight in the east. But these areas extend to the French coast; the weather in Dorset waters may differ considerably from that forecast for mid Channel. Whatever the direction or strength of the wind, it is always possible to get a dive in somewhere along the Dorset coast. The areas of Chesil sheltered by Portland may be particularly good when a strong easterly makes most sites impractical. Likewise, Swanage Bay is good when winds rise from the west.

# Divers and the fishing community

Throughout Dorset there is a history of co-operation between divers and those who make their living from fishing the sea. You will find crab and lobster pot markers all along the coastline. In places near the shore they will be particularly numerous. Do not dive near this fishing gear. Never, except in dire emergency, use pots as a mooring.

Maximum sizes for shellfish taken from the area are: crabs 12cm, lobsters 14cm, scallops 10cm. A copy of the local by-laws and minimum sizes for other species of shellfish can be obtained from the Chief Fishery Officer, Southern Sea Fisheries District at 64 Ashley Road, Parkstone, Poole, Dorset (tel. 01202 721373).

# Access to the water

Facilities for launching inflatables and small boats in Dorset are excellent almost everywhere a vehicle can approach the shore. There are, however, several popular beaches where diver overcrowding may occur on summer weekends. These are identified either at the start of the relevant area or under the individual site heading.

If you do dive from one of the popular holiday beaches try to adopt a caring and courteous attitude towards non-divers. Remember, the beach may be your base, but to other people it will be their final destination for the whole day. There will be others using various kinds of equipment from the beach: skiers, windsurfers, yachters and anglers will all be competing for space.

# Marine life

Dorset waters teem with underwater life. The lesser forms include anemones, many varieties of which may be seen in the clearer waters. A small white variety covers most overhanging sections of wrecks, while many other larger species are common, especially in stony or gravelly areas. Peacock worms will withdraw their gossamer filaments at high speed as a diver approaches. Jellyfish, some of which are brought in summer from warmer climes by the prevailing south-west winds, may also be encountered.

There are scallop beds off Lulworth and in Lyme Bay, and occasionally crayfish are to be found in the summer months on the western side of Portland, usually at a depth of 14m. Crabs are common everywhere and lobsters abound, especially in rocky areas. Off Anvil Point, near Swanage, is an area of shallow rocky gullies where swarms of young lobsters sometimes congregate. Wherever there are sandy bays there are flatfish of many varieties. Where there are extensive mussel beds, such as on the Christchurch Ledges or the Shambles Bank, there are lots of large plaice. There are areas of river bed in the upper reaches of Poole Harbour where young flounders form an invisible carpet just beneath the gravel surface.

On a first visit to Dorset the diver will be comfortably surprised at the warmth of the water. This is especially so in the eastern half of the area during the period July to October when the water in the bays is warmed by the sun. It is at this time that the sea becomes full of microscopic forms of life, which can be seen after dark sparkling and flashing with their own fluorescence. At these times the night diver glides in a cosmos of glittering life.

*Sea fan on the wreck of the Baygitano (Site 25).* Photo: Peter Glanvill

# Wrecks

The protection and shelter offered by Poole and Weymouth have helped to increase the number of ships that have come to grief off Dorset. Ships sailing to or from London and the other South Coast ports have encountered many a ferocious westerly storm off the shores of either Devon or Dorset. Suffering damage and unable to make further headway, they would often run with the storm hoping to find shelter and safe anchorage in Portland Roads, Weymouth or Poole. But in bad visibility, with no modern navigational aids, it was all to easy for an anxious captain to order a "turn to portside" too soon and finish up smashed to fragments on Chesil Beach or meet a lonely death against the desolate cliffs of The Purbeck.

The two world wars, with their tragedies of death and destruction at sea, have also provided divers in this area with many wrecks. Today, despite the use of modern technology, the sea is still claiming sailors and ships. Between 1980 and 1981, for instance, there were several major sinkings off Dorset and the Isle of Wight.

# Contacting the Coastguard

The whole of the Dorset coastal area is covered by the operations room of the Coastguard Portland Marine Rescue sub centre based at Weymouth. Their non-emergency telephone number – to obtain information on sea and weather conditions or to report intended journeys and expeditions – is 01305 760439.

*The distinctive red and white Sikorsky S61N search and rescue helicopter.*
*Photo: Roy Smallpage*

# Diving emergencies

Based central to the area, and within the Naval air base at Portland, is the Coastguard-controlled red and white Sikorsky S61N search and rescue helicopter. In the event of any possibly life threatening or serious diving incident, such as a diver lost or missing, or decompression illness or embolism, the Coastguard *must* be contacted direct and immediately. For a serious diving-related incident all other time absorbing procedures will be overridden and the helicopter will be on its way to you in minutes.

*Always call the Coastguard first.* Whether onshore or at sea, contact the Coastguard direct on VHF Channel 16, or by dialling 999 and asking for the Coastguard.

If less dramatic symptoms of decompression illness occur inland, a GP or hospital casualty department (or the Coastguard) should be contacted. Emergency transfer to the nearest available recompression chamber will be arranged for you if it is necessary. Make sure you carry the 24 hour telephone number of Portsmouth Naval Base (01705 818888), which you can pass to the doctor concerned so that specialist advice can be obtained from the Diving Medical Centre there.

# Decompression illness

Decompression illness symptoms vary between those that are so sudden that immediate air evacuation to a chamber is vital and those that might not become apparent for some hours. Some of these less dramatic symptoms, which may well be delayed, can be more serious and produce greater disability than the excruciating pain associated with a joint bend. Tingling and numbness are included in this category.

Air embolism or severe decompression illness symptoms require prompt but careful transfer of the subject to a recompression chamber. The victim should be laid flat on their back and, if possible, should be given 100% oxygen. If at sea, contact the Coastguard for help immediately: in a small boat, any attempt at speed may bounce the victim and almost certainly worsen the symptoms rather than help the situation.

# The Military Remains Act

The Military Remains Act 1986 may in the future affect the wreck diver much more than it does at present. Its main drive is to preserve the sanctity of "war graves" – the wreckage of military ships and aircraft known to contain remains of service personnel.

The wreckage of all military aircraft of any nation is automatically protected, but ships will have to be designated by the Secretary of State and will need a statutory instrument to do so. This means that ships to be named as "war graves" will have to be named and approved by Parliament in the same way that ships to be protected as historic wrecks need a statutory instrument passed through Parliament.

There seems no doubt that those who passed the Act had little idea of the number of ships that could fall under its terms, such as a merchant ship with a Navy gunner aboard – was he among the survivors? – and as a result no ships have yet been named under the Act. This does not mean that ships are not covered by the general thrust of the Act and divers should therefore treat all possible "war graves" with total respect.

However, once these ships have been named, the diver commits an offence only by tampering with, damaging, moving, removing or unearthing remains, or by entering an enclosed interior space in the wreckage. The punishment on conviction of an offence is a fine. Nothing in the Act prevents the wreck diver from visiting the site, examining the exterior or even settling on the wreckage. An offence is only committed if the diver disturbs remains or enters a proper compartment of the wreck. The punishment on conviction is a fine.

This is of course only a brief description, and serious wreck divers should study the Act itself. Your library or H.M. Stationery Office should be able to supply a copy.

# The Merchant Shipping Acts

The Receiver of Wreck is responsible for the administration of the Merchant Shipping Act 1894 and the Merchant Shipping Act 1906, which deal with wreck and salvage. It is a legal requirement that all recovered wreck (flotsam, jetsam, derelict or lagan – whether recovered within or outside United Kingdom territorial waters) is reported to the Receiver of Wreck. The Coastguard act as the Receiver, and it is to them that recoveries should be reported.

Finders who conceal items are liable to prosecution, so any object – even if it appears to have no monetary value – should be declared as soon as possible. The Receiver of Wreck can then make a decision as to the future ownership of the property.

Wreck recovered from within United Kingdom territorial waters that remains unclaimed at the end of a statutory one-year period becomes the property of the Crown, and the Receiver of Wreck is required to dispose of it. This may be through sale at auction, although in many instances the finder will be allowed to keep unclaimed items of wreck in lieu of a salvage award. This, however, is at the discretion of the Receiver of Wreck, and each case is judged on its merits.

For further information contact: The Receiver of Wreck, The Coastguard Agency, Spring Place, 105 Commercial Road, Southampton SO15 1EG (tel. 01703 329474; fax 01703 329477).

# The Protection of Wrecks Act

Divers who find a site that might be of historical, archaeological or artistic importance should leave everything as it is and report their findings, in confidence and as soon as possible, to the Department of National Heritage (or its equivalent in Northern Ireland, Scotland or Wales). If appropriate, the wreck can then be designated under the Protection of Wrecks Act 1973, in order to control activities on the site.

Designated sites may only be dived or items recovered if a licence for that purpose has been granted; failure to comply with this is an offence and can result in a fine. All recoveries from designated sites must be reported to the Receiver of Wreck. For further information contact: The Secretariat of the Advisory Committee on Historic Wreck Sites, 3rd Floor, Department of National Heritage, 2/4 Cockspur Street, London SW1Y 5DH (tel. 0171 211 6367/8).

*Cannon on the breakwater at Lyme Regis. Looking back towards the town it is possible to see the two slipways and the (now demolished) lifeboat station.*

*Photo: Roy Smallpage*

# AREA 1:

# Central Lyme Bay

Stretching from the Devon boundary in the west (just west of Lyme Regis) to Abbotsbury in the east, this is the least dived area off the Dorset coast. Road access is good. The A31 and A35 provide good routes from the east. From the north the main road connection from the M5 is through Chard and Axminster. This coastal district is well known as a busy family holiday area, characterised by small market towns and unspoilt villages.

Underwater, the story is completely different as far as visitors go, for vast areas have remained undived, but with the advent of excellent charter boats for divers now working out of the Cobb at Lyme Regis, the area is starting to be opened up. Long stretches of high cliffs between access points have left large areas of sea bed almost totally unexplored. Over the last few centuries, scores of sailing ships have been wrecked by the great gales that sometimes sweep these shores. Many of these wrecks still lie undetected in shallow water awaiting discovery. Silver coins found on the beach beneath Black Venn give a clue to the existence of just one.

Farther offshore is Dorset's richest area for modern wrecks that have not been salvaged. Many are lying on the sea bed with no further damage since that inflicted by the exploding bomb or torpedo that detained them in Dorset waters for ever. Many are still complete with their huge bronze propellers, portholes and telegraphs. Some lie in deep water, but many are within the capability of the average club diver and even the deeper sites are easily visited using the latest techniques, which take advantage of enhanced gas mixtures now readily available.

There are also other special attractions. Never more than 5 miles from the shore are a series of beautiful reefs, all with exceptional geology and all so richly endowed with almost every description of undersea life form. The jewel must be the East Tennants Reef with its massive sea fan forest and subterranean caverns and passageways. This reef is described, together with several others, all with their own individual special attractions. John Walker, owner of the Lyme Regis charter boat *Miss Pattie*, has made a special study of these reefs and the authors are most grateful for the information he has kindly provided.

There are many other fairly small reefs that we are unable to list: the easiest way to find and visit these is by using the services offered by John and his boat.

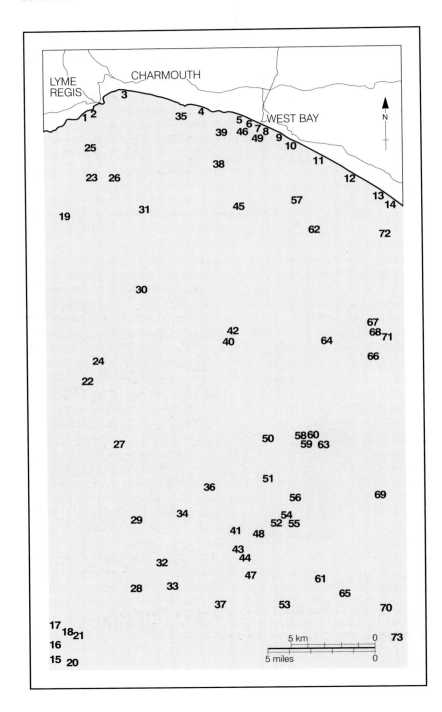

Nearer the shore, too numerous to mention as specific sites, are many other rocky areas of reefs and ledges for the diver to discover. Most of these are easily accessible by inflatable, or in some cases, by swimming from the shore.

Wherever access to the sea is possible, it is generally easy and convenient for both shore diving and boat launching. Tidal currents, especially at the immediate shoreline sites are weak. Offshore, particularly in the east, the currents are stronger, but not exceptionally so. The best times to dive in central Lyme Bay are generally between 5 and 6 hours after high water at Devonport.

Bad weather can affect shore dive sites badly. Because the coastline mainly faces south, a strong blow from the southern half can bring a swell on shore, which, particularly in the west, will stir up the dark silt of the eroded shale beds, reducing the visibility. In settled periods, visibility can be in excess of 10m, and much better when well offshore.

WARNING Between Lyme Regis and West Bay some sections of high cliff are slipping. Divers on the beaches should keep well away.

# Shore dive and snorkel sites

**1 Monmouth Beach and Poker's Pool** SY 337 915. *Snorkel site, free launching.* This site is just west of the harbour (called The Cobb) at Lyme Regis. At the western end of the town a road called Cobb Hill, with a gradient of 1 in 5, provides the only direct road access to this site. At the bottom of the hill it is possible to walk straight on to the beach. A second choice is to take the turning to the west along the sea front. After 100yds you will see the large buildings on the right, used as the Royal Air Sea Rescue depot during World War Two. Before this, on left and right, are small car parks, and beyond it on the right is another parking area. From this car park a wide track leads directly onto the beach. The nearest long-stay car park is the Holmbush car park at the summit of Cobb Hill.

Monmouth Beach extends from the wall of the Cobb in the east to just beyond the county boundary with Devon in the west. The beach at its upper levels consists of pebbles and stones with patches of coarse gravel. At low tide an extensive area of flat, rock ledges and weedy areas is exposed. Depths off the beach from mid-tide to high-water are rather shallow, usually no more than 3m. It is because of these shallow depths that this site is designated as a snorkel site.

So long as it can be carried across pebbles it is possible to launch a small inflatable boat from this beach when the tide is fairly high, but it would require a lot of awkward wading at anything near low water, even on neap tides. From opposite the former RAF buildings eastwards to the Cobb the beach is designated as a swimmers' beach. Boats are allowed to launch or approach the beach only to the west of this area. This site is ideal for children and beginners to practise snorkelling.

The nearest telephone kiosk is at the bottom of Cobb Hill, opposite the Cobb Arms Hotel near the quay. There are toilets between the lifeboat house and the old RAF buildings.

**Opposite: Dive sites in Area 1, Central Lyme Bay. This area is covered by Admiralty chart 3315 (Berry Head to Bill of Portland); Ordnance Survey Pathfinder maps 1316 and 1317.**

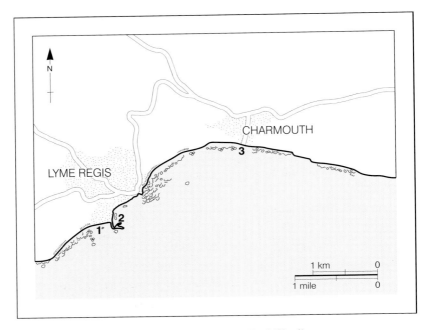

*Lyme Bay, showing Monmouth Beach and Poker's Pool (Site 1),*
*The Cobb at Lyme Regis (Site 2) and Charmouth (Site 3).*

**2 The Cobb, Lyme Regis** SY 338 916. *Launching point only.* To find this small harbour from the centre of Lyme Regis, drive westwards up the hill through the town on the A3052 (Broad Street). Take the first turning left towards the sea. This is Cobb Hill, a very steep 1 in 5 road, leading to the Cobb and its public launching facility. Immediately at the bottom of the hill is a quay with two adjacent launching ramps. Use the wooden one to the east, which takes weights up to 3 tons.

   At the lower states of the tide, the harbour almost completely dries out, but boats can still be launched as the firm sand bed of the harbour allows towing vehicles to be driven from the bottom of the ramp to the water's edge.

   Charter boats pick up from the quay on the offshore side of the harbour. Vehicles are *not* allowed to drive to this quay – there is a £25 fine for doing this. However, the harbourmaster is totally in charge of the harbour and can give permission to do almost anything if he considers there is a valid reason for the request. In return he asks that divers do not congest the small slipway area at the head of the launching ramps. A busy Saturday or Sunday will see up to 100 boats launched and recovered at Lyme.

   Near the launching ramps can be found the very modern lifeboat house and harbour office. There are parking areas to the west of this building and and vehicles should be left there. Personal diving gear not already in boats should be carried from the car park to boats after they are clear of the launching ramp. On

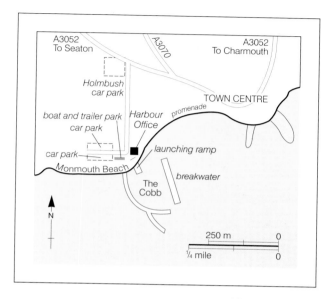

*Above: Lyme Regis.*

*Below: The two slipways at Lyme Regis – the one on the left is the one to use.*

Photo: Roy Smallpage

21

recovery of boats, gear should be transferred out of the boats, either before recovery up the ramp, or after recovery, when the boat is clear of the slipway area. Boat trailers, after launching, are also parked to the west of the harbour office, in a specially allocated area at the rear of the beach.

An all-in fee is charged for launching and trailer storage. This is payable in advance at the harbour office where dive group organisers should first report on arrival. At the same time they will be asked to fill in a special form detailing their group, boat and dive plan details. There is great emphasis on safety and safe procedures at Lyme Regis. Dive groups are advised to inform the Coastguard of their intended trip and expected time of return.

There is no spare mooring or anchoring room in the Cobb and all visiting boats returning to the Cobb at the end of the day have to be recovered and taken ashore out of the harbour. High water at Lyme Regis is Dover plus 4 hours 25 minutes or Devonport plus 52 minutes. There is a stand at high water of 1½ hours. The harbour office radio listens on channel 16 and works on channel 14.

There are local by-laws. Within the harbour and its immediate approaches, boats must keep dead slow. Power boats are not allowed on the landward side of an imaginary line drawn from outside the harbour mouth to the outward end of Church Cliff Jetty. This line encloses the town beaches and an area of sea reserved for swimmers.

One other point about Lyme Regis. There is no petrol outlet in the town; the nearest garage is 3 miles away at Uplyme. In emergency contact Rob Perry – see Area Information and Services – who will be able to fetch some fuel for you.

**3 Charmouth** SY 365 903. *Snorkel site, free launching.* This site is where the little River Char flows through a wide gap in the coastal hill line and then enters the sea through a wide pebble plain at the rear of the beach. To find it, turn off the main A35 into the centre of Charmouth village from where Lower Sea Lane leads, in less than ½ mile, to the beach.

Charmouth is still a quiet beach, but is fast becoming more popular. However, there is lots of room to spread out into the wide pebbly and grassy areas that are ideal for picnics and sunbathing. Farther to both east and west cliffs rise up. There are fossils to be found in the soft rocks, which regularly collapse onto the beach.

On the higher section of the beach is a spacious tarmac car park. From this, boats can be wheeled or carried directly to the sea, down a bank of pebbles onto flat firm, pebbly sand. The incline of the pebble bank, which varies with storms and spring tides, often hampers vehicular access to the lower levels of the beach. Dominating the scene at the beach is a large isolated stone building, which, in the eighteen hundreds used to be a cement producing workshop. Now it houses a café, a Heritage display centre and the office of the beach and car park superintendent.

The sea bed at Charmouth slopes away gently, giving a shallow area studded with low rocks. Mouth rocks are directly opposite the road end, approximately 100yds out. At low water springs these rocks dry out, but at other times they represent a definite danger to propellers. On leaving the beach, boats should steer a course well to the south-west where there is a clearer area of sandy sea bed stretching out into deeper water. It is because of the shallowness that this beach is recommended for snorkellers only. Around the rocks and on gravel patches in the area where fresh water percolates into the sea there should be some fair sized flounder to be seen. Visibility depends on calm conditions and is soon reduced when a southerly wind roughens the sea, disturbing the eroded black silt from the nearby collapsing cliff line.

Currents in this area are weak. High tide is high water at Dover plus 4 hours 25 minutes, or high water at Devonport plus 52 minutes. There are toilets near the beach and in the event of the beach office being closed there is a telephone (999 calls only) mounted in a small cupboard within the wall of the building near the office door. The beach office telephone number is 01297 560626.

**4 Seatown** SY 420 917. *Snorkel, aqualung, free launching.* Seatown is a small settlement built in a gap in the cliffs. Through this gap a small river soaks its way out to the sea through a wide shingle beach heaped up across its mouth by the sea. To find this site, turn south off the A35 in the centre of Chideock. This is the only southerly turning. It is called Duck Street and is directly opposite the church. A narrow lane ¾ mile long with very few passing places then leads to the beach at Seatown.

The road ends at the very edge of the beach, and a concrete slope enables small boats to be wheeled or carried on to the shingle. From here it is a short distance to the water's edge over very loose, deep shingle. There is a large grassy car park that extends to the edge of the beach. Its entrance is 50yds back from the sea front. The beach at Seatown is at the centre of a small bay. The headland to the west is formed by the 191m Golden Cap, the highest point on the

*The cannon site at Seatown (Site 4).*

*Seatown, a small hamlet nestling in a gap in the cliff line.* Photo: Authors

Dorset coastline. To the east is the high Ridge Cliff. There are excellent walks along these cliffs.

A good aqualung or snorkel dive can be enjoyed from any part of this beach. From the water's edge the sea bed slopes fairly steeply down pebble and sand terraces to a depth of about 5m. Here, the bottom levels out and slopes gently out to sea. Within 100yds of the beach, depths of 9m can be found. The sea bed is variable in character. There are large areas of flat rippled fine sand, but also some large rugged rocks. In recent years sand levels have risen considerably near the shore, almost covering a large area of what have been massive slabs of rock, standing 1.5m high and extending 100yds out from the beach, directly opposite the road end.

Marine life at Seatown is prolific. Crabs and lobsters live wherever there are rocky holes available, and large plaice are common. Flounders come up to the shallows where the fresh river water soaks through the beach. There is also a surprising variety of weed growth in the bay wherever there are rocks nearing the surface. For the wreck detective there is a mystery cannon site just offshore of Seatown. In 1980 a group of divers from Chelmsford and District SAC, led by Ed Cumming, lifted three cannon and other artefacts. These have been preserved and two of the cannon are on public display in the Deep Sea Adventure wreck museum at Weymouth.

Bar shot, cannonballs and lead shot can be seen on display at the Charlestown Shipwreck and Heritage Centre in Cornwall. One cannon has been dated around 1750, and a small breech chamber around 1600. Despite intensive searches through local records, the name and date of the wreck remain a complete mystery. Still lying on the sea bed are many cannonballs, scattered piles of musket shot and bar shot, all congealed by iron oxide crud, which probably contains many other artefacts.

To find this site, at a point exactly opposite the road end, swim directly out to sea for 100yds. This will lead to a spot beyond the unbroken rock area. The wreck material is spread out over at least 200 square yards of sea bed. But do not get over excited. In most seasons the wreck site is covered by a deep layer of sand. John Parker, a pot fisherman at Seatown, reckons that the wreck was probably the result of a large sailing vessel being driven by a south-westerly storm over the rocks off the base of Golden Cap, tearing out its bottom, but remaining afloat long enough to be driven into the bay before finally sinking.

There is still more intrigue at Seatown. A pile of cannon have recently been discovered to the east of the bay in the shallow water off Thorncombe Beacon, and to the west, off Golden Cap, a group are said to have recovered a small bronze cannonade. Then there is the Anchor Inn, just to the rear of the beach. Alan Miles, the landlord has accumulated many photographs and items of historical interest inside the pub, but, outside, on display is a huge iron anchor, claimed to be from the treasure wreck of the Dutch privateer *Hope*. A large notice gives many details of the wrecking and subsequent plundering.

The bay is slightly sheltered from the west and south-west, but a southerly or south-easterly wind soon brings waves onto the beach, spoiling the visibility, which can be up to 11m in quiet periods. Currents in the immediate bay area are weak, but become slightly stronger around the headlands. This site is excellent for any grade of diver, and makes a very convenient shore dive. Near the beach, beside the Inn is a small shop selling teas, ices etc. Toilets are adjacent. The entrance to the Golden Cap caravan and camping site (tel. 01297 589341) is 50yds back along the road. There is a public telephone at the entrance to the site.

**5 Eype Mouth** SY 448 910. *Snorkel, aqualung, free launching.* The simplest way to reach this site from Bridport is to leave the very centre of the town by the B3157 West Bay Road until reaching the traffic island at the crossing with the town bypass (A35). Turn west along the A35 for almost 1 mile, until just after a bridge crosses the road there is a left hand turning into a narrow lane signposted to Eype. Take this turning and then carefully follow the signposts for Eype Mouth at all junctions. The route, through typical Dorset sunken lanes, eventually comes to a dead end at the low cliff top where there is a small car park.

A short length of tarmac pathway leads from the road end to a 12m flight of steps that descends to the rear of a pebble and sand beach that the Eype stream soaks across into the sea. A keen, fit group will find it just possible to lug a small inflatable 40yds to the beach. This is not an easy exercise as the route is either down a short steep grassy bank or down the steps, which have right angled turns and high wooden hand rails on either side.

Underwater, the main interest is a series of low rock reefs that thrust up through a sandy bottom, each running parallel to the coast. A number of these can be found within ½ mile of the shore. Also, here and there, are piles of quite large rocks in isolated groups. After entering the sea, the beach terrace of pebbles descends near the shore to depths of 4 to 5m, but the slope becomes much more gentle out to sea; 100yds out from the shore, depths are little more than 6m. Visibility is normally good at Eype Mouth and large pollack can usually be seen around the rocks.

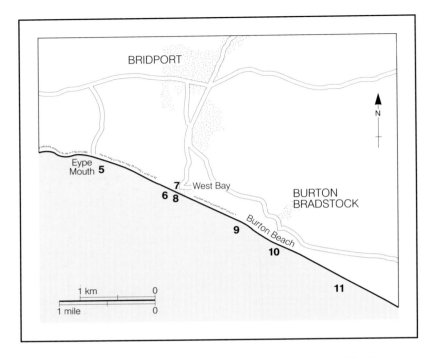

*West Bay and Burton Beach, showing Eype Mouth (Site 5), Table Rock (Site 6), the Harbour (Site 7), East Beach Car Park (Site 8), Burton Freshwater Caravan Park Beach (Site 9), Burton Bradstock Beach (Site 10) and Cogden Beach (Site 11)*

Currents are generally weak and run parallel with the shore. High water is high water at Dover plus 4 hours 25 minutes, or high water at Devonport plus 52 minutes. Rise and fall in this area on springs is about 4m. As this is a fairly open site, any wind from the southern quarter soon stirs up the visibility near the beach. The site is excellent for any grade of diver. Starting at Eype Mouth and extending eastwards, a by-law restricts speed to 8 knots for 200yds out to sea.

A short way back up the lane is Eype House tea-garden and shop, plus a pay-telephone. Caravans and camping are available at Eype House (tel. 01308 424903). The New Inn is in Lower Eype village.

**6 Table Rock (West Bay)** SY 459 904. *Snorkel, aqualung, free launching.* From Bridport take the B3157 to West Bay. Follow the road around the periphery of the harbour and drive along to the end of the sea front to the west. You can park here on a pay-and-display basis. Access to the sea from the high promenade and car parking area is by a choice of two points where flights of approximately 23 wide stone steps descend to the beach. Boats can only be launched if they can be carried down these steps.

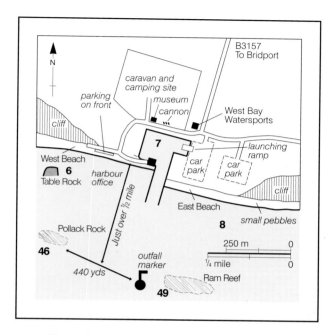

*The harbour and beaches at West Bay, showing Table Rock (Site 6), The Harbour (Site 7), East Beach Car Park (Site 8), Pollack Rock (Site 46) and The Ram (Site 49).*

The beach is of lovely ochre coloured coarse sand, and at high tide is almost totally covered by the sea. Sometimes, as a result of storms, the sand can be totally removed, uncovering a lower beach level of rocky substrata. The shore slopes gently away from the sea-wall to depths approaching 7m within 150yds of the shore. The sea bed has many interesting rock ledges running out at an oblique angle from the shore, but this is not the main item of interest. Recently discovered by local diver, Steve Marley (owner of the nearby West Bay Watersports dive shop), are the remains of a very, very old ancient forest. Petrified wood, in the form of tree stumps and roots are exposed, still in their original growing position on a clay sea bed. They are located at a depth of 5m, 90yds out from the beach and 50yds west of the harbour pier. A local expert has estimated their age at 30,000 years! Divers interested in viewing these unusual fossils should visit the site urgently as there are plans afoot to construct an outer harbour at West Bay, which will effectively destroy the site.

Beyond the western end of the beach and area of protective rock fill, just offshore is a large black rock with a flat top that shows at anything but high water. On springs, the rock dries completely. This rock is known as Black Rock, or Table Rock, and is used as an indicator by local boatmen of what depth of

27

*Steve Marley, owner of West Bay Watersports, displays an ancient stone anchor that he recovered locally.* Photo: Authors

water to expect when entering the nearby harbour. If more than about 2ft of vertical rock is showing, the tide is too low to enter the narrow passage between the piers. Out beyond this rock are other rocks and reefs, which make very interesting diving. There is plenty of short weed cover on submerged rocks, providing a suitable habitat for many territorial fish.

This site is easily disturbed in a swell. Any wind from the southern half can stir up the beach and completely spoil the visibility. Currents are fairly weak, especially on the ebb when the twin piers of the harbour give protection. There tends to be a stand on high water (Dover plus 4 hours 25 minutes, or Devonport plus 52 minutes). The site is both ideal for the beginner and interesting for the experienced diver. A local by-law restricts speed to 8 knots up to 200yds from the shore. Cafés, a public telephone and toilets are all available 200yds away at the harbour.

**7 Harbour at West Bay** SY 463 904. *Launching point only.* The B3157 from Bridport ends at West Bay, which is backed by a conglomeration of caravan sites, holiday homes, hotels and shops. The working harbour with its fishing trawlers and potting boats with their brawny crews contrasts strongly with the tourists and candy-floss stalls that throng its periphery. At the head of the harbour is a substantial slipway where vehicles can launch boats from trailers directly into the water. At low water, particularly on springs, the harbour dries, making launching impractical. Harbour dues and launching fees are payable to the harbourmaster, whose office is at the western pier.

*There is ample parking on the promenade at West Bay. The photograph shows the steps down to the beach.* Photo: Roy Smallpage

Although conditions in the harbour may appear deceptively calm, a swell can create tricky conditions between the two piers on the way to the open sea. Study these conditions by walking out on the pier before launching. If they are judged by the harbourmaster to be unsuitable for small boats the gate across the launching-ramp will be locked. During storms, pebbles from the beach to the east often clog the entrance of the harbour. This not only means the entrance can be very shallow, but as a result, causes incoming swells to steepen and accelerate between the two piers. Local by-laws forbid speeds of over 8 knots within 200yds of beaches in West Bay. High water is Dover plus 4 hours 25 minutes, or Devonport plus 52 minutes.

An area on the south and east walls of the harbour is reserved for visiting boats to tie up. Moorings in the season are normally all in use. You will find a public telephone and toilets near the George Hotel, approximately 40yds north of the slip way. For the harbourmaster's office, telephone 01308 423222. After launching, the best place to park is the long stay car park, situated 120yds back along the Bridport road.

**8 East Beach car park, West Bay** SY 464 902. *Snorkel, aqualung, free launching.* The B3157 from Bridport leads directly to the harbour at West Bay. At the harbour, take a left turn, which doubles back in an easterly direction. Down this street, on the right, approximately 30yds from the harbour, is the entrance to a very large area at the rear of the beach, which, during the summer months, is used as a pay-and-display car park. It gives direct access over a high bank of pebbles to the East Beach. With a struggle, small boats can be carried over the bank to the sea – a distance of 150yds.

A somewhat faster route onto the East Beach is from the harbour area and along past the Bridport Arms. However, on this route, any boat has to be lifted or negotiated around obstructions at the rear of the beach. To the east, a high, yellow sandstone cliff rises perpendicularly, giving shelter from the north, and, on sunny days, trapping the sun and reflecting its heat on to the beach. The sea bed slopes away from the beach in a series of small pebbly terraces to a depth of about 6m. After this, the slope is more gradual. Once clear of the pebble bank, the underwater scene is one of sand with scattered pebbles and outcrops and nodules of interesting rock. Large plaice and flounder can be seen here.

This site is the western extremity of Chesil Beach. After a calm period, visibility can be excellent. But a wind from the southern half soon piles up a swell that can make entry and exit difficult. This site is excellent for all grades of diver. There is an 8 knot speed limit in force up to 200yds from the shore. There are telephones, toilets and cafés in abundance at or near the rear of the beach over towards the harbour end.

**9 Burton Freshwater Caravan Park Beach** SY 476 896. *Snorkel, aqualung, free launching.* This is a private beach available only to people staying at the Freshwater Caravan and Camping Park. It is included because diving individuals or groups may wish to base themselves here and take advantage of the excellent facilities offered by the park. Besides large residential caravans, there are spacious areas for visiting touring caravans and for campers. The Park entrance is situated ½ mile west of Burton Bradstock on the B3157 Bridport road. Once inside and on the private roads of the site it is possible to drive a vehicle right onto the rear of the pebble beach to deposit gear or a small inflatable. The sea is then a 50yd walk across the loose, fine pebble beach. Heavier boats can be launched at nearby West Bay harbour and driven the one mile to Freshwater Beach.

Freshwater represents a wide gap in a sandstone cliff where the River Bride flows across the beach into the sea. In the river to the rear of the beach are deep, interesting-looking pools. The river has cut and maintains (especially when in full flow) a deep channel across the beach and has formed a delta of pebbles out from the beach underwater. The beach itself is formed entirely of fine pebbles with an occasional narrow band of coarse sand. Although the caravan-park extends to the very edge of the beach there is a sense of space, with a wide sweep of beach and yellow cliffs at either side of the ½ mile wide gap.

There is a variety of sea bed for the diver. East of the river, just along the cliff, there are many rocks and much life. West of the river, the sea bed descends a shallow terrace of pebbles to a mixture of sand and clumps of small rock outcrops littered with stones fallen from the eroded East Cliff. Also to be seen are the remains of World War Two concrete sea defences known as dragon's teeth, which storms have drawn down to the lower levels of the beach terrace. There is also a mystery. Local diver Steve Marley (owner of West Bay Watersports dive shop) has made a strange discovery diving from the shore here. On bare patches of sandy sea bed he found areas with lots of strange bones. Local villagers believe that the river Bride has disturbed an area of a Roman rubbish tip near the village, and has transported the bones from there out into the sea. Depths of 6m can be recorded fairly close to the beach in the western half, but it is shallower where the river has taken material out to sea and where larger rock-beds are situated east of the river. Crabs can be found in the rocks and flounder can be seen around the river mouth. Plaice can be found on sandy patches.

This site is sheltered only from the north and north-east. Virtually any other wind will bring a swell. Visibility is excellent, especially in periods of still weather. The tidal current flows parallel to the beach. This site is ideal for any grade of diver, especially the beginner, who can have a good dive very near the beach. There is a local by-law restricting boats to 8 knots up to 200m from the beach west of the mouth of the River Bride. The nearest public telephone is near the reception building. There are also toilets and a café.

**10 Burton Bradstock Beach** SY 490 887. *Snorkel, aqualung, free launching.* To reach this beach drive eastwards out of Burton Bradstock along the B3157. Once clear of the village the road crosses the River Bride and swings sharply to the left. Some 400yds farther on a turning on the right is plainly signposted to the car park and beach. Follow this turning for another 400yds to the beach at a place known locally as The Hive.

The National Trust owns the land adjacent to the sea, and in the lovely grassy area to the rear of the beach they have created a fairly small car park in a sloping paddock. Small boats can be easily carried or wheeled from the end of the road onto the beach. To do this it may, at times, be necessary to unlock a wooden pole across the beach entrance. The key is readily available from the car park attendant. From the rear of the beach to the high-water mark is a distance of 50yds over very loose fine gravel.

Above water, this site is very much like Burton Freshwater. To the west, the sandstone Burton Cliff rises up perpendicularly from the beach. But to the east a different geology shows itself in a sloping bank of clays and shales. Linking these two extremes in one magnificent clean sweep is the pebble beach. Underwater, the beach descends in a sloping terrace of pebbles and tumbled rocks, the contours of which depend on the severity and direction of the last storm to strike the area.

At a depth of 7m the pebbles and rocky terrain changes to flat rippled sand. Towards the cliff, a little west from the road end, the terrace becomes much rockier with a plateau of rocks extending farther out into the flat sand area. Very little weed grows on this site, but in the summer months shoals of young pouting gather and swim under and around the larger rocks. The occasional John Dory can also be observed. Once off the pebbles and rocks, plaice and sometimes sole can be seen cleverly camouflaged and partially covered in the fine sand. Large flounder occasionally make an appearance too.

This site suddenly became of serious archaeological interest in April 1990 when local diver Steve Marley (owner of West Bay Watersports dive shop), in the course of a casual shore dive, discovered 3 iron cannon, together with what are now thought to be piles of ballast stones. They were at a depth of only 6m, and only about 80yds out from the shore and, conveniently, exactly opposite the road end entry onto the beach. Astounded that the 3 cannon – 4, 6 and 9 pounders – had not been spotted before at this popular dive site, Steve subsequently organised their recovery. They are currently on view outside the harbour museum in West Bay. At least one other cannon lies still partially hidden in the pebbles of the underwater beach terrace, appearing briefly after storms.

On inspection it was found that two of the cannon had their bore plugged with corks. On removal, the barrels proved to be fully primed with wadding and black powder. They are thought to be of Dutch or French manufacture, and of a very early type. So far there are no known records of a shipwreck to account for this exciting find. Another extremely strange facet of this find was that after one of the cannon had been lifted clear of the crud encapsulated pebbles on which it lay, there, beneath it, within the crud, Steve discovered part of a belt of live World War Two 0.303 ammunition.

Burton Bradstock is well sheltered from the north and north-east. But any other wind direction (especially if above Force 4) will soon bring a swell pounding on to the beach. In quiet periods the visibility here is excellent. The tidal current is manageable and runs parallel to the shore. This site is excellent for beginners. It is an extremely convenient site for a shore dive, and the beach does not usually become overcrowded in summer. Immediately to the rear of the beach you will find a café and toilets. There is a payphone inside the café.

**11 Cogden Beach** SY 504 880. *Snorkel.* Cogden Beach is a remote place with no facilities. It can, out of season, also be a very lonely area. There is no telephone, and no dwellings nearby. To find this site, drive east from Burton Bradstock, along the B3157 towards Abbotsbury for approximately 1¼ miles, when the entrance will be seen on the seaward side. The National Trust have recently taken control of the area, and now prevent vehicles approaching the rear of the beach. A car park is provided just off the B3157, and then it is a good ½-mile walk down a steep track to the beach. It is because of this distance that diving gear has now to be carried that we advise this site as snorkel only.

The beach is part of the western end of the Chesil Bank and accordingly is made up of pebbles. Under the water, the sea bed descends quite steeply from the shore in a series of pebble terraces until, at about 7m, there is flat, rippled, clean sand. This is a good bottom to find plaice. The site is sheltered from the north and north-east, but is very much affected by south or south-west winds. Anything much above Force 3 can bring a heavy swell tumbling onto the beach. Visibility in quiet periods can be in excess of 10m. The tidal current runs parallel to the beach.

**12 West Bexington** SY 531 864. *Snorkel, aqualung, free launching.* At West Bexington there is a small car park on the pebble beach. If this is full, parking is also permitted on the approach road. From the car park it is an easy task to carry a small boat down the 80yds of gently sloping small loose pebbles to the sea.

To find this site, drive west along the B3157 coast-road from Burton Bradstock towards Abbotsbury. In a sharp dip of the road are the outskirts of the village of Swyre. In this dip, on the north side of the road, is the Bull Inn, and directly opposite the Bull Inn is a turning down a lane to West Bexington. Follow this lane to the car park on the beach.

On land, the scenery is typical of the western end of the Chesil, with the bank of pebble beach backed by a narrow strip of almost fen-type land. Behind this, cultivated farmland rises away from the sea to almost 220m in places. Underwater, the beach descends in a series of terraces until flat sand is found at about 9m and 50yds offshore. Plaice can often be seen lying on this sand. There is no weed off the shore.

This area is more or less sheltered from the north and north-east, but is completely open to other winds. A south or south-westerly wind of much above Force 3 brings a swell that will make exiting the water very difficult if it grows much over 1m in height. The visibility can be well in excess of 10m in quiet periods. The tidal current runs parallel to the beach. If a diving group does not mind a walk back, it is easy to drift-dive along the beach on the current. West Bexington is an excellent site for beginners, who can easily control their depth on the sloping terrace of the beach.

A little way along the road is an unusual establishment. Guy and Rita Wise have, since the late 1960s, run a village shop, café and tea garden. They sell everything from bananas to birthday cards, as well as snacks, hot and cold drinks and sandwiches. These can be consumed inside or at tables in the garden. Opening hours are anytime anyone requires anything, except on Christmas Day! A private telephone at this shop is available for emergency calls. The nearest public telephone is a kiosk 300yds up the road on the bend in the village. There are toilets at the rear of the car park.

**13 Abbotsbury Bomber** SY 546 852. *Snorkel and aqualung.* The pilot of the American Flying Fortress later described how, in 1943, he was coming in low towards the Dorset coast, and was unable to gain height because of damage sustained in a raid over the Continent. He spotted the yellow water along the edge of the beach at Abbotsbury. Judging this to be a sign that the water was only a few inches deep he ditched his failing aircraft, expecting that he and his crew could step out of the aircraft and wade ashore. Instead, they found themselves to be sinking in a depth of 11m.

The remains of the Flying Fortress are still lying on the sea bed at Abbotsbury. She provides an interesting target for divers who know where to look for her. The flat sandy sea bed sometimes shifts in winter storms and the wreck is almost covered, but at most times the whole width of the massive wing section, complete

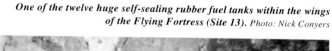

*One of the twelve huge self-sealing rubber fuel tanks within the wings of the Flying Fortress (Site 13).* Photo: Nick Conyers

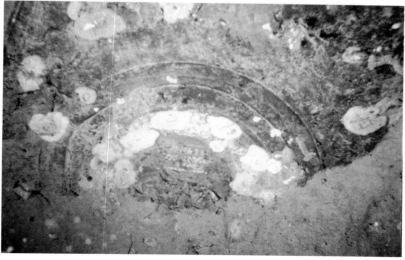

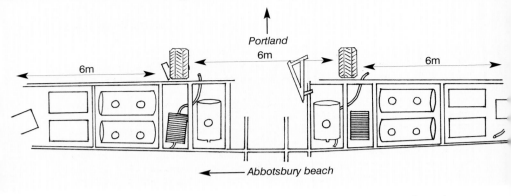

*An extremely accurate illustration of the wings of the Abbotsbury bomber, drawn in 1994 by diver Steve Jones.*

with its undercarriage wheels can be seen. The fuel tanks are all still in place. Steve Jones of Port Talbot, who specialises in diving and researching crashed aircraft, has recovered a filler cap from the top side of the tanks, proving, despite opinions to the contrary that the wings are not upside down. There is a minor mystery as to what has happened to the fuselage section and three of the four engines. One engine was recovered by divers in the 1960s.

To dive this site drive to Abbotsbury beach (Site **14**). It is then necessary to drive westwards following the narrow road, which deteriorates into a track along the rear of the beach, for ¾ mile. Lawrence Cottage, a detached thatched building will eventually be seen standing one field back off the track. Just past this cottage, standing on the beach is a World War Two concrete pill box. Pace out exactly 110yds westwards along the track from opposite this box. This identifies a place where the track starts to bend and rise, and there is an entrance to a field on the inland side (blocked by a heavy padlocked chain hanging between two steel gateposts). The aeroplane lies in the sea directly opposite this point – 140yds out at low water neaps. Due to untidy blocks of stone deposited all along the side of the narrow track, parking a vehicle is difficult.

WARNING This is an ideal site for the beginner or the experienced diver but see cautions for diving at Site **14**. This is part of Chesil Beach: do not enter the water if the waves breaking on the pebbles are more than 1m high. Getting in is easy, but getting back out is much more difficult.

*To establish an exact transit line to the Abbotsbury bomber, one person must stand between the two steel gateposts, in a position 2yds from the eastern post. A second person then moves along the edge of the sea until the first person's head is directly below a large patch of scrub on the hill behind, just below the horizon. This line, extended out to sea, leads to the wreck.*

**14 Abbotsbury Beach** SY 559 845. *Snorkel, aqualung, free launching.* To find this beach, leave the village of Abbotsbury by driving westwards along the B3157 coast road. About 400yds after passing the last few houses of the village, a left-hand turn is plainly signposted to Chesil Beach. This junction is at the point where the B3157 starts to climb the very steep Abbotsbury Hill. Follow the left hand turning until, in just under one mile, a large car parking area will be seen on the left and immediately to the rear of the bank of the pebble beach.

Launching involves carrying your boat approximately 90yds, over the crest of the pebble bank and then down several loose pebble terraces to the sea. The best place to start from is the end of the road outside the car park. For the shore diver, a wooden walkway from inside the car park to the summit of the bank makes carrying gear relatively easy.

From the end of the road, by the car park, a track extends along the rear of the beach to West Bexington. In the past it was possible to park vehicles at many places along its length, giving access to a total of 2½ miles of beach. Unfortunately, The Dorset Heritage Coast Service have deposited hundreds of untidy blocks of stone along the side of the track to prevent parking and, in effect, to force everyone to use the section of beach immediately adjacent to the car park. The best a diving party can do to use their "heritage coast" is to transport gear along the track to the desired site, but then return the vehicle to the car park, and carry out the reverse procedure at the end of the day.

There is access at many places from the track onto the beach either in places where the pebbles are level with the track, or where there are grassy slopes to scramble down. Wherever you choose to dive along this beach, the underwater scene is very similar. The sea bed at Abbotsbury descends in a series of interestingly-sloped pebble terraces whose profile changes with each storm. At a depth of 10m the pebbles abruptly cease. From here on there is flat, rippled sand. This change from pebbles to sand occurs about 90yds from the shore. Plaice sit on the sand, and if you look carefully you may spot the odd sole buried up to its eyes.

On the pebble terraces lie scores of anglers' lines, lost after breaking during over-energetic casting in an attempt to reach out to the sand where the plaice swim. At the end of each line is a nice lead weight, nylon trace and hooks. As a diver, you can salvage quite a collection of such items, but make quite sure they are not still attached to rods on the beach! Like most stretches of Chesil Beach, Abbotsbury has its tale of treasure. Local people tell of the day when a heavy storm moved the pebbles off the lower slope of the beach. At low tide the uncovered area was found to be scattered with Roman coins. This story is almost certainly true.

The beach at Abbotsbury is sheltered when the wind blows from the northern half, but a wind above Force 4 from the south or south-west soon produces a heavy swell that crashes on to the beach. Do not dive if the waves breaking on the beach are much over 1m high. Entry into the water is easy. Getting out can be difficult and sometimes downright dangerous. Always have help waiting on the beach with a throwing rope. Snorkellers can be of great help to the cumbersome aqualung diver by assisting him through the breakers at these times.

The tidal current flows parallel to the beach at Abbotsbury, but although it can be quite strong (especially on springs) it is not a serious hazard to the competent diver. This site is ideal for all grades of diver, but beginners should exercise caution in rough conditions. There are toilets in the car park but no telephone. While visiting this site – especially if conditions are not ideal for diving – your party may enjoy a visit to the nearby tropical gardens 200yds up the road from the beach.

# Offshore boat diving and wrecks

**15 Rotorua I** 50 18.47N; 02 59.73W. This is the wreck of a really big, triple-screwed ship of 11,130 gross tons. It is a long trip out to her, but worth every mile, and it takes more than one visit to even start to explore her inner spaces. The owners were the New Zealand Shipping Company, and it must have been a very sad day for them when their magnificent liner was sunk by a torpedo fired from the German submarine *UC-17* on 22 March, 1917 while she was sailing from London to Wellington. (The name of this ship was, after her sinking, transferred to another ship – the *Shropshire*, which became *Rotorua II.*)

The ship is whole, and, especially up forward, is fairly intact for the time she has been on the sea bed. She was built in 1910 at the Clyde shipyard of W. Denny Brothers at Dumbarton – the same yard that had launched the *Kyarra* only seven years earlier. They built the *Rotorua* to a specification that did not go short on brass fittings. She has three decks and a shelter deck. Her hull measures 484ft 2in long with a beam of 62ft 3in.

Around the area of her engine room she is somewhat collapsed, allowing her huge six-cylinder steam engine to stand proud of the surrounding structure. The wreck has been positively identified by the recovery of her bell. We thank Nick Chipchase of Wellington & Taunton SAC for the information on this wreck. He has dived her and says she makes a cracking good dive. She lies north-west to south-east at a sea bed depth of 55m. She stands up to 11m high. *Boats: Lyme Regis 25 miles.*

**16 Greta C** 50 21.03N; 02 59.20W. This wreck was first dived and identified in July 1996 by Nick Chipchase of Wellington & Taunton SAC, who surveyed and ascertained the wreck's identity to be that of the Isle of Wight Carrisbrook Shipping Company's 474 gross ton motor vessel the *Greta C*, formerly the *Westland Trader.* Only two days later, a second party of divers visiting the site totally confirmed Nick's identification of the wreck by recovering the ship's bell inscribed with her former name. The *Greta C* was lost on 7 September, 1974 when she foundered in force 7 seas when heavily loaded with a cargo of granite chips and dust. One member of the crew died.

The ship was built in 1963, measured 170ft long with a beam of 24ft. She is fitted with a 5 cylinder oil engine. The wreck lies perfect and totally intact on its starboard side, complete with its propeller. She lies north to south, bows to the south and there is even the table still in place in the galley. There is a trawl net jammed over the stern. Depth to sea bed is 55m and she stands up 5m. *Boats: Lyme Regis 22 miles, Weymouth 31 miles.*

**17 Bokn** 50 21.97N; 02 58.90W. Look along the bottom edge of Admiralty Chart 3315, just east of the 3° line. There is a long finger of more shallow sea bed, the contour line around which looks like a giraffe facing Devon. Along the lower side of its neck line, just above the body, are "three wrecks in a line", and are known as just that to the skippers and divers who venture out so far. They are some of the victims of convoy WP 183, which was attacked by E-boats on 9 July, 1942. No less than six ships from the convoy were lost in the immediate area. The most westerly of the "three in line" – at the above position – was thought previously to be the *Rosten*, but is almost certainly the 698 gross ton Norwegian collier *Bokn*. She measured 193ft long with a beam of 28ft. She was sunk by torpedo.

On a dive in the summer of 1996, Nick Chipchase of Wellington & Taunton SAC obtained measurements of 25ft across the deck rails of an upright fairly small ship lying with a midships-located engine. The ship lies north to south, with her stern to the south. A single boiler lies displaced and twisted from its mountings and slopes at 30° down to the sea bed level where there is a layer of debris and coal. Aft of the boiler, a small section of the casing of a triple-expansion engine can be seen within an area of twisted metal that rises higher than the boiler. Farther aft (south), is mounted a deck winch and the clear outline of a hold can be discerned. Sea bed depth 54m.

The hull of the stern half is intact and standing 3m high, but forward of the boiler the wreck is well broken down to piles of debris and coal. The highest part of the wreck is standing up 9m. *Boats: Lyme Regis 21 miles.*

**18  Rosten** 50 21.72N; 02 57.86W. This is the middle one of the "three wrecks in a line", all of which were part of convoy WP 183, and were sunk by an E-boat attack on 9 July, 1942. It was thought previously to be the wreck of the *Bokn* (that wreck lies nearby to the west) but is now thought almost certainly to be the wreck of the *Rosten*, a similar Norwegian ship, also carrying coal.

The wreck in this position is apparently lying on its port side, well collapsed and twisted. The stern is probably to the south and the wreck is well netted. Sea bed depth is 54m. Wreck stands up 6m. *Boats: Lyme Regis 22 miles.*

**19  West Tennants Reef** 50 38.82N; 02 57.70W. Roughly four miles south-west of Lyme Regis, the above position gives the centre of a reef composed of a big slab of raised bedrock. The reef extends 1½ miles east to west, but is very much narrower between its north and south boundaries. Depths on the top of the reef average 25m, with a surrounding sea bed at 29m.

Scenery on the reef is excellent with the occasional huge boulder, patches of sea fans, dead man's fingers and shoals of fish swimming above. However, the main features are a number of very interesting V-shaped gullies, some of which are up to 4m in depth, the reef is very pretty, with high vertical drops off to the sea bed of sand, especially on its northern edge. Scallops are in profusion in the surrounding areas. *Boats: Lyme Regis 4 miles.*

**20 Majorca** 50 20.13N; 02 57.48W. The *Majorca*, a small coaster previously known as the *Ida*, had been built in 1957 and was powered by a 395hp oil engine. She was carrying a cargo of fertiliser from Antwerp to Teignmouth. On 18 September, 1982, in rough conditions, when halfway across Lyme Bay, she suffered a catastrophic shift of cargo, which caused her to capsize and sink. She has been dived and, besides other items, the bell has been recovered. Depth to sea bed is 45m, wreck stands up 6m. *Boats: Lyme Regis 24 miles.*

**21 Reggestroom** 50 21.50N; 02 57.45W. The more easterly of the "three wrecks in a line" at the above position is thought to be the *Reggestroom*, a two-deck Dutch ship of 2,836 gross tons, built in 1923. She was fitted with two steam turbine engines. Her cargo is listed as produce from Douala. The only diving report is that she lies upside down and is well netted. She was part of convoy WP 183 and one of six ships sunk on 9 July, 1942. Sea bed depth 53m. Wreck stands up 9m. *Boats: Lyme Regis 22 miles.*

**22 HMS Clyde** 50 32.10N; 02 56.55W. The *Clyde*, a large trawler, had been hired by the Admiralty in 1915 and like many of the other small hired ships, was employed mainly to patrol the shipping lanes and carry out mine sweeping duties. Many of these ships were lost through enemy action, but, as the war dragged on in France, it must have seemed to the crew of the *Clyde* that she was turning out to be a lucky ship. It must have been a truly unexpected shock to them, when, on 14 October, 1917, she was involved in a violent collision at her stern end, and immediately sank.

Today she sits on the sea bed upright and complete, but with clear evidence of her demise – an extremely large dent over her iron hull, at the stern. The ship of 146 gross tons, was built in 1871 and was fitted with a small 45hp triple-expansion steam engine. She lies north-west to south-east on the sea bed at 43m and stands up a full 6m high. A small enough wreck to see most of her on one visit. *Boats: Lyme Regis 11 miles.*

**23 Heroine** 50 40.49N; 02 56.04W. In early December 1852 this wooden sailing barque had left London on a voyage to Port Philip in Australia. Like all ships of her day plying their trade "down under", she carried both cargo and a number of emigrants, eager to start a new life in a new land. The emigrants on the *Heroine* were said to be of a "poorer" class and were probably desperate people risking all, including their lives, to reach the then booming Australian gold fields.

By 26 December she was off the Devon coast and battling into an ever worsening south-westerly and heavy seas. So bad were the conditions becoming that her Captain was eventually forced to seek shelter in Torbay, hoping to ride out the storm in the lea of the headland. The anchors were set down – but failed to hold. Gradually, in the storm and darkness she dragged across the bay, ever nearer the opposite headland shore. Valiant attempts were made to escape the approaching trap, but unable to sail out she grounded onto rocks, tore off her rudder and badly holed herself.

She had been built in 1838 and had been certified as A1, which meant she was a vessel of top specification for her class. Possibly it was the quality of her timbers and the excellent workmanship of her Tyneside builders that now saved the day, for somehow she was miraculously lifted off the rocks by the heaving sea and taken around the headland and drifted helplessly out into Lyme Bay. By dawn of the 27 December she was in real trouble. All through the night, the by now exhausted crew had been working furiously pumping incoming water out of her damaged bilges. They were waging a battle that was slowly being lost. She was armed with two carronades, and it was to these that the Captain now turned. Each was loaded over and over again with black powder and fired at intervals – a well accepted method of signalling distress.

From out of the storm, the distant boom of the guns was plainly heard

*Above: The cargo of bricks
pinpointed the whereabouts of
the wreck of the Heroine.*
Photo: Peter Glanvill

*Right: The panel of
remembrance created with
bricks from the wreck of
the Heroine and built into the
wall of the new Lyme Regis
lifeboat house.* Photo: Authors

throughout the small Dorset town of Lyme Regis. Townspeople flocked out onto The Cobb, regardless of the breaking waves and spray that surged over the walls of their small harbour. They were all curious and eager to see what was happening. What they saw was a vessel four miles out to sea, slowly starting to sink. There were however, four local seamen who did not just stand there gawping into the gale – they knew full well what it must be like for those poor people on that sinking ship. They also knew there was no lifeboat at Lyme, and that they were the only ones capable of giving assistance. They quickly donned waterproof oilskins, launched, and bravely rowed out of The Cobb entrance intent on a rescue mission. No sooner had they left the shelter of the harbour, still in clear view of their friends and families in the crowd of gathered townsfolk, when an extra large breaking wave caught them up and flung them back against the outside of The Cobb wall. Three were killed instantly, the fourth was rescued, badly injured. Out at sea, the *Heroine* had completely disappeared, but, at the last minute, her crew had successfully launched her two longboats and together with all the passengers safely aboard were rowing for the shore. All were saved, one boat managing to enter the harbour, the other coming ashore farther to the east.

The *Heroine* was gone. During the next year, 1853, records show that Lloyd's sent a salvage boat to Lyme Regis with divers. They successfully located the wreck and "recovered valuable items of cargo". After this she was not disturbed again, but lay forgotten for almost 150 years, her wooden hull gently rotting and ever so slowly collapsing and disappearing into the sand, that is except for two items. Firstly, her two small cannon never seemed to completely sink beneath the surface, and an item of cargo also remained. One of her holds had been carefully stacked full, right up to the underside of her deck with firebricks. When eventually all the timber of her superstructure and hull had disappeared, these remained above her grave, as a great big cairn and a damned nuisance to Lyme Regis fishermen who kept hitting that strange isolated "reef" with their scallop dredgers. Gradually, more and more bricks became dislodged and scattered, but a pile 12yds long and 1.5m high is still there.

In November 1991 Richard Greenaway and a diving colleague, both members of Swindon BSAC, were carrying out a drift dive. Drifting with the current across a sandy plain at a depth of 24m, they started to see a scattering of copper nails, rivets and other bits and pieces. Immediately suspecting a nearby wreck, they recorded the position and returned on several subsequent occasions to search the area. It was into the 1992 season when at last they discovered the iron cannon, and then, not far away, the huge pile of bricks.

The discovery could not have been made by a better group or club, for Swindon branch, over the years, have a record of being well capable of organising underwater projects and recoveries, and on this occasion they excelled. Joining up with John Walker, who is both an Advanced diver of 30 years experience, and owner skipper of charter boat *Miss Pattie* at Lyme Regis, and six other members of the Swindon club, Richard Greenaway formed a dedicated archaeological group, which was named Lyme Bay Heritage. This group was to subsequently research, investigate and finally excavate the wreck and to eventually present all the recovered artefacts to the Town Museum at Lyme Regis. Richard was lucky in one respect, for one of his team members was Jeff Bryant, an experienced underwater archaeologist who had been part of the *Mary Rose* Project. Jeff was to oversee all the archaeological aspects of the work.

The bulk of the work was carried out in the 1995 season, when over 1m of overburden of sand and gravel was removed, using a 4in diameter airlift, powered by a Compair road compressor, mounted on the deck of *Miss Pattie*. Soon laid bare, after all those years, were the lower surviving timbers and keel of the *Heroine*, and there, lying spread out in the sand, was the hull's copper sheathing. Gradually, more and more of the ship was uncovered the sand giving up many artefacts that had settled right into the very bilges.

Items recovered include 28 telescopes, a compass, a sextant and an octant, and two carronade cannon. The ship's iron pump, a silver comb, many bottles, shoes, keel pins, wooden sheaves, sawn bones and fish bones, and of course bricks. The bricks have the name "RAMSAY" on them and a selected number have been brought ashore and presented to the RNLI. They form a commemorative panel built into the interior wall of the recently completed lifeboat house at The Cobb and are a permanent reminder of the three men who bravely gave their lives attempting to render assistance to their fellows in distress at sea.

The main work is now complete and Richard Greenaway says divers are welcome to visit the wreck. Obviously to be seen is the brick pile – with no less than 8 resident congers, one an 8ft giant, but also the ship's timbers can be seen over the total 100ft length of the boat. They stand up to almost 1m above the sand in places. The wreck lies bows facing south. Around the stern area – to the north of the brick pile – can be seen coal among the stern frames. Currents are manageable, and the wreck can be dived at any stage of the tide. Depth 25m. *Launching and boats: Lyme Regis 4 miles.*

**24 Unknown wreck** 50 33.00N; 02 56.00W. A wreck is known to exist at this approximate location: divers working from Lyme Regis had it on their echo sounder, but lost it again. Searches of the area continue. *Boats: Lyme Regis 11 miles.*

**25 Baygitano** 50 41.76N; 02 55.97W. This wreck is situated 1½ miles offshore almost due south of The Cobb at Lyme Regis, and is plainly marked on the chart. A large British steam-driven collier of 3,073 tons, she lies at a depth of 18m. This ship, formerly the *Cayo Gitano*, was victim of a torpedo fired by the German submarine *UC-77*, and was sunk on 18 March, 1918, when on a voyage in ballast from Le Havre to Cardiff. Her crew escaped ashore in her lifeboats, but 2 were killed in the explosion when the torpedo slammed home.

She measured 330ft long with a 45ft beam and is still recognisable as a whole ship. She makes a very accessible and interesting dive. The wreck is surrounded by a gravel sea bed at 18m and stands up to 5m high. Her power plant of 3 steam boilers is easy to recognise amidships as is her triple-expansion three-cylinder engine, still upright, just to the rear of the boilers – so it is easy to find her stern from her boilers, by swimming eastwards past her engine, across a gap and then between two winches to where a large, spare propeller is mounted

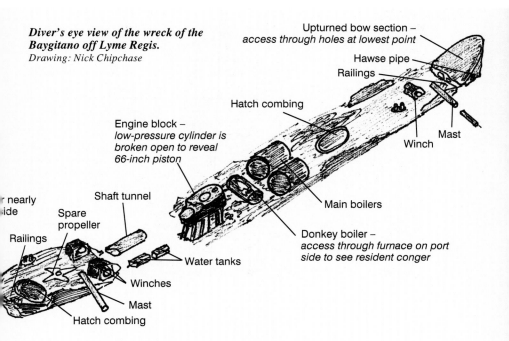

*Diver's eye view of the wreck of the Baygitano off Lyme Regis.*
*Drawing: Nick Chipchase*

Upturned bow section – access through holes at lowest point

Hawse pipe

Railings

Hatch combing

Engine block – low-pressure cylinder is broken open to reveal 66-inch piston

Mast

Winch

Main boilers

Shaft tunnel

r nearly ide

Spare propeller

Railings

Donkey boiler – access through furnace on port side to see resident conger

Water tanks

Winches

Mast

Hatch combing

on the stern deck. The remains of a mast can be seen, both at the stern and near the bow, where they have collapsed to her starboard side. Her bow area has partially collapsed, leaving a steep incline up to its point. The wreck is home to shoals of fish life.

The *Baygitano* is regarded as a good dive, and is highly recommended by those who know her well. The period of high water is the best time, but she can be dived at any period of the tide. *Launching and boats: Lyme Regis 1½ miles.*

NOTE When planning to launch at Lyme Regis, it is essential to read details given for Site **2**, which cover The Cobb and the harbourmaster's arrangements for launching and diving.

**26 Lanes Ground Reef** 50 40.44N; 02 55.00W. The above position gives the centre of an area of raised, rough, cobbly ground, barely 3 miles south of Lyme Regis, and only 1½ miles east of the *Heroine* (Site **23**). There are no ledges, but lots of boulders, up to 0.5m high. Because of the coarse material of the surrounding sands that also overlay onto the reef area, the visibility here is usually the best in the bay, and is usually first to settle down after a blow.

The rocky area is large – extending to 02 55.40W in the west and 02 54.75W in the east – and is probably named after a local fisherman who constantly fished here and who was obviously no fool, for the area is the habitat of a profusion of sole, brill and skate. The fauna is a photographer's dream, with boulders covered in all manner of sponges with a full range of colour from yellows through to purples and blues. Sea fans and corals abound with scallops all around the surrounding sea bed. Depths average out at 24m with 29m off the edges of the reef. The area has been studied by the Devon Wild Life Trust and there is a proposal to create an offshore conservation area. *Boats and launching: Lyme Regis 3 miles.*

**27 King Charles** 50 29.45N; 02 54.57W. There is a distinct lack of information about the origins of this wreck. Previously thought to be a working Brixham trawler, she is now believed to have been requisitioned by the Admiralty during the World War One, and while carrying out her duties, was sunk by the Germans.

The wreck consists of a hull, boiler and engine, but has lost her timber deck and wheelhouse. She is starting to break up and bits and pieces are becoming dispersed. Depth 44m and rises up 3m. *Boats: Lyme Regis 13 miles.*

**28 Nyasaland** 50 23.50N; 02 53.66W. This wreck was identified in May 1998 when Chris Lewis of Clifton SAC recovered the builder's plate. This small 383 gross ton Norwegian steam-driven collier, previously called the *Diamante*, was on a voyage to Le Havre after being fully loaded with Welsh coal at Cardiff. She was built at the yard of J. C. Tecklenborg at Geestemunde in Germany. Her measurements are 148ft long with a beam of 26ft 1in. The machinery fitted was a triple-expansion three-cylinder engine.

Making her way steadily along the English Channel, she had arrived, by 8 April, 1918, at an area in Lyme Bay where German U-boats, by audacious use of their torpedoes, had sunk so many vessels before her. But her demise was to be different, for she was confronted by the surfaced *UB-33*, which proceeded to sink the hapless *Nyasaland* by firing salvo after salvo into her from her deck gun.

The wreck lies at a sea bed depth of 50m. The hull has sunk well into the sandy bottom but still stands 3m high. The stern is oriented to the north – it is intact but sections of the hull on the port side are collapsed or missing.

Outlines of holds and a winch can be discerned. A single boiler is easily seen towards the stern. Farther forward there is an area of collapsed plates with portholes. *Boats: Lyme Regis 20 miles, Weymouth 27 miles.*

**29 Unidentified wreck** 50 26.23N; 02 53.51W. Previously, the wreck in this position was thought to be that of a tank landing ship (LST), one of the losses from the disastrous American *Tiger* exercise, but these losses have now been accounted for in other locations. Research and diving surveys carried out by Nick Chipchase and his friends from the Wellington & Taunton SAC, now show that this is a steamship. The unidentified wreck had previously been given the nickname of the "Tower Wreck" because of the sonar profile, which seemed to show such a structure. This turned out to be the wreck's two boilers (one a donkey boiler), which stand high in the middle of a mass of low and flattened wreckage.

The wreck looks as though it has become pretty well smashed to pieces and collapsed. Investigations by the Wellington divers are proceeding. Nick Chipchase had tentatively identified the wreck as the *Edison*, a 469 gross ton steamship, but on subsequent dives in July, 1996, he managed to inspect the engine and found it to be a two-cylinder compound. This now totally rules out the *Edison*, which was fitted with a triple-expansion engine. It is now thought the wreck is that of either the *Bamse* or *Borgund I*. As the top cover is off one of the engine cylinders, Nick intends, at the next opportunity, to measure the diameter of the piston, and once armed with that information, it should be possible to identify the wreck. *Boats: Lyme Regis 18 miles, Weymouth 24 miles.*

**30 Gibel Hamam** 50 35.85N; 02 52.95W. The *Gibel Hamam* was a small British steamship of 647 gross tons, measuring 180ft long with a beam of 29ft. She was built at Newcastle upon Tyne in 1895. On 14 September, 1918, when on voyage from Swansea to France with a cargo of coal, she was hit amidships on the port side and sunk by a torpedo from the German submarine *UB-103*. Twenty-one of her crew, including the captain were lost and only one man survived – the coxswain, who was later washed ashore at Abbotsbury. The wreck is upright on a sandy sea bed with stem and stern intact, but much damage amidships where the torpedo struck. Her boiler is partly exposed. Somewhere below the stern deck is a triple-expansion engine. Depth to the sea bed is 31m and the ship is 8m high.

For many years, her whereabouts were unknown, and the identity of this wreck was a mystery until her 48lb bell was recovered from within the wreck with her former name *Bamburgh* on it. One of the group of Taunton divers who now own the wreck is Paul Streeton. Depth 31m, depth to top of wreck, 24m. *Boats: Lyme Regis 7½ miles.*

**31 East Tennants Reef** 50 39.12N; 02 52.75W. This reef area is not only the loveliest reef dive in Lyme Bay, but possibly ranks as the finest along the whole of the Dorset coast. Situated in an area of outstanding visibility, the reef exhibits an extremely varied scene, containing masses of both static and free swimming life forms. To cap it all, there is a geological aberration that allows entry of the gloomy natural habitat of the many conger eels to be found below the sea bed. One fact is certain, no matter how many times you come here, the life is so diverse that every dive is guaranteed to be different.

The reef is not very extensive, being ½ mile from east to west and a mere 400yds north to south, but what a jewel of a place within these dimensions. The position given is virtually the centre. At the western end are piled boulders the size of small cars, moving eastwards these reduce in size and frequency and when the centre of the area is reached, give way to a covering of slabby rock, which is best described as a pie crust for it is strangely hollow with holes here and there through its surface, which give access to a dark subterranean area beneath. Underground channels are the habitat of fish, conger eels, lobsters and crabs, and allow the inquisitive diver to enter and explore a secret world, and travel below the "pie crust", and exit back to his sunlit world at a choice of places distant from his entry. To describe such a journey as spectacular is to make a gross understatement.

The surface of the reef is equally amazing, especially along the areas forming its northern edges – there is a spectacularly beautiful display of closely packed sea fans. In one place, a biological study is being pursued. John Walker, skipper of Lyme Regis charter boat *Miss Pattie*, has assisted a marine biologist to set up a grid 4 sq m in area. This grid contains no fewer than 80 sea fans. The southern boundaries of the reef are covered densely with dead man's fingers, but the other areas of the reef are like a garden – giving a never ending change of scene, consisting of sponges, corals and anemones of all shades of colour.

Above the reef swim crowds of pollack and separate shoals of pouting. Among the rocks and corals hide many territorial fish with the ever present iridescent blue cuckoo wrasse always attempting to escort the visiting diver away. The average depth of 25m allows the reef to be generally covered in a dive, but virtually all visitors will require to return and study the area's beauty in far greater detail. Surrounding the reef, at 29m, is a sea bed of gritty sand to the north, and fine sand to the south – abounding with scallop. *Boats: Lyme Regis 4 miles.*

**32 Pontoon** 50 24.46N; 02 52.21W. At this position, at a depth of 50m, on a sandy level sea bed, lies a pontoon or barge like vessel. It is thought possible that this may be another remnant of the American *Tiger* convoy. In the convoy, which included no less than eight tank landing ships, *LST 58* was towing a pontoon causeway when the convoy was attacked by German E-boats in the dark hours of the morning of 28 April, 1944. No doubt to improve her manoeuvrability, *LST 58* jettisoned her tow. *Boats: Lyme Regis 20 miles, Weymouth 25 miles.*

**33 Unidentified wreck** 50 23.58N; 02 51.36W. The wreck of what appears to be a small coaster was previously suspected of being the *Nyasaland* but now remains totally unidentified after the latter was proved to lie at Site **28**, 1½ miles to the west. The sea bed depth at the wreck is 50m. The bows and forecastle are upright and intact, but her midships and stern are much the worse for wear. Her boiler is clearly in place in front of her engine, with its mounted reversing wheel. Forward of the main boiler stands an upright donkey engine boiler. Divers of

Wellington & Taunton SAC discovered an engine steam gauge with the German inscription "Fabrik Merke", and other German made engine fittings. *Boats: Lyme Regis 20 miles, Weymouth 24 miles.*

**34 Avalanche** 50 26.56N; 02 50.65W. She was an iron, three-masted sailing ship, unusual and interesting on a number of counts. She had been built in 1874 in an era when iron construction had only just become the norm, and when sail power was fast giving way to steam. Built entirely as a sailing ship, she had much in common with the *Royal Adelaide*, swept onto the Chesil five years earlier. It is possible that they may both have had a common source of iron from the renowned iron smelting works of Abraham Derby at Ironbridge.

Like the *Royal Adelaide*, she had set out down the Thames on a journey that should have taken her to the Antipodes. In an age when new colonies were almost totally dependent on the supply of manufactured goods from Britain, she contained her fair share of the trade – her holds were stuffed full of goods, tight up to the underside of her decking. Indeed, there is a theory that she may have been sailing badly overloaded. Also, like the *Royal Adelaide*, together with manufactured goods she had a complement of passengers, some were new emigrants but most were colonists going back home.

The *Avalanche* set sail in early September, 1877, and made her way along the Downs without incident. By 11 September, 1877, she was off the Dorset coast, and fighting her way through one of those nasty storms that so often seem to come in out of the Atlantic during September. By the evening of 11 September, she had cleared the Portland Race area, and, still tacking to and fro, was well across Lyme Bay.

*An exquisite sugar bowl and jug from the wreck of the Avalanche (Site 34) after lying on the sea bed for more than a century. Photos: Authors*

In the gathering gloom and driving rain the lookouts aboard the *Avalanche* apparently completely failed to see another ship heading towards them – on the opposite tack. It was the 1244 gross ton wooden ship *Forest*, which came straight on and rammed the *Avalanche* at full speed. The *Avalanche* sank immediately, taking all but 3 of her 63 passengers and 34 crew with her to the sea bed. Relations and friends of the victims later suggested that a memorial be built on Portland. Through public subscription in Britain and New Zealand a total of over £2,000 was raised and it was decided to build a church. This was built at Southwell on the island.

The wreck lay on the sea bed, an undisturbed time capsule, for 107 years until in April 1984 divers from Bingham SAC in Nottingham came upon her remains. With specially obtained permission from her owners – the Shaw Saville Line – a quantity of beautiful pottery, some still in a perfect state of preservation, was recovered from her. They also brought up one of her great anchors. These

*The iron anchor raised from the wreck of the Avalanche, now displayed at the Avalanche Memorial Church at Southwell on Portland.*
*Photo: Authors*

were presented to the church and now appear there on permanent display. The church is kept locked, but the keys can be obtained from the Warden at a nearby house. A visit is very much recommended.

The wreck lies on a silty, sand and broken shale sea bed at 52m and stands up a maximum of 4m – the highest point being her bows. She is upright but with a 20° list to her port side. There is a badly damaged area on her port side, approximately 18ft back from her bow. The section of her bow forward of this, although upright, is pushed round to starboard and possibly broken off. There is a definite gap of 20ft between this section and her deck. Is this where she was rammed?

There are at least two large 13ft square open hatches into her holds amidships with their combing intact. There are many barrel type objects with congealed contents piled inside the holds, almost completely filling them up to the level of the hatches. The deck planking has gone, but the under framework is still there with sandy silt between the frames lying on the top layers of cargo. Her stern half is lower and more collapsed than her forward half.

The stub of her centre mast, located just aft of her centre section, stands up 4 to 5m high. While diving this wreck, if you find yourself in an area of champagne bottles, you are in the area approaching the stern end of the ship. These are thought to be Don Perrier Company – still with wire and lead seals with stamped numbers still in place. Her stern mast has fallen outward to the starboard side. Some divers claim to have seen another small vessel along her port side. This may be the remains of a steam pinnace, which was being carried as deck cargo.

She was 1,210 gross tons and measured 214ft 6in long with a beam of 36ft. She makes a good dive. Surrounding her in the sand, particularly on her port side, are many items of pottery and glass spilled from her holds, and divers also report seeing exceptionally large brill around, and large crabs and lobsters within her. The visibility can be excellent, but the soft deposits around the site are easily disturbed. *Boats: Lyme Regis 21 miles, Weymouth 23 miles.*

**35 Golden Cap Boulder Field** 50 43.12N; 02 50.20W. In a wide area around the above position, both inside and outside the 5m line on the chart is a sea bed covered in boulders of all sizes, which, over thousands of years, the sea has eroded from the base of the high cliffs on the side of Golden Cap. This makes an ideal end of the day shallow dive on the way home.

The scenery is good and crustacean life is prolific. The visibility of this area can be quickly spoiled by an onshore blow, but it is very sheltered if winds are from the northern half. Depth 6 to 10m. *Launching: Seatown 1 mile, Lyme Regis 4 miles.*

**36 Broomhill** 50 27.61N; 02 48.87W. The previously unidentified wreck is almost certainly that of the *Broomhill*, a steam-driven collier. Identification is made possible by diving surveys done by Nick Chipchase of Wellington & Taunton SAC. Nick reports a vessel completely on its port side lying north to south. The whole ship is remarkably intact, but has a large hole in the hull near the keel. The propeller, or at least the blades, are missing.

Topside amidships is one boiler, almost totally exposed and free of its mounting. A second boiler nearby lies halfway up the hull and is almost hidden by plates. Nick saw something else too on this wreck. He and his buddy report being "absolutely horrified" by an enormous conger eel that reared up above them in an unnatural stance – like a huge sea serpent – with half its body still hidden within the dark confines of the wreck. Just the part of it they could see was larger than any conger they had ever encountered before and they gave it a very wide berth. The wreck is at 47m, standing up 10m from a firm sea bed of sand and chalk.

The *Broomhill* was one of a fleet of ships owned and employed carrying coal by Broomhill Collieries Ltd. She had been built in 1909 and measured 243ft 3in long with a beam of 36ft. She was 1,392 gross tons.

Disaster struck when she was fully loaded with coal, and on voyage from Penarth to Sheerness. The German submarine *UC-61* surfaced and attacked the unarmed and helpless ship with gunfire. Once having thoroughly terrified and subdued her civilian crew, an armed party was put aboard. Not only were they carrying arms, but came equipped with a very large scuttling charge, which was fixed and detonated near the ship's keel. It did not take long for her to fill with enough water to sink. Two members of the crew died during the attack.

Nick Chipchase is confident that the hull measurements he has carefully made, together with the number of amidships positioned boilers and the large neat hole in the hull, by her keel, positively confirm that this is the *Broomhill*. Boats: *Lyme Regis 17 miles, Weymouth 21 miles*.

**37 Algarve** 50 22.71N; 02 48.40W. In this position lies a British armed steamship. She has been positively identified by the recovery of the builders plate and her bell as the collier *Algarve*. The ship was working under the auspices of the wartime shipping controller and was in ballast, on her way back to Swansea from Rouen to collect more coal. Using the usual inshore shipping lane across Lyme Bay, she fell prey on 20 October, 1917 to a torpedo fired by the German submarine *UB-38*. No less than 21 crew members and the Captain died.

She was built in 1899 by Lobnitz & Company at Renfrew, and was fitted with a triple-expansion engine. The vessel was of 1,274 gross tons and measured 229ft 4in long with a beam of 34ft. The depth to the sea bed is 54m and the wreck stands 9m high. Boats: *Lyme Regis 21 miles, Weymouth 23 miles*.

**38 Saw Tooth Ledges** 50 41.09N; 02 48.06W. Only two miles south of West Bay harbour there is a dive of immense interest, named because of the pattern of edges of rock that run north to south across this reef and give it the look of a giant saw blade – but this is not the cause of this reef's fame. The place to seek out is its northern edge, for which the above position is given, where over a short distance of 400yds, a very sharp drop off occurs with vertical and overhanging ledges up to 6m high.

On the underside surface of the overhangs and on the parts of the vertical surfaces of the underwater cliff, where they are not subject to direct sunlight, grows a very rare and beautiful coral. Only recently discovered here, the sunset coral (*Leptopsammia*) is virtually unknown around the British coast, except for isolated specimens around Lundy and the Channel Islands. The coral slightly resembles the Devonshire cup coral, but with the light of a torch it looks like a brilliant egg yolk. As if this rare and dazzling display is not enough, the rest of the vertical faces of the rock are covered with tightly packed patches of jewel anemones, each patch a different shimmering colour from that of its neighbour.

*Sunset coral, rare in British waters, but in profusion
on Saw Tooth Ledges.* Photo: Peter Glanvill

In addition to the cliff and display of rare coral, the gigantic saw tooth indentations extending across the tide are spectacular in their own right. These can easily be found 200 to 300yds south of the northern drop off and they form an extensive area. Surrounding this reef on all sides are prolific scallop beds. Depth to the top of the reef is 23m. Depth to surrounding sea bed is 29m. *Launching: West Bay 2 miles. Boats: Lyme Regis 6 miles.*

**39 High Ground** 50 42.50N; 02 47.80W. Less than a mile off Eype Mouth, and plainly shown on the chart is an extensive shallow reef that is a favourite place for local angling boats from West Bay. The best way to find this reef as you motor away from the shore is to keep the church spire at Lower Eype in a vertical line with the beach access at Eype Mouth. After about ¾ mile the sea bed becomes generally rocky. The highest point of the rocks is just 400yds to the west of this line, but the most spectacular part to dive is the offshore southern boundary of the reef where a high drop off occurs.

Depths are around 6m, with 15m off the edges of the reefs. Crab and lobsters live on these rocks, with skate and plaice found around the reef on sandy patches. Farther to seaward, scallops can be found. This is a convenient site and makes a good, easy dive for a beginner, though it is also excellent for the experienced diver. Tidal currents are mainly weak. *Launching: Eype Mouth ¾ mile, West Bay 1½ miles.*

**40 Ailsa Craig** 50 33.66N; 02 47.46W. This British steamship, built in 1906 and of 601 gross tons, was on a voyage carrying coal from Cardiff to Granville when torpedoed and sunk by the German submarine *UB-80* on 15 April, 1918.

She was sunk just under 4 miles due west of the *Pomeranian*, and on the same day. Were the vessels in convoy? She is still a whole ship and sits more or less upright, standing 5.5m high, but her bows are twisted over to the starboard side. Her stern is intact with her boiler and engine at her aft end plainly exposed. She lies facing west. The sea bed, at a depth of 35m, is silty. The wreck of the *Moidart* is only 650yds away to the north-east. *Boats: Lyme Regis 11 miles, Weymouth 21 miles.*

**41 Gorizia** 50 25.72N; 02 47.38W. This wreck lies exactly 1 mile to the west of the wreck of HMS *Boadicea*. Captured by a German submarine, she was scuttled on 30 April, 1917 while sailing from New York to Le Havre. Despite being an unexplored wreck, the interest now is twofold. Firstly, she was unusual for the English Channel. The *Gorizia* (formerly the *Glenmount*) was a Great Lakes type steamship built in 1907, with accommodation and bridge section right up on the bows and all her machinery aft.

She was 1,957 tons gross and measured 249ft long by 43ft wide – and could be described as a very large self propelled barge. The other point of interest is her cargo of steel and brass – so interesting that the now defunct Southampton based salvage company, Risdon Beazley, had a go at her and, finding her lying upright, are recorded to have recovered, by grab, 104 tons of brass! To facilitate this operation, they blew off her bow section.

Late in the 1996 season, Nick Chipchase of the Wellington & Taunton SAC dived on the midships section of the wreck. In that area he found the hull reduced (probably by the salvage work) to a height varying from 2 to 3m, with the area littered with brass ingots – thick disks 6in across and ½in thick. There are also larger steel ingots. Sea bed depth 46m. Sand and gravel bottom. *Boats: Lyme Regis 18 miles, Weymouth 22 miles.*

**42 Moidart** 50 34.02N; 02 47.22W. This vessel was an armed merchant steamship – or at least she was before her gun was lifted long ago by divers from a "special projects" group lead by Peter Cornish. The *Moidart* was torpedoed amidships by German submarine *UB-77* on 9 June, 1918, while carrying a cargo of coal from Barry. Fifteen of her crew died. She was built in 1878, measured 243ft 8in long with a 32ft beam and was 1,878 gross tons.

She is not as long today though, for her stern is completely detached and lying on its starboard side 20yds to her rear. The break occurred in the area of her engine room – the engines and boiler are clearly visible at a point that now forms the back end of her front half. The port wall of the engine room is still intact and in racks mounted on it, plain to see, are the engineer's spanners. One is a monster, being over 3ft long and probably weighing over 1cwt. She lies north-west to south-east on a sandy gravel sea bed, at a sea bed depth of 33m, height of wreck is 6m.

A strange feature is that one of her great anchors, instead of hanging downwards on its chain below her hawser port, has somehow become lifted up and is hooked by its flook over the gunnel, directly above the stem. When you see this freak feature you can be sure you are diving the *Moidart*. The ship's bell was recovered in 1992 by divers from the charter boat *Channel Chieftain*. It was found alongside, in the sand. Only 650yds away to the south-west lies the wreck of the *Ailsa Craig* (Site **40**). *Boats: Lyme Regis 11 miles, Weymouth 21 miles.*

**43 Unidentified wreck** 50 24.98N; 02 47.08W. In this position lies a well broken vessel, possibly a collier. The portholes suggest a British built ship; Wellington & Taunton SAC divers are still studying it. *Boats: Lyme Regis 19 miles, Weymouth 21 miles.*

**44 Unidentified wreck** 50 24.72N; 02 46.73W. At the above position is a small vessel with a boiler amidships and this is the only information to hand, but it is on the "to be investigated" list of the Wellington & Taunton SAC divers. *Boats: Lyme Regis 19 miles, Weymouth 21 miles.*

**45 Unknown wreck** 50 39.30N; 02 46.70W. Steel wreckage has been trawled up in this approximate position, and it is now suspected that a barge type vessel exists in the vicinity. It may turn out that the trawled up artefacts, which included a torpedo carriage, were cargo scattered from this barge. Divers from the Lyme Regis charter boat *Miss Pattie* are investigating. Depth 26m. *Launching: West Bay 3 miles. Boats: Lyme Regis 7 miles.*

**46 West Bay – Pollack Rock** 50 42.11N; 02 46.50W. Just over ½ mile offshore from the west beach at West Bay is a rocky area. Within this area a mound of rock comes within 5m of the surface. Surrounding depths on the seaward side are 15m, but are much shallower towards the shore. The top of the rock is covered in kelp, but this thins out at greater depth. Many fish live around this rock, including the many pollack that give it its name. The peak of the rock lies 400yds approximately north-west of the nearby outfall marker buoy. Pollack Rock is a good beginner's dive. *Launching and boats: West Bay ¾ mile.*

**47 L.H. Carl** 50 23.96N; 02 46.48W. It was 20 July, 1917, almost four years into World War One, when the British steamship *L.H. Carl* made her way eastwards across Lyme Bay with her holds full of Welsh coal. She had set out from the docks at Barry and was to take the much needed fuel up the River Seine to Rouen. Unknown to her captain, the German submarine *UB-40*, lay quietly lurking in the ship's path.

No more than one hour earlier, the submarine's captain Oberleutnant Howaldt had fired one of his torpedoes and sunk one of the largest ships of his career – the P&O liner *Salsette*. The hue and cry from this attack had scarcely got going and Howaldt, having managed to sneak away from the death and destruction he had caused six miles to the north, must have been hesitant to give away his location by attacking another, relatively small ship. But he took the risk, fired another of his torpedoes, and scored a direct hit on the *L.H. Carl* – killing two of her crew and sending the ship straight to the bottom.

The *L.H. Carl* was a ship of 1,916 gross tons and measured 280ft in length. Her owners were Lambert Brothers of London. The wreck lies on a shingly sea bed at a depth of 53m, lying south-east to north-west. The very experienced deep diver Chris Collins of Highbridge, Somerset is lucky to have dived this wreck several times in good visibility. He reports that she is upright and very intact. She rises some 9m from the sea bed and only her superstructure, which may have been of wood, is missing. Her decks are still complete with no sign of collapse. *Boats: Lyme Regis 20 miles, Weymouth 21 miles.*

**48 HMS Boadicea** 50 25.70N; 02 45.90W. Death was never far away in Lyme Bay during either of the World Wars. The successful deployment of the torpedo by the Germans led to a large loss of shipping tonnage and, on most occasions, to a cruel loss of life. The terrors that men were subjected to are now almost impossible to appreciate. A visit to the *Boadicea*, a war grave, will remind us of the sacrifices made by those young men so long ago.

The World War Two destroyer *Boadicea* (H65) had seen an action-packed career. She was completed and commissioned on 2 June, 1931, and immediately went to the Mediterranean and among many other duties, was involved in evacuating British Nationals at the start of the Spanish Civil War. She missed the Dunkirk evacuation because of a refit, but was operational by 9 June, 1940, when she went to Le Havre to protect the evacuation of the 51st Highland Division. The next day found her off the French coast between Fécamp and Dieppe and being heavily attacked with bombs from nine Ju 87 dive bombers. The first attack missed by 30yds to starboard, but the second attack obtained three hits. The first penetrated her deck, entered the engine room and burst without exploding, a second bomb penetrated into her after engine room and exploded, killing all the

*The Boadicea (Site 48) was sunk off Portland in 1944 and lies undisturbed in deep water. Photo: Wright & Logan, Portsmouth*

engine room personnel except one. A third bomb entered the after boiler room and passed straight through the ship's bottom without exploding. The third attack missed to port. Orders were given to abandon ship. A skeleton crew managed to stem the flow of water into her and she was later towed into Dover – and later still was repaired at Portsmouth.

Fully operational by February, 1941 found her at Scapa Flow, taking part in the hunt for the *Scharnhorst* and *Gneisenau*. In November, 1942, off Oran, she engaged a French destroyer and in this action received a direct hit with a 5.1in shell. Three days later she rescued 425 survivors when the troop ship *Viceroy of India* was torpedoed. Following this was a period escorting convoys to and from north Russia, where she was extensively damaged by ice. July, 1943 found her on further convoy escort duties in the South Atlantic, during which she saved 220 survivors from the MV *Incomati*. Later she was again at the forefront of the action, escorting the initial assault convoys for the Normandy landings.

Escorting a follow-up convoy across Lyme Bay turned out to be her final duty – she was again the target of the Luftwaffe and suffered a direct hit by a torpedo dropped from a German aircraft on 13 June, 1944. The explosion of the torpedo detonated her own ammunition in the forward magazine – blowing her virtually in half. She immediately sank taking with her over 150 of her crew. Less than a dozen men were saved. Today, her main section lies upright on a sandy sea bed at a depth of 52m. She stands over 6m high and lies on a small reef, which causes her to slope upwards slightly towards her front end, which, without her bows, presents a yawning gap, which is in fact the forward part of her engine room. She has a large gun on her stern and other anti-aircraft guns, some of which must have been firing frantically at her aerial attacker in the last moments of life. The bow section has yet to be discovered. Her bell has been recovered. *Boats: Lyme Regis 18 miles, Weymouth 21 miles.*

WARNING There are items of unexploded ammunition, including depth charges around this site.

**49 The Ram** 50 41.95N: 02 45.50W. The position given is the highest point of a fairly extensive rocky reef only ½ mile off East Beach at West Bay. The reef extends eastwards – almost to Burton Freshwater. The area is easily found by motoring straight out from the beach. Anywhere in the reef area you will find a rough, rocky bottom. The highest and most rugged part of the reef lies just east of a direct line out from the beach, opposite the westerly summit of East Cliff.

To just south of west from the high point of the reef, ½ mile away, is a large yellow outfall marker buoy. The rock area changes to a rather plain, gravely, sand sea bed approximately 100yds inshore of an east–west line drawn through this buoy. Depths on the reef are about 7m; but they drop off rapidly on the seaward side to about 15m. An ideal site for the inexperienced. *Launching: West Bay harbour or East Beach, both within a mile.*

**50 Minerva** 50 29.60N; 02 45.31W. This iron wreck should not be confused with the *Minerve*, the French submarine that lies under the cliff near Portland Bill (Site **121**). The wreck lies at a depth of 44m and is located almost at the centre of the compass rose on Admiralty chart No. 3315. In the past, this wreck was thought to be that of either the *Perriton* (now thought to be off the Devon coast at 50 24.19N; 03 01.31W) or the *Polkerris* but, mainly due to investigative diving and research carried out by members of the Wellington & Taunton SAC led by Nick Chipchase, the wreck has now been shown to be almost certainly the three-masted iron screwed Norwegian steamship of this name.

The Minerva, formerly the *Marie*, was sunk by a German submarine on 10 May, 1917. She was built in 1864, with a gross tonnage of 518 and measured 182ft 3in with a beam of 25ft. She was built in a German yard at Stettin, a port today in Poland. When sunk she was carrying only ballast, being on a journey back from Caen to Swansea to collect another cargo of Welsh coal.

The German builders must have put some thick plates of iron into her hull, for today she still sits upright and complete, lying north to south, facing south on a sand and shell sea bed and rising up 6m. The hull is unusually complete except for damage amidships on her starboard side. She has an unusual clipper bow – which, together with her two-cylinder compound engine and nearby reported position of sinking, virtually clinches her identification. The framework of her hatches and deck beams are still in position together with the clear access opening to the engine room. There is also some damage at the very stern end and the propeller has a blade missing. The Wellington & Taunton divers say she makes an excellent dive with lots of fish in and around her. *Boats: Lyme Regis 15 miles, Weymouth 19 miles.*

**51 Ull** 50 27.98N; 02 45.14W. The wreck at the above position has now been tentatively identified. This is primarily the result of diving surveys carried out by Nick Chipchase, and his fellow divers, of Wellington & Taunton SAC. Based on careful measurements of the hull, observation of the boilers, and type and size of engine and cargo, together with his research into the reported position of losses in this general area. Nick now thinks he has amassed enough evidence to be able to state fairly categorically that the wreck is that of the Norwegian Steamship *Ull*, a ship with three previous names: *Ole Lea, Peritia* and *Tosca.*

Built in 1880, she was not a large ship, being only 543 tons gross, measuring 168ft long with a beam of 26ft 6in. She was carrying a cargo of coal from Glasgow to Nantes when struck by a torpedo from a German submarine on 4 July, 1917. Today the ship lies upright on a sandy gravel sea bed at a depth of 50m. In places her structure stands up 5m high. The steel hull has collapsed in places but was still intact enough for precise measurements to be taken in May, 1995. On an earlier dive, in April of that year, before the successful identification, a steam whistle had been recovered, which had led to the ship becoming known as the "whistle wreck". She has a four-bladed propeller. Her midships engine and boiler, with remains of a funnel on top, plus forward and stern winches are easily seen. A certain amount of debris surrounds the wreck, particularly on her port side. She lies north to south, bows facing north. *Boats: Lyme Regis 16 miles, Weymouth 19 miles.*

**52 LST 531** 50 26.05N: 02 44.65W. This is the more southerly of the two LSTs lost by the Americans during exercise *Tiger* in the dark early hours of 28 April, 1944; the other is at Site **56**, approximately two miles to the north-east. [This information differs from that given in the 1995 edition of the companion volume *Dive South Devon*, but based on more recent diving reports the authors believe that it is correct at the time of going to press.]

The *LST 531* was hit by two torpedoes during a surprise attack by German E-boats. The second hit caused ammunition to explode, following this, she turned over and sank within 7 minutes. A total of 424 of the American navy and army personnel aboard perished. Today she lies on the sea bed upside down in 50m. Her open bow doors are pointing to the south. Swimming into her hold, the visiting diver will see a paraphernalia of lorries and military equipment – a time capsule, undisturbed since that terrible disaster. *Boats: Lyme Regis 19 miles, Weymouth 19 miles.*

**53 Trito** 50 22.60N; 02 44.40W. The *Trito* was a coastal steamship of 1057 gross tons, employed in the coal trade, when she was bombed and sunk by a German aircraft on 20 September, 1940. On board she had a cargo of coal, loaded at Port Talbot for Shoreham in Sussex.

After the attack and sinking there were only two survivors out of her crew of 23. She had been built in Holland in 1921 and was fitted with a triple-expansion steam engine. Sea bed depth is 58m and she stands up to 10m with her bows blown off. *Boats: Lyme Regis 23 miles, Weymouth 21 miles.*

**54 Recoil** 50 26.37N; 02 44.02W. Lying midway between the two LSTs lost by the Americans in the *Tiger* convoy is a previously unknown small wreck. Nick Chipchase of Wellington & Taunton SAC has devoted a lot of time and research into the wrecks in this area, and after diving this wreck in 1995, he states that all the evidence points to it being His Majesty's requisitioned trawler, the diesel driven *Recoil*, formerly the *Blakenburgh*. She went missing while out on anti-invasion patrol on 28 September, 1940, and nothing was ever found of her except a smell of diesel in her patrol area. A loud explosion had been heard just after 9 that evening.

In late October of that year a crew member was found dead in the sea. From the evidence, it is assumed she struck a mine. The wreck, which Nick has surveyed, is on a sandy sea bed at a depth of 52m. It stands several metres high and is orientated north-west to south-east There seems to be a gap in the middle of the wreck, so Nick says the stern section could be broken off and lying separated by some 20 or 30ft. *Boats: Lyme Regis 19 miles, Weymouth 19 miles.*

**55 Remindo** 50 26.17N; 02 43.64W. At this position is a wreck that up to now has been an unknown. Early in the 1996 season, Nick Chipchase of Wellington & Taunton SAC carried out a series of survey dives onto this wreck from the Lyme Regis charter boat *Miss Pattie*. He found a small coaster of approximately 250 gross tons with a triple-expansion three-cylinder engine and one boiler situated amidships. An unusual feature of the engine is that the largest (low pressure) cylinder is broken open on the port side exposing the piston. The wreck is upright and fairly intact, except for two broken down sections of hull on the starboard side, one on either quarter. Both the high bow and the low stern are intact.

Together with obtaining precise measurements of the hull, Nick recovered two important clues to the ship's identity – one a live round of 303 ammunition, the other a part of an electrical insulator marked "Admiralty Patt. 463A" and thought to be part of a voltage reducer. On the deck area, at either side of the boiler room, are two curious circular hatches of 1m diameter, possibly coaling holes. No winches were apparent anywhere. From his observations, measurements, and artefacts, Nick matches the wreck to the 256 ton *Remindo*, a trawler hired by the Admiralty in 1917, measuring 117ft with a beam of 27ft 5in and lost on 2 February, 1918 – cause unknown, yet another mystery awaiting patient investigation. The wreck, in Lyme Bay, lies east–west with bows to the west, on a sand and gravel sea bed, at a depth of 50m, and rises up 3m. *Boats: Lyme Regis 18 miles, Weymouth 18 miles.*

**56 LST 507** 50 27.15N; 02 43.55W and 50 27.10N; 02 43.46W. The first position above is where the bow section of this vessel lies. Her stern section lies at the second position some 200yds to the south-east. [This information differs from that given in the 1995 edition of the companion volume *Dive South Devon*, but based on more recent diving reports the authors believe that it is correct at the time of going to press.]

This is one of the World War Two wrecks of the American *Tiger* exercise, which was caught by German E-boats during the early hours of 28 April, 1944. The Americans were carrying out a full scale simulated operation, which was to culminate in a landing across Slapton Sands in Devon. Steaming across Lyme Bay in darkness, the LSTs were packed tight with thousands of men and scores of vehicles, all carrying copious amounts of live ammunition and fully fuelled up.

As we now know, many things went wrong and almost a thousand men perished. Of these, 131 were accounted for when *LST 507*, after being hit amidships by a torpedo, became a roaring furnace of vehicle fuel spilling from the fully fuelled tanks of the 13 trucks on her outside deck and the 22 amphibious DUKWs in her hold. We are indebted to Nick Chipchase of Wellington & Taunton SAC for information on this and other casualties of this convoy, together with much information on adjacent wrecks. Nick has dived these wrecks many times to carefully ascertain their identity and has gone on to contact American survivors of this tragedy.

*LST 507* now lies at a depth of 50m on a sandy sea bed, her bows are upside down with her ramp to the west. Her stern section, best preserved, is also upside down, showing her twin propellers and massive beach landing skegs on her bottom. Now that she is lying silent on the sea bed, it is perhaps the duty of any visiting diver to pause and reflect on the death and destruction that took place here. *Boats: Lyme Regis 18 miles, Weymouth 18 miles.*

**57 Unknown wreck** 50 39.50N; 02 43.17W. Despite searches, no wreck has so far been found in this area, so the location is approximate. There are however, continuing reports of debris and spoil being found. Depth 25m. *Launching: West Bay 3 miles, Lyme Regis 8 miles.*

**58 Salsette** 50 29.66N; 02 43.02W. It is not necessary for us to extol the virtues of a dive on this wreck, for, if the reader is approaching a stage of experience that allows a deep offshore dive, they will already have encountered at least several divers with a sort of glazed look in their eyes who go around constantly raving about there experience of diving the *Salsette.*

Why is this? Primarily, this is the wreck of a huge ship. Despite her depth she causes a boil of water at the surface at most stages of the tide. Built in 1908, in Scotland by J. Caird & Company, she measures 440ft long, has a beam of 53ft, and was a massive 5842 gross tons. Her steam engines developed a colossal

*The P&O liner Salsette (Site 58) was custom built for a fast run between Britain and India. From a depth of 48m in Lyme Bay she is now yielding many items.*
Photo: Imperial War Museum

*One of the two solid gold*
*Edwardian watch chains*
*recovered from the wreck*
*of the liner Salsette.*
Photo: A. Smith collection

10,000hp, delivered to two giant bronze screws (one still on her). She was and still is owned by P&O, and had been built to run the express mail service between Aden and Bombay, but during the years of World War One, this very fast liner was used on the London to Bombay service.

It was on such an outward journey – on 20 July, 1917 – that she was hit on her starboard side by a torpedo fired by the German submarine *UB-40*. Fourteen men died almost instantly, and she was gone in an amazing 28 minutes. For a graphic description of the history of the *Salsette* and the dreadful events of that day there is no better source than Volume 2 of *Great British Wrecks* by Kendall McDonald. The ship is on her port side and lies on a line north to south, bows to the north. Her starboard rails are therefore mainly her uppermost part, at a depth of 32m. She had at least three hundred portholes on each side and only a very small number of those on her uppermost side have been removed. Her sloping decks give many choices of access to her mainly untouched interior with its plethora of luxury fittings, mandatory for a vessel of her class. Anglers also rave about this wreck – not about the fancy brass fittings, but about the torpedo-sized pollack that abound here.

The usual method employed to dive the wreck by local charter boats is to drop a shot amidships just up tide of her highest point. Depending on the direction of tide, the last of the current before the slack will push the line either across the hull to the upper rail, or alternatively, across her deck and again to the upper starboard rail. The descending diver can then be quite sure to find the highest point of the wreck and easily choose the depth to dive. The only negative item is that the bell has already been recovered! *Boats: Lyme Regis 15 miles, Weymouth 17 miles.*

WARNING The sea bed is at a depth of 44m, but beware of the scour at her bow and stern that gives an extra 5m of depth. This wreck is an advanced dive, and it is easy to be tempted to a much deeper depth down the sloping deck than was planned. Another feature to beware of is lost monofilament fishing lines.

**59  Grane**  50 29.23N; 02 42.78W. This Norwegian steamship was carrying coal from Swansea to Rouen when sunk by a torpedo on 9 March, 1918. She lies north to south, only 300yds to the south-east of the *Salsette*. The depth to sea bed is 45m and the fairly well broken wreck stands up to 7m high. The *Grane* was built by Bergens MV of Bergen in 1899. A three-cylinder triple-expansion engine was fitted. Her measurements were 230ft long with a beam of 30ft. She was 1122 gross tons. The wreck has been positively identified by the recovery of her bell by a London diver. *Boats: Lyme Regis 16 miles, Weymouth 17 miles.*

**60  Unidentified wreck**  50 29.46N; 02 42.78W. Lying approximately 250yds due north of the Grane (Site **59**), and very near the huge wreck of the *Salsette* (Site **58**), is another small wreck very rarely dived. It consists of ribs and frames sticking out of the sea bed. There is a lead keel and probably brass fittings remaining. It is said to be the remains of a French yacht, and may well predate the wrecks nearby. Depth to the sea bed is 44m. *Boats: Lyme Regis 16 miles, Weymouth 17 miles.*

**61  Unidentified trawler**  50 23.80N; 02 42.00W. In this position, at a depth of 52m, lies a small steam-driven vessel, thought to be a trawler or tug. Little information is available, but divers of the Wellington & Taunton SAC are investigating. *Boats: Lyme Regis 21 miles, Weymouth 19 miles.*

**62  St Dunstan**  50 38.27N; 02 41.98W. Sunk by a mine on 23 September, 1917 with the loss of two lives, this 200ft iron vessel now stands 8m proud of the sea bed at a depth of 27m. Although built as a bucket dredger, the *St Dunstan* is believed to have been working as a minesweeper at the time of her sinking. Divers report that she is upside down, but a strange feature is that all her engine gauges are the correct way up. Perhaps she has broken and twisted. *Launching: West Bexington 2½ miles, West Bay 5 miles. Boats: Lyme Regis 10 miles.*

*The tug Buccaneer (Site 63), here seen berthed in Portland Naval Base, was accidentally sunk in Lyme Bay.*

**63 Buccaneer** 50 29.37N; 02 41.70W. This wreck is the 840 gross ton British armed tug *Buccaneer*. She was one of the resident tugs of the Portland Naval base. On 26 August, 1946 she was out in Lyme Bay towing a floating target for gunnery practice by the new destroyer HMS *St James*. During firing, a 4.5in shell from the destroyer hit the *Buccaneer* instead of the target – badly damaging and sinking her.

The tug, built in 1937 by Flemming & Ferguson, measured 165ft long with a beam of 32ft. She was equipped with a three-cylinder triple-expansion engine, transmitting power to a single screw. Her armament consisted of one 3-inch gun, mounted on her bow. After all this time she still sits upright and intact on the sea bed. Depth to the sea bed is 44m. The wreck stands up 8m and lies east to west. Her bell has been recovered. *Boats: Lyme Regis 17 miles, Weymouth 17 miles.*

**64 Pomeranian** 50 33.57N; 02 41.33W. In many a crowded bar, particularly in the Dorset area, a chance conversation on diving and shipwrecks will quickly lead to someone speaking up and asking: "Have you dived on the ship at Weymouth with all the diver's helmets on it?" For somehow, probably helped by past media attention, the *Pomeranian* and her cargo have caught popular imagination and become firmly established in Dorset folklore. But then it is true that the manifest of her cargo of Government stores included 16 diver's helmets.

Ted Nicklin of Weymouth recovered one of these in 1970 and on the same dive Brian King (formerly of the Weymouth Scuba Centre) discovered a second one, but his lifting line became detached and the helmet never surfaced. It was never seen again, nor have the other 14, unless someone somewhere harbours a large collection and a very deep secret! There are other items of cargo, which, for the diver, are very collectable, and can be found within her hull or scattered on the sea bed. These are smelting crucibles, manufactured by the famous

*This diver's helmet, recovered by Weymouth diver Ted Nicklin from the wreck of the Pomeranian, has drawn much attention to her listed cargo of 16 of these items. The other 15 have still not been found.*
Photo: Authors

pottery company, Royal Doulton, and have the company's name embossed into the base. They are beaker shaped with a pouring lip. There are three sizes, the smallest being 9½in high and having a 7in diameter at the top. The small sizes were packed inside the larger ones, the largest being approximately three times bigger.

This is a large ship of 4,241 tons gross and was owned by Canadian Pacific Ocean Services Ltd of Montreal. She had been requisitioned by the Government and was under the control of the Allan Line Steam Ship Company when, sailing from London to Newfoundland, she was torpedoed on 15 April, 1918, by the German submarine *UB-77*. No less than 55 of her crew, including the Captain were killed. The *Pomeranian* (formerly the *Grecian Monarch*) sits 7m upright, but with a heavy list to starboard on a flat rock sea bed. There are times when this rock is clear and clean, but there seems to be long cycles of time when she is quite deep in very silty sand, which covers the lower parts of the hull. It was during a clear period that the helmets were spotted when access was gained through a hole, deep down on her hull. Was this where the torpedo hit?

She lies roughly east to west. Now, after all this time lying on the sea bed, she is slowly starting to collapse. This has become most apparent on her centre section in recent years. There is a large chunk of her off to the north-west, this can just be discerned from the main wreck during periods of good visibility. Depth 33m. An excellent dive. A bell has been recovered. *Boats: Lyme Regis 13 miles, Weymouth 16 miles.*

**65 Romsdalen** 50 23.22N; 02 40.06W. This is a single screwed, armed British steamship of 2548 gross tons, measuring 300ft long with a beam of 40ft. She had been built in 1895 and was sunk on 17 February, 1917, by the German submarine *UB-84*. Eleven of her crew were lost. She was on a voyage from Swansea to Calais with a cargo of patent fuel – pieces of coal marked with an insignia.

It is this cargo that now helps with her identification, because the large upright wreck at the above position – which in the past was sometimes confused with the *Lord Stamp* – has holds full of this fuel and a gun on the stern. Divers report she is intact, except for her superstructure, which has either been swept or is collapsing. Sea bed depth is 54m, height of wreck is 14m. *Boats: Lyme Regis 22 miles, Weymouth 19 miles.*

**66 Sidon** 50 32.96N; 02 38.43W. The British S class submarine sank twice. The first time was in Portland Harbour on 16 June, 1955 after an explosion in her torpedo bay, while moored alongside other submarines. Valiant attempts by members of her own crew and crews from other boats to evacuate the injured and trapped crew from her smoke filled interior were only partially successful for she flooded and sank within 20 minutes, taking 13 men with her and leaving some of the would be rescuers themselves to be rescued out of the water.

The *Sidon* was later raised and sunk again – intentionally – in 1957, in her

*A graphic illustration of a tragic accident in 1955. The torpedoes on the submarine Sidon were driven by hydrogen peroxide; this propellant caused an explosion in the torpedo bay and she quickly sank, inside the Portland Naval Base. Thirteen crew were lost. Photo: Authors' collection.*

*The S-class submarine Sidon (Site 66) as she was before her catastrophic sinking inside Portland Naval Base.*

present position, for use as an ASDIC target (ASDIC is a device for detecting submarines). She lies north-west to south-east at a sea bed depth of 34m and rises 8m off the sea bed. She is intact and makes an excellent dive. *Boats: Lyme Regis 15 miles, Weymouth 15 miles.*

**67 Scaldis** 50 34.27N; 02 38.34W. The *Scaldis* was an 80ft motor fishing vessel. Both the ship and crew were from Brixham in Devon. She went missing in a stormy period while trawling in the Lyme Bay area between 25 and 29 January, 1974. No distress signal was ever picked up and despite intensive searches, no sign of the vessel or her crew could be found.

Over twelve months later, a Weymouth fishing boat snagged her nets into an obstruction where none had existed in the past. Divers from the BSAC Special Projects Group were called in by the fishing boat's skipper to recover his valuable gear, which was left buoyed off. The Special Project divers – one of whom was Brian King, formerly of the Weymouth Scuba Centre – investigated what had snagged the nets and there, at a sea bed depth of 32m, they discovered the *Scaldis* sitting perfectly intact.

Subsequently, Brian participated in an investigation of the wreck for the Devon and Cornwall Police. The vessel's life rafts were recovered and her hull inspected, but no apparent reason could be determined for her sinking, until it was noticed that her beam trawling wire was deployed. It took a relay of three divers to swim that wire, each tying a surface marker onto the wire at the end of the section he had swum. Brian explained, it should have taken only two men to swim the distance, but the second man down, went the wrong way only discovering his error when he arrived back at the wreck!

The third man down got to the trawl end of the wire and almost certainly discovered the cause of the vessel's loss – for there, snagged into the vessel's trawl was a World War Two German aircraft. It was assumed that the sudden weight of the aircraft on the beam trawl, in rough surface conditions, had caused the *Scaldis* to spin round and immediately capsize, giving her crew no time to escape or send an SOS message.

The wreck is still as she was found, lying on her starboard side at an angle of 35°. The aft positioned wheelhouse is intact with a toilet a feature of her interior. Above the wheelhouse is the remains of what may be a gantry. There are small round windows low down on the rear of the wheelhouse. Her propeller can be seen easily, located in a nozzle, forward of an intact rudder. Alongside, on the sea bed, on the port quarter, is a trawl beam and net. The boat itself is clear of any nets. Diving reports say her starboard side is a mass of beautiful plumose anemones. *Boats: Lyme Regis 13 miles, Weymouth 16 miles.*

**68 Barge** 50 33.90N; 02 38.06W. Almost midway between the wrecks of the *Scaldis* and the *Landrail*, at this position is what is best described as a barge. It sits level, rising up 1m from a fine sandy sea bed at 32m. The strange feature of this vessel is the fact that it has a wooden deck, very unusual for such a craft.

Nick Chipchase of Wellington & Taunton SAC investigated this site in 1996. He recorded that the box like section measures 30ft by 12ft. A heavy chain is fixed to an eye at one corner and runs back over the deck and off to the sea bed at one side. Years ago, the Navy had floating targets moored in this area. This may be one that stopped floating. *Boats: Lyme Regis 15 miles, Weymouth 15 miles.*

**69 Martha** 50 27.25N; 02 38.05W. This wreck is a steamer of 653 gross tons. She was launched in September, 1905 at Grangemouth, and became a World War One casualty. When she was hit by a torpedo from a German submarine she was reported to have sunk extremely rapidly on 7 March, 1918. She measured 185ft long with a 27ft beam.

She is upright on a sand and shale sea bed. Her sides and bulkheads are still intact. Her highest point is 5m above the general sea bed depth of 50m. Weymouth charter boats *Tiger Lily* and *Channel Chieftain* dive her fairly regularly. Visiting divers report an abundance of lobsters, many portholes still on her, and that she is more intact than would normally be expected of a wreck of her age. *Boats: Weymouth 15 miles.*

**70 L24** 50 22.50N; 02 37.79W. This British submarine was lost with her full complement of 36 men on 10 January, 1924 in a very sad peace-time accident. On Fleet exercise off Portland, she had surfaced and found herself directly under the bows of the battleship HMS *Resolution*, which, being under way, came straight on and rammed her forward of the conning tower. She immediately sank to the sea bed.

She was discovered in 1984 by Andy Smith, when he was called out by a fisherman whose trawl net had snagged an unknown object. Andy was very surprised to find an apparently undamaged submarine lying upright with all hatches closed, except the front torpedo loading hatch, which was wide open. Soon, however, he noticed a deep cleft in the upper part of the hull forward of the conning tower on the starboard side. This looked as though the submarine had been hit by a giant axe. This damage obviously helped with the wreck's identification.

The *L24* was less than four years old, having been completed by Vickers in 1920, her construction having begun under the Emergency War Programme of 1916. She measured 239ft long with a beam of 24ft and had a displacement of 1,080 tons. Her armaments included a 4in deck gun and four 21in torpedo tubes at her bow. She was powered by a Vickers diesel engine. She lies at a sea bed depth of 55m, but divers report an extra 2m (which must be a scour) around her bow and stern. The conning tower stands up some 5 to 6m. *Boats: Weymouth 20 miles.*

**71 HMS Landrail** 50 33.74N; 02 37.51W. There has been, in the past, a lot of confusion as to the large steel wreck in this position. At first everyone agreed it was HMS *Hazzard*, until research showed she was on the sea bed to the east of the Isle of Wight. The then consensus of opinion, after diving reports, was that it was HMS *Bittern*, a C class torpedo gun boat. Both ships had been lost through collisions in 1918. Further research and diving reports indicate that this wreck is definitely HMS *Landrail*. The *Bittern* has yet to be found and is probably in very deep water – in excess of 50m.

HMS *Landrail*, of 790 gross tons, was built in 1886 at Devonport dockyard, one of the Curlew class of steel gun vessels. The ship measured 195ft long with a beam of 28ft. She was fitted with a reciprocating steam engine of 350hp that enabled her to achieve 14½ knots. Her armaments, besides guns, included one bow torpedo tube and two torpedo launching carriages on her deck. At the time of her sinking, she was based at Portland Naval Base, and was being used as a target ship. When needed she was towed out into the Lyme Bay firing range area.

It was after such a firing exercise when, on 4 October, 1906, while on tow back to Portland Harbour, that she suddenly sank, claiming the life of one man. She still stands 6m high and makes a good dive. Her hull lies north-west to south-east, with her bows listing well over to port side. Sea bed depth is 31m. *Boats: Lyme Regis 15 miles, Weymouth 15 miles.*

**72 Reef off Abbotsbury** 50 38.15N; 02 37.30W. Almost one mile due south of the end of the road to the beach at Abbotsbury is an extensive reef. The area is also known as the Swyre Ledges. The position given is a high point clearly shown on the chart. The reef and rock outcrops form a band almost ¾ mile wide, which extends eastwards for many miles, finally approaching Chesil Beach at a shallow angle. The reefs are not continuous along the entire length, but disappear here and there under a flat, gravel-and-sand bottom. Depths are in order of 22 to 26m.

The section of the reef directly off Abbotsbury is easily identified by the pot-markers along it. It is well fished by inshore boats from West Bay, and is, needless to say, a good ground for crab and lobsters. Scallops are also found sheltered between the reefs. Tidal currents run up to 1.5 knots at times on springs. *Launching: Abbotsbury Beach, 1 mile.*

**73 Unidentified wreck** 50 21.30N; 02 37.22W. The wreck at the above position, which is just 11 miles south-west of Portland Bill, has, in the past, been listed as the British submarine *L24*, but that vessel is now known for sure to lie 1½ miles to the north. The wreck is now said to be a small coaster or trawler, but there seems to be no reliable diving reports – or is there a secret and a surprise here? Sea bed depth is 57m. *Boats: Weymouth 19 miles.*

*Now on show in the Nothe Fort at Weymouth, this propeller from an RAF Mosquito lost in 1944 was recovered 50 years later by divers from the Dive Dorset Adventure Sport Diving Club. This exciting discovery was featured in the national press, after which a number of relatives of missing World War Two RAF air crew contacted diving officer Mike Bowles (back row, fourth from left) in the hope of at last finding out where their loved ones had died – a poignant reminder of the sacrifices and loss of life that many artefacts on the sea bed represent.*

**Portland Bill lighthouse.**
*Photo: Roy Smallpage.*

# AREA 2:

# Chesil, Portland and Weymouth Bay

The area between Abbotsbury in the west and White Nothe in the east takes in Chesil Beach, the Isle of Portland, Portland Harbour and Weymouth Bay. The coastline is dominated by Portland and the large holiday town of Weymouth, where there are popular holiday beaches, but elsewhere, even in the peak holiday season, there are many stretches of almost deserted beach and cliff.

For the diver, this is Dorset's most popular wreck area. West of the Bill are many almost untouched modern vessels that fell victim to the two World Wars. Divers from all over Britain come to visit these sites – and to cater for them a flotilla of extremely well equipped boats with first class skippers has grown up over the years.

For the shore diver, Chesil Beach is a graveyard of ancient sailing ships and the eastern end of the beach gives some of the most convenient – and possibly the finest – shore diving that can be found on the South Coast. Portland Harbour, with its sheltered wreck sites, is all that a diver needs when the inevitable gales rise from the south and west.

Included in the text of many sites in this section are further reminders about tidal currents. These should be read and carefully noted. Tidal predictions for Portland can be obtained in table form from Admiralty Tide Table NP 200 or in extracted form from local dive shops. High water at Portland is, on average, one hour after high water at Devonport, and four hours forty minutes before high water at Dover.

---

**SAFETY WARNING**

Divers contemplating diving from the shore of Portland Island or taking boats into Portland waters, especially off the Bill, are advised to study in advance the Admiralty Tidal Stream Atlas *Approaches to Portland Shore* (NP 257). However, shore divers should note the caution on page 3 of this atlas and are advised to read the booklet *Tidal Streams between Portland Bill and St Albans Head* (Boldre Marine, 1998).

---

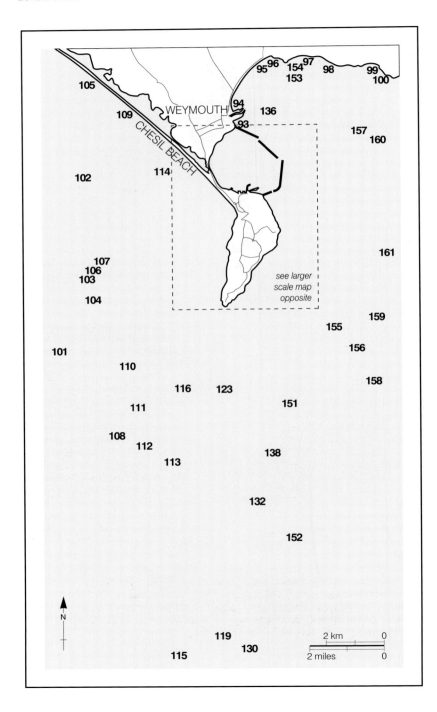

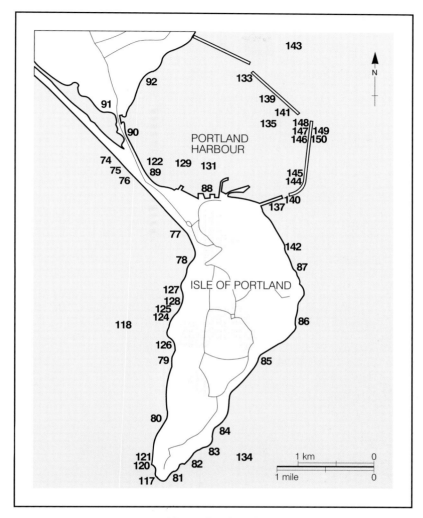

**Above: Detail of Portland and the harbour sites.**

Opposite: Dive sites in Area 2, Chesil, Portland and Weymouth Bay. This area is covered by Admiralty charts 3315 (Berry Head to Bill of Portland), 2255 (Approaches to Portland & Weymouth), 2610 (Bill of Portland to Anvil Point), 2268 (Portland Harbour); Tidal Stream Atlas: Approaches to Portland NP 257; Outdoor Leisure Map No. 15.

The average tidal range on springs is about 2m. There is a marked double-low throughout the area east of Portland Bill. An extremely important fact to note is that the height of the tide – or whether it is ebbing or flowing – bears no obvious relationship to the strength or direction of currents around Portland. Watch out, the unexpected can often happen in these waters.

For almost eight miles, CHESIL BEACH is divided from the mainland by the Fleet, a shallow channel of water. Most of the Fleet and the offshore area of Chesil is designated an area of scientific interest. From the beginning of April to the end of August parts of Chesil bank and beach become nesting areas for many birds including the little tern, a Grade I protected species.

From the beginning of April to the end of August, diving parties planning to cross the Fleet or approach close to Chesil Beach between Abbotsbury and Wyke Regis Bridging Camp from the sea should obtain clearance in advance. This may be done by contacting the Tern Warden on 01305 760579. It is illegal to walk on many areas of the bank during this period, and divers are asked not even to land on the beach except at the following three designated landing points. Here, small boats may be rowed across the Fleet, but the use of an engine is prohibited.

*Langton Herring* From the village follow a potholed road leading in 1 mile to the old Coastguard cottages and the shore of the Fleet at OS reference SY 606 813. Crossing the Fleet here gives access to the sea at a point adjacent to the wreck of the *Vera* (Site **105**).

*Moonfleet Hotel, Fleet* From Weymouth, take the B3157 Bridport road to Chickerell. At a small road island and large sign for the Moonfleet Hotel, turn

*Divers emerging from a shore dive at Chesil Beach. Getting out of the water here is not always as easy as this.* Photo: Roy Smallpage

left, and keep straight ahead down narrow roads for 1½ miles to the hotel. It is possible to use the hotel car park and, with permission, to carry a small inflatable through the courtyard of the hotel and down a path to the shore some 50yds away. The launching point is SY 616 805, which gives access to a point on the Chesil Beach ½ mile north-west of the *Hope* cannon site (Site **109**).

*Chickerell Crossing* From Weymouth Harbour follow the B3157 Bridport road towards Chickerell village for two miles. Turn down the lane on the left, immediately after passing the Army camp. This is Fleet Lane, a privately owned road. After just 400yds, and opposite a terrace of former Coastguard cottages, a gate leads onto a gravel track across farmland to the Fleet's shore at Hive Point. (Do not enter this farmland, but first carry straight on for a farther 300yds to East Fleet Farm. Permission has to be obtained from the farm to take vehicles to the shore.) Directly opposite the end of the track is a channel across to the Chesil Bank, between the flats that dry on low water springs. This channel was last dredged out in the 1940s and has now silted up to such a degree that it is difficult to row even a shallow inflatable at low water. Launching point is at SY 637 791. Cars should be left parked neatly at the side of the track. Crossing the Fleet here gains access to the Chesil Beach ¾ mile south-east of the *Hope* cannon site (Site **109**). East Fleet Farm (tel. 01305 785768) also operates a small touring caravan park for visitors. There is a reception office, a small shop and a public telephone kiosk.

# Shore Dive and Snorkel Sites

The map of Portland Harbour also shows the positions of site numbers 74 to 92 (see page 69).

**74 Royal Adelaide** SY 664 755. *Snorkel and aqualung.* If approaching by boat, the chart reference is 50 34.65N; 02 28.50W. The year of 1872 was a landmark in maritime folklore. On 5 December the *Marie Celeste* was discovered bereft of her crew, yet sailing uncannily along her appointed course. Meanwhile, in England on 14 November – seven days after the *Marie Celeste* had left New York – another ship was setting sail, this time from London, bound for Sydney. She was one of the latest of a new generation of huge iron sailing ships designed to carry goods and passengers around the world. Her name was the *Royal Adelaide*. It is pure coincidence that these two ships were at sea at the same time and that both were carrying large amounts of alcohol. Had fate not taken a cruel hand, the two ships would have crossed routes. They may even have been in sight of each other, for the *Marie Celeste* was bound for Gibraltar.

Whether or not alcohol had any bearing on what happened aboard the *Marie Celeste* we shall never know. But in Dorset, especially around Weymouth, they still talk of the part that Dutch gin played in the great tragedy that took place after the *Royal Adelaide* was wrecked on the Chesil on 25 November. There had been no large wreck there for some time, so when the 235ft ship came plunging along in a gale in plain view of the shore it was not long before wreck fever began to grip the whole district. The ship was eventually hurled on to the pebble beach shortly after dusk and all but five of those on board were rescued by breeches buoy. Still

*Vicki Hinchcliffe lends scale to the huge deck winch on the Royal Adelaide (Site 74).*
Photo: Authors

battered by the surf, the ship soon began to disgorge her contents on to the beach where a crowd of 3,000 now waited. Virtually the first items to be cast up and spread for almost a mile towards Portland were dozens of gin casks. The crowd went mad. Holes were punched in the casks, and men, women and boys drank long and deep. By dawn it is said that no less than 20 people lay dead on the beach having succumbed to exposure after falling senseless on to the cold wet pebbles.

The design of the *Royal Adelaide* is of interest as she was one of two sister ships (the other was the *Royal Sovereign*) built by William Patterson at Bristol in 1865. Launch reports noted that the hull was perfectly smooth, almost approaching enamel, due to a special coating. The part that remains of the hull today is being rapidly eroded by the Chesil pebbles during storms. Around the wreck usually swims a large shoal of pout whiting, and many pollack can normally be seen. Large crabs and a few lobsters make their home on the wreck, particularly in the first half of the year.

To dive the wreck of the *Royal Adelaide*, take the A354 Portland road from Weymouth. After crossing the Fleet at Ferrybridge, continue along the Chesil Beach road for 400yds before taking the first turning on the right into the large pay-and-display car park sited at the rear of the beach. Park near the entrance and kit up. The wreck may be found by following the transit diagram opposite. The sea bed descends steeply in a series of pebble terraces much like those on the beach above the water line. The wreck is situated at the point where the slope changes to being almost level. There are many other pieces of wreckage nearby, but you will know when you have found the main hull because of the huge foredeck winch

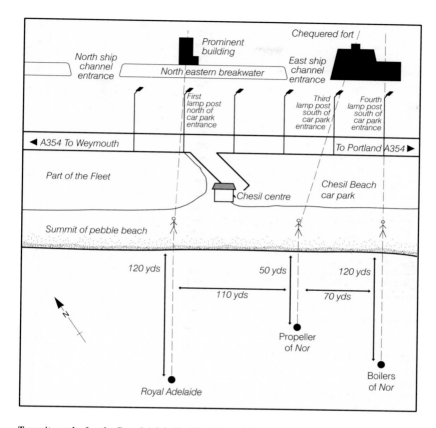

*Transit marks for the Royal Adelaide (Site 74) and the two parts of the Nor (Site 75) off Chesil beach. First line up on the transits at the summit of the pebble beach. In each case, following a line from this point – taking care to keep precisely at right angles to the sea edge – will lead to the site.*

perched high up within the wreck. This intact section is the chain locker lying on its starboard side, with the port side and decks eroded away.

In calm conditions this site is ideal for all grades of diver. The currents can be moderately strong, especially on springs, but they run parallel to the shore. The visibility can be anything up to 13m. Snorkel divers can choose whether to attempt deep dives to the wreck, or whether to dive the much shallower pebble terraces nearer the beach. Any wind above Force 3 from the south or south-west will usually preclude diving here. But an easterly or north-easterly, even up to almost Gale Force, will leave this site virtually unaffected. There are toilets in the car park, and a café provides refreshments. The nearest public telephone is 400yds along the road towards Weymouth.

**75 Nor** SY 665 775. *Snorkel and aqualung.* Before the days of modern electronic navigation, fog presented a terrible danger for shipping, and nowhere more than in the area of Portland and the Chesil. The reaction of damp air flowing in from the Atlantic over the cold waters of Lyme Bay can quickly precipitate very dense fog. Such a day was Tuesday, 18 January, 1887. The *Nor*, a Norwegian schooner rigged steamer, was on voyage from Cadiz to her home port of Bergen with a full cargo of salt. Of 943 tons register, she had a crew of 20 aboard. Her captain thought he was taking a course that would have put the steamer well clear of Portland Bill, and then was intending to turn around the island into Portland for coals.

The first inclination that all was not well was when the steamer suddenly came to a grinding and very swift halt impaled on the Chesil Beach. She had hit the pebble bank at a place very close to where the *Royal Adelaide* had met her end only fifteen years earlier. A continuous blowing of her steam whistle soon alerted the Coastguard and with their help all the crew, together with a cat and dog, were soon safe ashore.

Later, a heavy swell began to lift and bump her on the submerged bank. By late afternoon of the next day she had broken and completely disappeared, having been drawn down into the great maw of the ocean by the enormous undertow of the breaking surf. Her remains lie about 100yds south of the *Royal Adelaide*, at 12m at the base of the submerged terrace of the beach, but her great iron propeller lies much closer to the shore, halfway up the slope of the underwater pebbles. The massive propeller shaft which is usually covered by the pebbles, points straight to her boilers. On a bright day, at a depth of only 7m, besides being an interesting snorkel dive, the propeller, with one blade pointing directly to

*The Nor (Site 75) became a total wreck, another victim of Chesil Beach.*
Photo: Weymouth and Portland Museum

74

the surface makes a great subject for photography. To find this wreck from the *Royal Adelaide*, see the transit drawings on page 73.

WARNING  Like the adjacent *Royal Adelaide* (Site **74**) and tank landing craft (Site **76**), this is an extremely convenient shore dive and is excellent for any grade of diver, but do not enter the water if the waves are breaking on the beach any more than 1m high. In rough conditions getting in is still easy, but getting out becomes much more difficult.

**76  United States Tank Landing Craft**  SY 669 750. *Snorkel and aqualung.* If approaching by boat, use 50 34.41N; 02 28.22W. Friday 13 October, 1944, is still remembered by some in Weymouth and Portland district as a day of disaster. At this time, with the nation at war, there was a multitude of small military craft at sea off the south coast. The *United States Tank Landing Craft No. 2454* was one such vessel. Her fate was to be caught in a cruel gale with her two diesel engines failed. Driven helplessly on to the Chesil Beach, she went down with the loss of nine of her twelve crew and two local Coastguards who went to her aid.

Today, half the vessel is still where she finally sank 100yds off the beach. Her other half is now broken into relatively small pieces which are 75yds to the

*Transit marks for the United States Tank Landing Craft (Site 76) off Chesil Beach. The observer must stand on top of the beach and line up the tops of the car park boundary posts, then walk 12yds along the summit of the beach towards the north-west (away from Portland). The wreck is then directly opposite, 100yds from the shore. The compass bearing is 240° magnetic.*

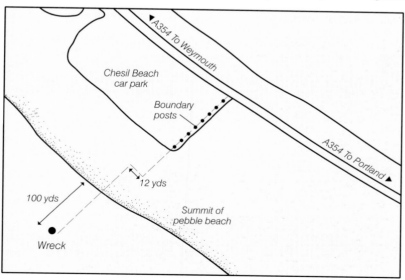

75

north-west and although above high water mark are buried under tons of pebbles beneath the beach. The main half of the craft, containing her twin engines and other machinery, now lies 12m down, and is covered in short weed and mussels. She stands upright, rises 6ft high off the sea bed, and makes a splendid dive.

To dive this wreck, park as recommended for the Royal Adelaide but leave your car at the Portland end of the car park. The wreck may be found by following the transit diagram on page 73. The underwater terrace of the beach descends at an angle of about 30°. The wreck is situated near the bottom of this terrace, where the angle of descent is much shallower. If you reach a point where the bottom starts to level out and sand patches start to occur, you have gone out beyond the wreck. In calm conditions this site is ideal for the beginner. Currents can be moderately strong, especially on springs, but they run parallel to the shore. Visibility off the Chesil is usually better when the tidal current is flowing. It can be anything up to 13m, but tends to drop around the slack, especially the low slack. Any wind above Force 3 from the south or south-west will usually preclude diving on this site. But an easterly or north-easterly, even up to almost Gale Force, will leave it virtually unaffected.

**77 Chesil Cove** SY 683 733. *Snorkel and aqualung, free launching.* This dive site area is huge. It consists of the last ½ mile of Chesil Beach before it joins the western cliff and shoreline of Portland Island and is one of the most popular and convenient shore dive sites on the South Coast. To reach the area, leave Weymouth on the Portland road, the A354. Cross the entrance to the Fleet at Ferrybridge, and keep straight along the Chesil Beach road towards Portland. At the roundabout system at the foot of Portland there is a choice of three car parks.

The large car park on the right is the Masonic or Victoria Square Car park – otherwise known as Parry's after the Subaquatics dive shop and air station run by Ian Parry. From here you carry your gear over the pebble bank to the sea. Fifty yards farther on is another large car park, next door to the Little Ship pub, again built right up against the rear of the pebble beach. From this car park an unsurfaced track leads shortly to another smaller car park at the side of the Cove House Inn, which gives direct access to a promenade and the beach. A fourth alternative is even farther along the bottom road towards Portland, where there is a car parking area in the centre of Chiswell (sometimes called Chesil). From here a short road, also with parking along it (Brandy Row), leads to the promenade on the summit of the beach.

For launching, the latter car park is best as it is closest to the summit of the beach and therefore also nearest the water's edge. Boats have to be carried over the promenade, down a short ramp and across the steep terraces of the pebble beach. It is easy to get an inflatable down to the water, but make sure members of your group do not go sneaking off home before they help to carry the boat back up-hill at the end of the day. Only boats that can be carried can be launched here.

Below water at Chesil Cove, by far the best area to dive is that between the Cove House Inn and where the pebbles give way to the rocks of Portland. Here the pebbles are very large, with patches of larger rocks among them. The sea bed descends in a series of terraces gradually levelling out at about 15m some 150yds from the shore. Here the scenery changes abruptly to clean, rippled sand inhabited by plaice and occasionally sole.

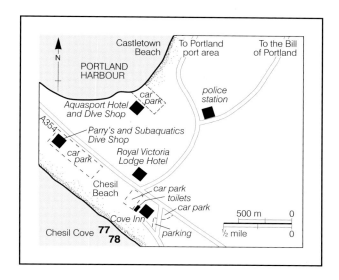

*Above: Chesil Cove and Castletown.*

*Below: Chesil Cove is completely sheltered from east winds by the western cliffs of Portland.* Photo: Authors

The best scenery is, however, found among the rocks and pebbles at 8 to 14m. In summer, many kinds of weed grow here giving a perfect habitat for a wide variety of life. Cuttlefish with their spaniel-like eyes can be seen, and John Dorys are not uncommon. Crabs and lobsters hide beneath the large rocks and under the large chunks of iron ships wrecked here. On a good day, with visibility up to 13m, this site can only be described as an underwater fairyland.

Currents are weak or almost absent at Chesil Cove. The site is ideal for any grade of diver and is thoroughly recommended for novices on their initial few open-water outings. They are able to have a very controlled dive here by being able to choose exactly what depth to go to, and never having to stray far from the beach. Snorkellers will find much to see among the rocks at the Portland end, where pebbles give way to huge boulders.

This site is extremely sheltered from the north and east, but anything above Force 3 from the south or west soon brings a swell crashing on to the beach and will probably preclude diving. In rough conditions, entering the sea is usually fairly easy, but getting out can be difficult and even dangerous. Boats can be swamped and badly scuffed on the beach. Shore divers on choppy days should always leave a lookout on the shore with a throwing rope to assist them through the surf at the end of their dive. Snorkellers can be of great assistance at this time in helping the cumbersome aqualung diver to get clear of the waves.

Coxswains of small boats need to keep a sharp lookout for pot lines, for the main potting area of the Chesil fishermen extends south from the beach, down the side of Portland. Within this area are many good and heavily dived sites, but relations with the fishing community here are excellent – *and it will be in the interest of all divers if we can keep them this way.*

The nearest public telephone is in Victoria Square outside the Royal Victoria Lodge Hotel or just 40yds up the hill from Chiswell, there are toilets in the middle car park and on the Portland end of the promenade.

**78 Tar Rocks** SY 681 727. *Snorkel and aqualung.* As with most of the Portland shore sites, reaching the water at Tar Rocks entails some expenditure of energy. Park in the village square at Chiswell, follow the promenade to its southern end, then take the footpath that runs parallel to the shoreline. At the end of the made-up part of this path just before a flight of stone steps is the start of a beach of football-sized white pebbles. From the car park to the beach is a 10-minute walk.

Within 100yds of the shore depths of 14m are found. At this depth a gravelly area is studded with huge rocks, some of which are the size of a double-decker bus. The scenery is exceptional, with kelp growing profusely on the upper sections of the rocks only. Here, large wrasse can be seen swimming in and out of the waving weed. Another attraction to divers on this site are the large crawfish that sometimes appear here in the summer months. This site is the most eastern in the English channel where crawfish are reported by divers. It is exposed to the south-west, and entry and exit are difficult through the boulders except when the sea is calm. Excellent conditions can be found here in a north or easterly wind – even one strong enough to prevent diving on almost every other site in Dorset. Snorkelling is excellent, but entry may prove difficult for a beginner using an aqualung.

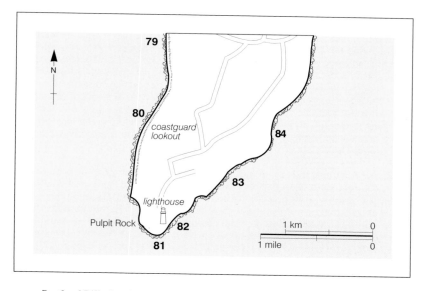

*Portland Bill, showing Mutton Cove to Wallsend Cove (Site 79), Solaway (Site 80), the Tip of Portland Bill (Site 82), Sandholes (Site 84) and the locations of the Lendora (Site 81) and the Marguerita (Site 83).*

**79 Mutton Cove to Wallsend Cove** *Snorkel site only.* Along the western shoreline of Portland, exposed to the Atlantic storms that sweep in across Lyme Bay, are the most spectacular cliffs in Dorset. There are three steep footpaths where it is possible to scramble down the cliffs to a shore composed of immense boulders. The names and locations of these paths are Barnes Tip Path (SY 680 711), Goat Track Path (SY 680 708) Barrow Hill Path (SY 679 705). Access to the water is through very large rocks, which tend to be slippery with short weed growth. In the water, the snorkel diver will immediately find depths of 8m with a further gradual drop to about 11m within 50yds of the shore. The sea bed is studded with huge blocks of stone that have split from the cliff face. The fish life is prolific, with fair-sized bass and pollack to be seen. Kelp grows thickly on the upper surfaces of the shallower rocks.

**80 Solaway** SY 676 692. *Snorkel site only.* This is reached by a precipitous path down the cliff near the old Coastguard lookout. There is convenient parking 600yds away, in the large car park near the lighthouse at Portland Bill. The safest times to snorkel at Solaway are 4 to 6 hours after high water at Portland. The time to hitch a lift on the ferocious current around the shoreline is in the last hour before high water at Portland. *Do not, however, attempt this hair-raising exercise unless accompanied by a local expert.* This site is for the experienced snorkeller only. The nearest telephone is a public kiosk a few yards south-east of the car park at the Bill, near the cafés.

**81 Lendora** SY 677 682. *Snorkel and aqualung.* On 8 September, 1951, a white yacht was noticed to be in trouble just off Portland. She had picked up a pot line on her propeller. Before any assistance could be organised, she drifted onto a close-in ledge of rock which juts out from the shore at a place known as Bill Point, offshore of the obelisk, near the lighthouse at Portland Bill. She was the 15 ton *Lendora.* Her keel can still be found lying in a deep gully close to the beach. Currents are weak close inshore, but inexperienced snorkellers should be carefully supervised for there is, only a very short distance away to the west and for many hours each day, a fearsome current running southwards down the western side of the island and at the tip of the Bill. Any who stray into it are carried directly offshore and out to sea.

**82 Tip of Portland Bill** SY 678 683. *Snorkel and aqualung site, free launching.* From the very tip of The Bill for a distance of about 500yds north-eastwards there is a shoreline of low cliffs with beaches varying from tumbled rounded boulders to expanses of bare, flat rock. It is possible to scramble down to the water's edge in quite a few places, including several directly opposite the lighthouse. In addition, two sets of rough steps are cut in the low cliff. It is just possible to carry and launch a small inflatable if the sea is dead calm.

Shore divers and snorkellers should not swim more than about 40yds offshore, and should keep to the east of the lighthouse where the tidal currents are comparatively gentle. The water is very clear, with depths down to 6m on the rocks and ledges of the immediate shoreline. Crabs and occasional lobsters are often seen here. Kelp grows around the shoreline but is not thick enough to prevent exploration of the gullies.

*Off the tip of Portland Bill there is a triangle of still water.*

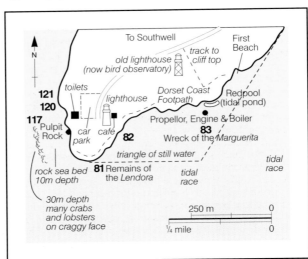

It must be emphasised that very strong currents are to be encountered only a little way out from this shoreline, and the safest time to dive is between 3 hours before and 3 hours after high water at Portland. Diving at any other time can be extremely dangerous, especially if you stray offshore or west of the lighthouse. This site is ideal for divers disciplined enough to stay among the rocks on the shore's edge. Car parking here is good, with a large car park by the lighthouse only a few yards away from the shore.

**83  Red Pool and the Marguerita**  SY 683 688. *Snorkel and aqualung.* Red Pool is a beautiful little site, ideal for beginners and more experienced aqualung divers. It is a very exciting place for snorkellers. Besides this, on a warm summer day it is an ideal venue for a young family. To find this beach follow the road across Portland, through Weston to Southwell, and leave Southwell as though heading for the Bill. Approximately ¾ mile short of the Bill, just before passing the old lighthouse, there is a track leading down between small fields to the cliff top 100yds away. Once at the cliff top, an easy path leads straight onto the beach. Access to the sea for the cumbersome aqualung diver is easy at all stages of the tide for smooth ledges can be walked down.

There is a triangle of sea at Portland Bill, the base of which is on the shoreline. It extends roughly from 400yds to the north-east of Red Pool and in the opposite direction for ½ mile to the south-west, to a point on the shore opposite the lighthouse – the apex of the triangle being approximately 200yds offshore. Within this triangle, especially at the Red Pool end, currents are negligible at all states of the tide. Up to 100yds from the shore, the sea off Red Pool is almost always still. But beyond this mark, a great swirling current runs south-westwards out to sea for 11 out of every 12 hours. You can see this current from the cliff top. On springs it thunders over Portland Ledge just to the east, hits the very base of the cliff and is deflected out to sea leaving the still patch of water off Red Pool. It hardly needs saying that a diver who carelessly swims out into this moving maelstrom will be taken rapidly out to sea and beyond the help of fellow divers on shore. Depths off Red Pool run down to 9m, especially to the north-east. There are wide, bare rock ledges with small drop-offs and, where the ledges are heavily undercut, long, shallow caves. Kelp grows profusely in places, but there are patches of almost white gravel. Pollack abound on this site, and crabs and the occasional lobster are also seen.

Because Red Pool faces south-east it remains sheltered and reasonably calm even when a strong south-westerly is blowing. The beach can, however, be affected by swell if the sea is rough or a wind is blowing from due south or east. In these conditions entering the water with an aqualung is hazardous. But with care snorkellers can safely dive here even when a large swell is running (making the beach a favourite place for local surfers). Diving at Red Pool is ideal at any state of the tide. The visibility is excellent, even after a storm.

The wreck found here is that of the *Marguerita*, a single-screwed fishing trawler that sank in fierce seas on 11 December, 1946. Built in 1919 at Thorne in Yorkshire, she was first registered at Hull in 1919 before being transferred to Milford Haven in 1929. She was later sold to her last captain, Bruno Nielson, who was planning to sail her back to his native Denmark. The *Marguerita* is easily found. On low spring tides the propeller and its shaft partially dry and can be seen up against the rock ledge.

*The propeller and engine parts and boiler of the*
*Marguerita show on low water springs.* Photo: Authors

**84 Sandholes** SY 687 692. *Snorkel and aqualung.* Follow the road across Portland and through Weston to Southwell. Take the only road to Portland Bill until, ½ mile along on the left, a pair of crane winches will plainly be seen on the rim of the cliff a field's length away. Park off the road at the top of a public footpath, which leads directly to the two cranes. Just 70yds to the east of the easterly crane is a scramble down a boulder and scree covered slope to a beach of boulders where, if the sea is calm, it is possible to enter the water.

WARNING For only a very short time in each tide cycle is it possible to dive at Sandholes. The best time is around three hours before high water at Portland, but do not attempt a dive here of any description without a local guide. Caught by the current, a diver will not be taken along the coast, but carried straight out to sea.

Needless to say, the underwater scenery at Sandholes is terrific, with ledges of rock stretching out from the cliff-base to deeper water. Fairly close to the cliff depths run down to 7m, making an ideal spot for snorkellers. There is plenty of life, including a profusion of large crabs. Immediately south-west of this site is a

*There is beautiful underwater scenery at Sandholes, but it is not an easy shore dive.* Photo: Roy Smallpage

*The ketch Reliance drove deep into a sea cave near Portland Bill in 1949 and later broke up.* Photo: Weymouth and Portland Museum

large cave. It was here that the ketch *Reliance* impaled herself on 3 June, 1949. Part of the engine, a twin cylinder diesel, can still be seen lying on the sea bed with other bits and pieces within the mouth of the cave.

**85 Church Ope Cove** SY 687 710. *Snorkel and aqualung.* To find this site, drive across Portland to Easton and continue straight on down the wide street called Wakeham. At the southern end you will see the Mermaid Inn on the left. Park on the road here, or continue 75yds to a car park on the right. The route to the cove is near the Portland Museum just before the right-hand bend, and is clearly marked. It consists of a narrow road (Church Ope Road) which first winds between cottages and then, after a metal barrier barring vehicles, leads between high stone walls to the top of a long flight of steps descending to the beach – a walking distance of ½ mile.

The cove itself can look like a scene from the Greek Islands in summer, with clear water, and white rocks gleaming in the sun. Access to the water is over a beach of large, rounded stones, which give way to rippled white sand at low tide. On either side of the cove are large rocks, studding the sand and providing islands of weed inhabited by many wrasse. Flatfish can be seen on the sand in the centre of the cove, and mullet and bass are a regular feature too. The sea bed descends to 10m within the cove, but goes deeper farther out.

Beyond the confines of the cove's small headlands there is a current which for 10 hours out of 12 runs towards the south-west, roughly parallel to the shore. This current can be quite strong at times, but is weak within the cove. Diving is always theoretically possible at Church Ope, but the best time is between three hours and one hour before high water at Portland. The main draw-back at this site is the tendency, in anything but very calm weather, for a swell to roll on to the stony shore. This can make entry or exit difficult or downright dangerous on a rough day. The beach faces south-east and so is sheltered from the west or north-west. Nevertheless, if the sea is rough offshore there is likely to be a sharp swell breaking on the beach.

A close study of tide tables may give the snorkeller the opportunity to ride the tidal currents out and back to the site. On the way to the Cove, among the cottages is the excellent Church Ope Café, run by Brian and Heather Hendy (tel. 01305 820451) where roast lunches are provided on Sundays, if ordered the previous day. Their private telephone, which is the nearest one to the beach, is available in emergency.

**86 Durdle Pier** SY 705 717. *Snorkel site only.* This site is one of the old Portland piers where stone from the quarries was loaded onto barges. The crane here is now used to lower local fishing and potting boats into the water. The site is of no use to the aqualung diver owing to its distance from the nearest road. There are two routes to Durdle Pier. The first is from Church Ope, a distance of almost 1 mile over footpaths; the other, which is slightly shorter, is by the cliff top path from Grove Road. Access to the water is by climbing down and between large rocks.

Depths at Durdle Pier are 12m fairly near the shore line. There are plenty of fish to be seen, and the shallower rocks are covered in kelp. Beware of the currents which are strong, even fairly close to the shore. For 10 hours out of 12 the tide runs south-westwards roughly parallel to the shore. About two hours before high water at Portland a north-easterly current sets in and flows comparatively weakly almost until high water This site is usable only when the sea is fairly calm, and is very exposed to easterly winds.

**87 Grove Point Beaches** SY 705 727. *Snorkel and aqualung.* Below the cliffs at Grove Point are four rocky beaches. The OS reference above is for the most northerly of these beaches at a point where the path from the summit of the cliff arrives on the fore-shore. The other beaches occur south of this point. To get to these sites, drive across the island towards Easton. About ½ mile before the centre of the village take the left-hand turning to Grove. Continue along this road and turn left along the cliff top for a short distance. There is a well marked footpath leading from the road down the cliff. It is a fairly easy walk down to the beach but a long slog back to the top of the 325ft cliff.

These sites are suitable for all levels of experience, but beginners should be carefully supervised with regard to currents. The nearest telephone is just inside the front main entrance of the borstal at Grove Road. There is also a public telephone kiosk 150yds farther along Grove Road to the west.

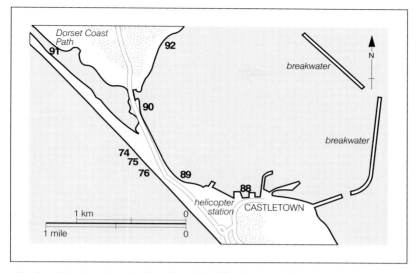

*Portland Harbour, showing East Fleet (Site 91), Castletown Beach (Site 88), Oil Tanks Beach (Site 89), Ferrybridge (Site 90), Sandsfoot Castle Cove (Site 92); also the Royal Adelaide (Site 74), the Nor (Site 75) and the United States Tank Landing Craft (Site 76).*

**88 Castletown Beach (Portland Harbour)** SY 688 744. *Free launching only.* This is a small shingle beach tucked away between the large Aquasport Hotel building and the entrance to Portland Port Business Centre. Take the A354 along Chesil Beach, and after passing the Royal Victoria Lodge Hotel follow the road to the left at the next two junctions. The large Aquasport Hotel will soon be seen on the left, with the entrance to the beach just beyond it. Across the beach there is a concrete slope extending down to mid-tide level, enabling easy trailer launching. This public facility is free. Vehicles or trailers cannot be left on the beach or the road at Castletown, but there is a pay-and-display car park. This is a very sheltered site, situated between piers, and is ideal as a launch point for diving either inside or outside Portland Harbour. Diving from the beach is prohibited.

---

**PORTLAND HARBOUR DIVING REGULATIONS**
The Navy has withdrawn from Portland harbour; responsibility for administration was handed over to Portland Port Ltd on 1 January, 1998.
    Permits to dive are necessary and are issued only to recognised sub-aqua clubs on request, and on payment of a fee. There are some areas within the harbour where diving is restricted and others where it is prohibited. Details of these should be obtained from and application for a permit made to: The Harbour Master, Portland Port Ltd, Castletown, Portland, Dorset DT5 1PP (Tel. 01305 824044).

---

*Divers at Castletown Beach. Photo: Roy Smallpage*

**89 Oil Tanks Beach (Portland Harbour)** SY 675 747. *Snorkel site, free launching.* This site is easy to find and makes a convenient launching point for diving anywhere in the harbour. From Weymouth follow the A354 along the Chesil Beach road towards Portland. Halfway between the Ferrybridge and Portland, on the left, will be seen a double row of large oil tanks. Almost opposite the first tank at the other side of the road is a wide tarmac parking area, which is clearly marked for emergency vehicles only – do not park here. At the Weymouth end of the emergency parking area is a small patch of pebbly ground, by an electric sub-station, where it is possible to park unofficially. The harbour beach is then accessible directly across the road.

The beach is of coarse shingle and is up to 50yds wide at low water. Under water, the harbour bed is almost pure sand. Depths are very shallow and this is why aqualung diving is not recommended. An interesting snorkel dive can be carried out by swimming to the right, off the beach and continuing along the rocks which form the protection of the shore line of the harbour, to the south-east. Many small fish and other marine life abound here. The sea off this beach is well sheltered from the south and west, but an east wind will produce choppy little waves and spoil the otherwise usually excellent visibility. It is an ideal site for a beginner's first snorkel expedition.

**90 Ferrybridge (Portland Harbour)** SY 667 761. *Snorkel, aqualung and launching.* Ferrybridge is the point where the A354 crosses the entrance to the Fleet at Smallmouth. There are several possibilities for snorkelling, aqualung diving and launching in this area of Portland Harbour. At the Weymouth side of the bridge is the Ferrybridge Inn (providing food and accommodation for divers). A road at the side of the Inn leads to its rear and a wide parking area, also the bank of the Fleet, west of the bridge. Entry into the water is very easy by walking down a 45° brick slope forming the bank. Small boats which can be carried, can be launched here, but notices ban the launching of heavier boats involving trailers and vehicles.

There is an excellent area for diving and snorkelling at the Fleet side of the bridge, especially at the Weymouth side. Care must be taken, however, with the heavy current, which on the ebb rushes out through the narrows of the bridge into the harbour. Depths are as much as 6m on high water. The bottom varies in different areas from shingle to clay and silts and sand. Life is abundant with many young fish, shrimps and prawns and tube worms to be seen. Slack water is high water at Portland plus 1½ hours and high water at Portland minus 4 hours. But much fun can be had and skill gained by both divers and snorkellers in learning how to use the currents and back eddies when the water is moving.

On the Portland side of the bridge is the boat yard and launching ramp of Ferrybridge Marine Services (tel. 01305 781518). Within the yard is a shop selling chandlery, hot food and drinks. There are toilets for customers and a telephone in the shop which could be used in an emergency.

**91 East Fleet** SY 652 772. *Snorkel and aqualung site, free launching.* This site is on the mainland side of the Fleet adjacent to the Royal Engineers Bridging Depot near Wyke Regis, and can be found down Camp Road. Take this road and keep straight on to the gates of the Army Engineering Bridging Camp. Here, a grassy track on the left leads over the last 60m to the gravel and clay beach of the Fleet. Cars can be parked on the road just before the start of the track. The Fleet at this point is known as East Fleet. Especially on the ebb, there is quite a strong current, which runs in a south-easterly direction down and out into Portland Harbour at Ferrybridge a good mile away. It is possible to enjoy an exciting drift dive using this ebb current to carry you to Ferrybridge, where a vehicle can be left parked.

The area is almost totally sheltered and unaffected by adverse wind and weather conditions. Depths in the Fleet run down to 7m in places, with a bottom of clean gravel and sand. This is a good area to see flounders and plaice. In the vicinity of the Bridging Camp, the Fleet is ideal for a beginner's dive or a winter dive when rough conditions prohibit diving elsewhere. Unless you intend doing the drift described, choose a time when the currents are slack. Around the time of, and just after, high water at Portland is best, and also gives the greater depth and fresh, clean water. Visibility can be good at such times. Launching is possible at this site, but entails a carry down a steep earth bank.

**92 Sandsfoot Castle Cove (Portland Harbour)** SY 673 772. *Snorkel and aqualung site, launching.* Follow the A354 south along the backwater section of Weymouth Harbour. Following the signs for Portland keep straight on across a large road island and up to Boot Hill. Keep straight on across a mini roundabout, but then, after another 200yds, where the A354 swings sharply right, turn left down Old Castle Road, which is a public road, including its very end section onto the beach.

A shore dive is best started from the section of beach near the public road end. Underwater, the sandy sea bed slopes very gently away from the shore. Currents are weak and this site is good for the beginner, except that to find any depth requires a fairly long swim. Visibility, even during winter, is usually excellent. From the road end, a private track leads immediately to the Weymouth Sailing and Activity Centre and the Scuba Shack Diving Centre (tel. 01305 788832). Here there are three excellent launching ramps besides parking and facilities such as food and hot showers, all of which are available to visitors.

**93 Newton's Cove** SY 683 784. *Snorkel and aqualung.* This site is only ½ mile from the main shopping centre in Weymouth. From the harbour bridge, turn left and follow the road along the quay into Hope Square. Keep more or less straight on through the square, leaving by Spring Road. In a few yards Newton's Road will be seen on the left. The cove is at the end of this road. To find the best and easiest access point onto the beach, climb the concrete steps onto the footpath that crosses Newton's Road on a small bridge. Follow the footpath to the east until a path descends through pleasant public gardens to the beach via a short flight of steel steps down a low sea wall. This is a good beginner's site. It can be dived when a strong south-westerly is blowing, but it is open to the east and south-east, and winds from this direction soon reduce the visibility to virtually nil.

*Weymouth Bay, showing Newton's Cove (Site 93), Weymouth Harbour (Site 94), Overcombe Corner (Site 95), Bowleaze Cove (Site 96), Osmington Bay or Shortlake (Site 97) and Osmington Mills (Site 98).*

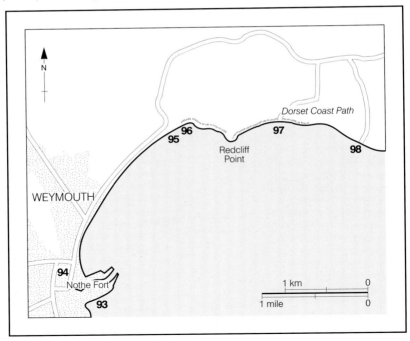

**94 Weymouth Harbour** SY 677 789. *Launching only.* On the town side of the part of Weymouth Harbour known as The Backwater there is an excellent, wide concrete launching ramp. Access to the ramp is from Commercial Road, which follows the harbour on the inland side of Town Bridge. The ramp is ideal for launching even very large boats because vehicles can easily reverse their trailers into the water. There is always some water on the ramp, even on springs. A launching fee is charged; the distance to the open sea from the ramp is about ¾ mile.

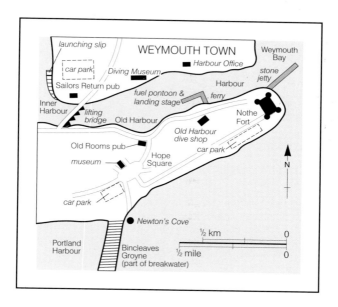

*Newton's Cove (Site 93) and Weymouth Harbour (Site 94).*

**95 Overcombe Corner** SY 696 815. *Snorkel site, free launching.* This site lies in Weymouth Bay at the point, 1 mile north-east of Weymouth, where the A353 turns inland away from the shore. The beach is of fine pebbles and sand, with pure rippled sand extending beyond the low water mark. Small boats can be launched easily, but they have first to be lifted from the road over a 1 metre high sea wall, or carried down a rock slope from a café car park. Aqualung shore diving is not advised here owing to the shallow depth and plain sandy sea bed. There is, however, one feature well worth a snorkel dive: a reef 40m out from the shore, which starts approximately 100yds on the Weymouth side of the café. It extends parallel to the shore for many hundreds of yards north-east towards Bowleaze Cove and is made of Portland stone, dumped here in the early 1900s. Depths along the reef are about 2 to 3m, but the weed covered rocks make an excellent beginners snorkel dive. Visibility can be good, but any blow from the south or east will soon stir up the sand in the shallows near the beach. There are no currents.

**Weymouth Harbour.** *Photo: Roy Smallpage*

**96 Bowleaze Cove** SY 703 818. *Snorkel site, launching.* This is an ideal family site. Next to the beach is a grass and hard standing area where cars and trailers may be parked. Adjacent is a café and restaurant. A wide concrete slip enables vehicles to reverse trailers straight into the water at high tide or onto and across the firm sand at low water.

Bowleaze Cove lies in Weymouth Bay, 1½ miles north-east of the town. Beginners will enjoy snorkelling off this beach. Off-shore towards Weymouth there is a rocky reef with surrounding depth of 2 to 3m (*see* Site **95**). This reef extends parallel to the shore towards Weymouth. Generally, though, the sea bed is sandy and shallow, and therefore unsuitable for aqualung diving. The proprietor of the café controls the car park and the slip. Divers are very welcome to use the facilities, but must remember that this is primarily a family area. Charges are very reasonable.

**97 Osmington Bay or Shortlake** SY 720 819. *Snorkel and aqualung.* This site is included for those divers who spend a family holiday at the Osmington Bay Holiday Centre. Access to the remote beach is along the centre's private road and through the grounds of the holiday camp itself, which is situated on a cliff-top site 4½ miles east of Weymouth. From within the holiday camp a path leads to the cliff top where a substantial concrete path and steps lead to the beach, a total distance of some 150yds. The long beach is backed by high cliffs and steep, gorse-covered slopes, and is often deserted.

Underwater, the sea bed slopes gently away from the fine shingle and sand beach, with several straight and narrow reefs running parallel to the shore. To the east of the beach access point some of these dry at low water and are so straight they look almost like pipelines. About 100yds off the beach at a depth of 5m is a similar straight band of rock running parallel to the shore. It rises out of the sand to a height of 1m. Otherwise, the bottom is mainly sandy with rocks here and there, and lots of eel-grass in summer. The site is good for beginners but is open to southern quarter winds, which spoil the visibility. The nearest telephone is in the holiday centre.

**98 Osmington Mills** SY 735 816. *Snorkel and aqualung.* From the village of Osmington take the lane opposite St Christopher's Garage, which leads to the cliff top. The access point to the beach is down a short, but rather steep and narrow, path. Launching is possible, but carrying an inflatable down here is very difficult. The snorkeller will find much of interest around the shallow rocks, where it is also possible to have an interesting aqualung dive. Strong winds from the southern quarter can bring waves on to the beaches in this area, although some shelter from the south-west is afforded by Portland Island. In quiet periods or when the wind is from the north the visibility can be very good, even close to the rocky shore.

About ½ mile east of the access point, only 50yds out from the cliff, is the substantial wreck of the steam-powered coal barge *Minx*. She ended up here after breaking free from her moorings in Portland Harbour in November 1927 and drifting during the night with no crew aboard. Her ribs protrude above the water at low tide.

**99 Ringstead Bay, Site A** SY 751 813. *Snorkel and aqualung, free launching.* To find this site, take the A353 eastwards from Weymouth to a point 1 mile beyond Osmington. Take the turning to the south – signposted Ringstead 1½ miles. This lane leads down into a shallow valley before rising up a long hill. Almost at the summit, a wooden signposted right hand turning leads to Ringstead Bay. This last mile of road is private and a combined parking and toll charge is made at the Ringstead end. This toll road, although fully made up, is shown on the OS map as only a public footpath.

The main parking area is 100yds from the beach, but it is possible for vehicles to tow trailers down the track to the low cliff top and reverse down a paved ramp to the beach. Permission to do so, and the key to a locked barrier at the top of the ramp, has to be obtained from the shop at the car park. Small trailers with inflatables can be hand wheeled around the barrier and down the ramp to the beach. All trailers and vehicles must, after unloading, be returned to the car park. The distance to the sea from the bottom of the paved ramp, across the beach, is only approximately 25yds, but crossing this with a vehicle is not practical, owing to the very loose shingle.

Approximately 50yds offshore, the Ringstead Ledge rises abruptly from the sea bed and then dips its wide, weed covered surface gently seawards. The top of the reef dries out at low water and shelters the strip of water between it and the beach, forming a lagoon where a few small boats are anchored. Here, depths only reach 3m at high water. Small boats can easily be launched into this calm strip of water, and although they can just pass out to sea over the reef at high water, it is much safer to motor eastwards for 50yds to a clear passage to avoid propeller damage.

For the snorkeller, there is ample scope for a short or extended expedition around and over the reef. The serious aqualung diver will find depths of 5m out beyond the reef, with a large, rocky area extending far out to sea. This site is

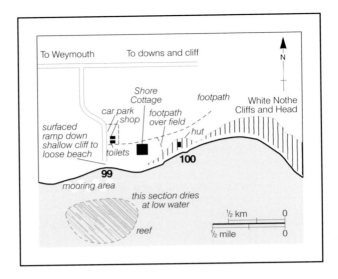

*Ringstead Bay (Sites 99 and 100).*

sheltered from virtually all winds from the northern quarter, but a blow from the south or south-west soon brings a swell over the reefs. Visibility is not easily affected over the rocky ground. Virtually no tidal currents exist in the bay.

**100 Ringstead Bay, Site B** SY 757 814. *Snorkel site only.* This site is excellent for the trainee snorkeller. Within 30yds of the beach depths of 6 to 7m can be found, but the ½-mile walk from the car park makes it unsuitable as an aqualung shore dive. After arriving at the car park by the route described for Site 99, walk east along the track immediately to the rear of the caravan shop. Keep on until you pass the last house, which is Shore Cottage, on the right. A short distance after this, climb the stile on the right and walk diagonally across the field on a footpath to the cliff top. Here steps cut into the low cliff lead down onto the beach. Just to the east of this point a large hut is set back in the cliff. The best diving area is opposite here. The sea bed consists of shingle, small rocks and shale outcrops. This is a quiet area, and the beach is usually virtually deserted, even on a warm, sunny day.

# Offshore boat diving and wrecks

**101 Inisinver** 50 29.35N; 02 35.13W. There is an unexplained mystery in this site. This small 127 gross ton motor vessel sank on 9 September, 1930, after ripping her bottom on a "submerged obstruction". The depth to the sea bed here is 43m, so one thing is definite: it was not a rock. The question of hitting another wreck, however improbable, is always worth considering – particularly in this case, for just 5 miles to the west and slap bang on the route which the *Inisinver* must have taken, is the wreck of the huge P&O liner *Salsette*. If the *Salsette* were upright in 1930, her mast heads would have been very near the surface. But the most likely explanation is that she struck a submerged submarine; maybe in some dark corner of an archive is a report that could give a definite answer.

The *Inisinver* now lies on the sea bed north-east to south-west and still stands up 3 to 4m high. Her cargo was china clay. She was built in 1913, fitted with a two-cylinder oil engine by A. Jeffrey and Company at Alloa and owned by Coastal Motor Shipping Company. *Boats: Lyme Regis 20 miles, Weymouth 14 miles.*

**102 M2 Submarine** 50 34.60N; 02 33.93W. This 296ft vessel sits complete and upright on a sandy sea bed. Were it not for the brightly coloured sponges that cover her upper superstructure and the forest of plumose anemones on her forward deck, the diver could be excused for thinking this was an operational submarine. The *M2* was built by Vickers in 1918 and sank on 26 January, 1932 with the loss of her full crew of 60 officers and men. A massive but abortive operation to lift her started as soon as she was located 8 days after her sinking. It was to last until 8 December, but was finally beaten by the weight of the vessel, strong tides and bad weather.

She originally had a 12in gun on her forward deck, but this had been removed in 1927 when she was adapted to carry a small folding-wing seaplane manufactured by Parnall, and named the Parnall Peto. A small hangar was fitted forward of the conning tower. Still plainly visible is the jib of the winch over the hangar door which was used to lift the aircraft back onto the launching ramp after landing on the sea. The hangar doors are wide open and it is possible to look into the silty interior. This wreck makes a splendid dive. Sea bed depth 30m. The height of the conning tower is 9m. *Boats: Lyme Regis 16 miles, Weymouth 13 miles.*

*A rare photograph of the submarine M2 (Site 102) with the crew busy on the ramp around the Parnall Peto folding-wing seaplane. Photo: Rodney Conyers collection*

**103  Anworth** 50 31.58N; 02 33.70W. This wreck, discovered in 1988, is of a steam-driven steel ship of some 150ft in length, and an approximate beam of 25ft. She sits upright on the bottom on a sandy sea bed at a depth of 38m and rises up a full 8m. The ship – identified from the name on her bell, though this may be a former name – is mainly complete, but with heavy damage at her stern where the hull and decking are broken open displaying her aft located engine room with its machinery, a boiler, condenser and lots of other bits and pieces. The midsection forms the highest point of the wreck. The cargo hold is approximately half full of a cargo of bags of cement.

The wreck lies north-west to south-east. A strange facet is that the bridge and accommodation superstructure, which was aft mounted, is lying complete but detached on the sea bed near the bow on the port side to the north-east. How could this large section have moved the full length of the ship? It was not long before the *Anworth* was a regular destination for several of the Weymouth charter boats, not just because she was a new wreck, but because of the massive lobsters with which she is infested. Indeed she has become better known to some divers as the "lobster wreck". Despite extensive searches, no record of this vessel or of her sinking has yet been found. *Boats: Lyme Regis 18 miles, Weymouth 12 miles.*

**104  Submarine P555** 50 30.87N; 02 33.43W. She was never given a name, but could well have been called "the submarine that no one wanted". She was completed at the Bethlehem Yard in the United States in 1922 and immediately joined the US Naval Fleet (as the *S24*) with others of her class already in service, but her design was not considered satisfactory. She was loaned to the Royal Navy in 1942 and became the *P555* after the war. The Americans did not want her back, so rather than send her to the breakers yard, the Royal Navy sank her on 28 April, 1947 for use as an ASDIC target. This submarine, of 1,062 tons displacement, measures 219ft long and has a beam of 21ft. Her armaments include four 21in bow torpedo tubes and she had a 3in AA gun. The deck is at a depth of 33m. The surrounding sea bed is 39m. She is upright and complete and lies east to west. *Boats: Lyme Regis 14 miles, Weymouth 12 miles.*

---

NOTE See the instructions and local access restrictions at the beginning of this chapter before attempting to dive Sites **105** or **109**.

---

**105  Vera** 50 37.43N; 02 33.39W. On 18 March, 1889, this 2,019 ton steamer was stranded on Chesil Beach opposite the village of Langton Herring. Aboard were 25 crew, 3 passengers and 2 stowaways – and all were helped ashore by a local Coastguard. The remains of the wreck are still to be seen today at the base of the pebble terrace in 10m of water. Over the years winter storms have caused the remaining iron framework of the ship to begin to collapse, but it is still well worth a dive. Currents run parallel to the shore and are not too strong. The visibility is excellent in calm periods, but the site is open to southerly and westerly winds. *Launching: Abbotsbury Beach (Site 14) or via the Fleet.*

*The Vera (Site 105) became a total loss after stranding on Chesil Beach. Her remains can still be dived there.* Photo: Weymouth and Portland Museum

**106 UB-74** 50 31.82N; 02 33.34W. This German submarine, after ravaging Allied shipping in World War One, was finally destroyed on 26 May, 1918, by a depth charge dropped from the armed yacht *Lorna*. The submarine had a displacement of 670 tons and measured 182ft long with a beam of 19ft. She is said to have been heavily salvaged; certainly she is well broken up. Since World War Two the Royal Navy have used her – together with the submarine *P555*, one mile away to the south – as a small ASDIC target. The bell has been recovered. The wreckage stands well proud of the sea bed at 34m and makes an interesting dive. *Boats: Lyme Regis 18 miles, Weymouth 12 miles.*

**107 Frogner** 50 32.02N; 02 33.06W. This Norwegian steamship of 1,476 tons gross, measuring 260ft long with a 37ft beam, was built in 1907 and sunk by torpedo on 29 April, 1918. She lies north to south at a sea bed depth of 35m. She has been extensively salvaged and her bell has been recovered. *Boats: Lyme Regis 18 miles, Weymouth 12 miles.*

**108 Stancrest** 50 26.80N; 02 32.50W. Because divers had recovered a bell bearing the letters "G.S.N.C.", it was thought that this was the 350 ton *Mallard* of the General Steam Navigation Company Line. However, a builder's plate recovered in 1997 proved the wreck to be that of a 462 ton coaster built and launched at Lowestoft in 1920 by Colby Brothers for the Glanmor Shipping Co and named *Glanmor*. Records show that in 1922 she was sold to the General Steam Navigation Company and renamed *Sheldrake*. In 1937 she was again sold, this time to the Stanhope Steam Shipping Co, and given the name *Stancrest*.

On 27 February, 1937 she left London bound for Bridgwater with a cargo of cement. The following day she was reported to be off the Isle of Wight, but after this nothing had been seen or heard of her again. Still complete with her cargo and aft-located machinery, she now lies upright in 46m and is one of the least dived wrecks in the area. *Boats: Weymouth 13 miles.*

**109 Hope** 50 36.50N; 02 32.00W. The place off the Chesil Beach at SY 623 794 where 26 large iron cannon lie is the wreck site of the *Hope* from Amsterdam. This privateer returning home from the West Indies was blown onto the Chesil and wrecked on 16 January, 1749. She carried coin, gold and jewels valued at the time at over £50,000. The word spread like wildfire that gold was to be had for the taking, and the army was eventually turned out to control a jostling, raging mob of over ten thousand would-be looters, all along the Chesil Bank. Little of her wealth was saved and the bulk of the treasure is probably still within the pebbles of the underwater terrace.

In the late 1970s a group led by Nowell "Chippy" Pearce recovered one of the cannon from the Chesil site, using a Royal Navy helicopter instead of a lifting bag. Trial excavations also led to the recovery of a number of items, the strangest being a huge plug of tobacco, still miraculously preserved beneath the pile of cannon and crud since 1749! Although all this was freely divulged by the divers at the time, one fact was kept a secret. The authors are therefore pleased that Nowell has allowed us to report that a number of Dutch silver coins were also recovered, which almost certainly identify this wreck as that of the *Hope*.

Like most Chesil wreck sites, the main bulk of the remains are to be found at a depth of around 11m, lying 120yds offshore, where the pebbles start to fade into a sandier sea bed. The cannon, cannonballs and crud forming a mound are easy to see. A recovered cannon is now on public display in the Nothe Fort at Weymouth.

Diving this site is safe and easy in calm weather. Currents run parallel to the shore, providing a good drift dive at times. The visibility is usually excellent, but a blow from the southern half of anything above Force 3 can quickly lead to difficult conditions. The site lies slightly under 1 mile to the north-west, along the beach from the Fleet crossing point at Chickerell. *Launching: Chesil Cove 5 miles, Abbotsbury Beach 4 miles.*

WARNING On Chesil beach, do not enter the sea if the waves breaking onto the pebbles are any higher than 1m. Getting into the water is easy, but getting out through the breakers onto the beach can be extremely difficult with diving gear on.

**110 Unidentified wreck** 50 28.90N; 02 32.00W. In the above position, 3 miles roughly south-west of Portland Bill, the Admiralty chart shows a wreck symbol. It is said to be that of a steam-driven coaster with a triple-expansion engine. A number of shell cases have been seen around here. Depth 36m to sea bed. *Boats: Lyme Regis 20 miles, Weymouth 10 miles.*

**111 Unidentified trawler** 50 27.55N; 02 31.50W. Just over 4 miles roughly south-west of Portland Bill, at a depth of 46m, rising up to 6m, lie the remains of a small trawler or tug. Diving reports are hard to come by for this wreck. It is in an area of fierce currents with little slack time. *Boats: Weymouth 12 miles.*

**112 Amy** 50 26.43N; 02 31.20W. Very little is known about this wreck, believed to be a small sailing ship that sank while making a film in 1928. The position may be well worth investigation. Depth 46m. *Boats: Weymouth 13 miles.*

**113 Gripfast** 50 25.97N; 02 29.95W. A member of the decimated convoy WP 183, she had earlier – during daylight on 9 July, 1942 – miraculously avoided being directly attacked by the E-boats in Lyme Bay. She had managed to go to the aid of the crew of the *Rosten* (Site **18**) when that ship had been sunk, and had picked up survivors. She was still moving eastwards with the remnants of the convoy, now harried by German aircraft, when a bomb hit her, killing five crew and three survivors from the *Rosten*. So bad was the damage to her hull that she sank immediately, off Portland Bill.

She was a British merchant steamship of 1,109 gross tons, measuring 225ft long with a beam of 35ft and had been launched in 1910 by J. Crown and Sons of Sunderland with the yard number "139", which must still be on her builder's plate somewhere on the wreck. The ship had a single deck with 4 holds, a poop deck and forecastle. She was fitted with a three-cylinder triple-expansion engine. As she was on a voyage from Barry to Sheerness, it is reasonable to assume her cargo was coal. Her owners were Newbiggins Steam Shipping Company and she was registered at Newcastle on Tyne.

Reported positions of her sinking and present whereabouts vary but the wreck at the position given is the most likely to be the *Gripfast*. Consistent with having been bombed, the wreck is badly damaged amidships, and lies bow to the east at a sea bed depth of 48m, with the wreck standing up 9m. Obviously, more surveys need to be done here, but be careful in this area – it is part of the Portland Race, with strong currents and little slack water time. *Boats: Weymouth 10 miles.*

**114 Stennis Ledges** 50 34.73N; 02 29.91W. Stennis Ledges are easy to find. Motor a good ½ mile out, due south from Chesil beach, from a point directly opposite the Army Bridging Camp near Wyke Regis. You should then be over the ledges. The current runs parallel to the shore and crosses the ledges at almost a right angle, so it is a simple matter to move up-tide, either north-west or south-east, and then start the dive and drift back onto the rocks. The ledges extend due south for just over a mile.

Underwater life is prolific. Lobsters and crabs are almost always resident, together with a wide variety of other fish. Depths are down to 27m. Visibility, in calm periods is excellent at well over 10m. Stennis Ledges make an exciting yet safe dive but are very exposed when a south or westerly wind rises above Force 3. *Launching: Chesil Cove (Site **77**) 3 miles.*

**115 Merchant Royal** 50 20.05N; 02 29.68W. Eleven miles, almost due south of Portland Bill, she is easy to find on Admiralty Chart 3315 as her wreck symbol is cut by the chart's southern margin at 20°N. Here lies this magnificent British cargo steamer (formerly the *Goodwood*) of 5,008 gross tons. She was involved in a collision and sunk on 3 July, 1946 – she was carrying a cargo of steel and wood. Tugs were dispatched from Portland to assist, but they could do nothing to prevent her sinking. The ship measures 416ft long with a beam of 55ft and was built in 1920 by J. Redhead & Sons at Sunderland. She was fitted with a huge Doxford triple-expansion three-cylinder steam engine. Her owners were Drake Shipping Ltd.

Although she had settled on the bottom with a heavy list to starboard, her upper samson post came within 18m of the surface on low water springs until demolition in 1969. Today she lies with her bows blown off, but her mid section and stern are upright with a heavy list to starboard. The sea bed is sand and shale with a scattering of 12in boulders – at a depth of 57m. The highest parts of what remains of her superstructure stand up a full 15m. An extra bonus for diving her is that this particular area gives very good visibility. The ship's bell was recovered by a diving group in 1984 – it had the inscription "Goodwood 1928". *Boats: Weymouth 17 miles.*

**116 HMS Fisgard II** 50 28.23N; 02 29.44. Built by Napier & Sons of Glasgow, and of 6,010 tons displacement, this ship was completed in 1870 and named *Invincible*. She measured 280ft long and had a beam of 54ft. Later, between 1901 and 1906, she operated under the name *Erebus,* but was then converted to a training ship and again renamed. With a crew aboard of 64 ratings, she was in the care of two tugs that were towing her from Portsmouth to Scapa Flow. Her engines had been removed and she had no steering gear. The weather was very rough and on approaching Portland she had started to ship water through her hawse pipes, and despite efforts aboard to shift machinery around to alter her trim, the situation steadily worsened.

A decision had been made to take her into Portland for shelter, but this was prevented by heavy seas and lack of steering gear. Off Portland Bill, the tugs gradually fought their way through the tremendous waves generated by the Portland Race, but the ship slowly listed and heeled over onto her beam ends. The ship's boats were launched, but one was smashed immediately, before it could get clear of the ship, which foundered at 4.20pm on 17 September, 1914, with the loss of 21 lives.

She lies completely upside down and is against a high reef. Even though she is still in good condition, her highest point is still at a depth of 47m. Her depth and position make her a difficult, dark and hazardous dive. Two charter boats that occasionally visit the site are *Skin Deep* and *Channel Chieftain* (both from Weymouth). *Boats: Weymouth 11 miles.*

**117 Pulpit Rock** 50 30.80N; 02 27.80W. Situated on the south-west corner of the tip of Portland Bill is the well known and well photographed feature of Pulpit Rock. Standing on the edge of a low line of cliffs, the rock towers above the restless waves that batter its base. Beyond the rock is a superb reef diving site. From the shore, the rock sea bed slopes away fairly gently, reaching 10m at a distance of 100yds offshore. After a flatter section, the angle of descent steepens and plunges in a series of rock faces and ledges to a depth of 30m. Thickly inhabiting the rocky ledges are dozens of crabs and lobsters. The reason why this position is congregated with so much life is also the reason why, for most of the day, diving is entirely prohibited. For 11½ hours out of every 12 a searing current of up to 5 knots thunders across this site. The only time when diving is possible on this site is approximately four hours after high water at Portland. Portland Bill offers slight protection from north-east winds, but otherwise this site is totally exposed. *Launching: Chesil 3 miles or, if conditions are very calm, from the tip of Portland Bill. Boats: Weymouth 8 miles.*

WARNING To dive this site the following rules are essential. The dive must take place from a boat (or if a shore dive is made a boat must be in attendance on the dive site). Divers must carry large, easily seen surface marker buoys – one each unless they can guarantee that they will not become separated from each other. The site should be dived only under the control and guidance of someone with good knowledge of it.

*This view of Pulpit Rock off Portland is on a postcard dating from about 1920. Despite the battering of the Atlantic storms this rock has changed little in the intervening years.*
Photo: Authors' collection.

**118 Chesil Ledge** 50 32.90N; 02 27.70W (approximate). Launch at Chesil Cove, then motor out to the south-west for ¾ mile, to a point 400yds beyond a line drawn between Blacknor Point and the radio masts at Wyke Regis. In this position an exciting gully extending across the sea bed in a north-west to south-east direction can be found. This gully has formed on a major fault in the bed-rock. Over perhaps thousands of years, the sea has undermined the rock, causing it slowly to collapse and break into square sections. The whole area along the northern side of the wide gully resembles a giant chocolate bar broken into square pieces, with the deep cracks between the squares providing excellent cover for crustaceans. The whole broken area swarms with crabs, and clouds of fish swim in the gully. The general depth is 28m, with an extra 2m to the bottom of the gully. The visibility can be 10m or more in calm periods. The currents, while not exceptional, are strong enough at times to prevent swimming up-tide. Chesil Ledge is reasonably sheltered from the north, north-east and east.

**119 Athen** 50 20.68N; 02 27.64W. This is a big wreck. The *Athen*, a British steamship of 2,199 gross tons, sank on 18 March, 1906, when on a voyage from Cardiff to Rio Grande do Sul, after a violent collision with the British Steamer *Thor* of Glasgow. She was carrying a cargo of patent fuel. The ship had been built in 1893 in the Stockton on Tees yard of Richardson, Duck & Company and measured 227ft 6in long with a beam of 37ft 5in. The *Athen* was fitted with a triple-expansion three-cylinder engine driven by two boilers. This wreck is upright, with the hull intact. Her decks have mostly collapsed inwards and the engines are visible midships. There is a quantity of pottery around, as well as her cargo of blocks of compressed patent fuel. Each block has the name "Cardiff" and the emblem of a crown or a phoenix. Her position is 20 miles south of Portland Bill and only 1½ miles north-east of the wreck of the *Merchant Royal* (Site **115**). Sea bed depth is 56m and the wreck stands up 11m. *Boats: Weymouth 17 miles.*

**120 Bournemouth** 50 31.00N; 02 27.58W. Many ships have driven themselves hard ashore on to the western coast of Portland during periods of thick fog. At such times one point seems to have had an uncanny attraction. Despite there being almost 3½ miles of coastline, almost every stranding in fog has occurred within 200yds of Blacknor Point. Virtually the only "fog wreck" found near the tip of The Bill rather than at Blacknor is that of the paddle steamer *Bournemouth*. On 27 August, 1886, she drove on to the rocks near Pulpit Rock. Aboard were 197 passengers who had been on a day trip to Torquay. All were rowed ashore in the ship's boats or in local fishing vessels.

Over the years, the steamer has become a total wreck, but her remains can still be found close inshore below the former Admiralty Weapons Research Establishment, which is on the cliff just over 400yds north of the lighthouse. There is no telling what a sustained search could turn up on this site. Wreckage of the submarine *Minerve* (Site **121**) is approximately 200yds to the north. This site is sheltered from the north and east, but exposed to the west. Divers should beware of the strong current that runs for many hours of the day just offshore. *Launching: Chesil, 3 miles; if calm, The Bill, ½ mile.*

**121 Minerve** 50 31.10N; 02 27.58W. This Free French submarine was wrecked on 19 September, 1945, while under tow in Lyme Bay. The towing cable parted and she drifted onto the rocky western shore of Portland, just north of the Bill, and soon she was a complete wreck. The wreckage is concentrated at a spot at the base of the cliffs, halfway between the lighthouse and the Coastguard radio aerials. The cliff top point which marks the site is the end of the wire perimeter fence at the northern side of the former Admiralty establishment. *Launching: Chesil 3 miles; if calm, The Bill ½ mile.*

*Another Portland fog victim: the paddle-steamer Bournemouth (Site 120)*
*wedged on the rocks.* Photo: Weymouth and Portland Museum

*The Free French submarine Minerve (Site 121) was wrecked at*
*Portland. The Cross of Lorraine is clearly visible on the conning tower.*
Photo: Weymouth and Portland Museum

**122 Haytion (Portland Harbour)** 50 34.68N; 02 27.52W. This shallow but substantial iron wreck has been known to divers as the "Ham Wreck". The *Haytion* established a name for herself by sinking three times around the local area! The first occasion was in 1937 after a collision. Raised, she sank again in 1940, to be raised again and later towed to her final resting place, where she can still be found on the outside edge of the Small Mouth Sands. Her plates have long ago gone, but her ribs and deck beams, below which a diver can easily swim, are still there.

The wreck is an interesting shallow dive and is ideal for underwater photography, for her shallowness and the reflective white sandy bottom provide excellent light penetration. Her position is sheltered with no current and she is situated on flat sand that slopes out gently from the shore – it is possible to wade most of the way out to her. Immediately on her offshore (east) side, the harbour bed slopes steeply to 8m.

To find the wreck, look for a patch of greenery on the back slope of the Chesil Bank. This patch is located exactly 100yds beyond the end of the Portland end of the Chesil beach car park, and is composed of scrub and grasses growing around the concrete boxes that formed the Portland end of the old firing range. Choose the only street light on the adjacent A354 that, if lined up with the green patch, gives a transit line extending at right angles across the road and then into the harbour. This is the line the wreck is on. Depth 3m. *Launching: Any site in Portland Harbour.*

WARNING This dive is possible from the shore, but because of the high density of windsurfers, especially on windy days (this is their allocated patch), a boat should be anchored above any diving party exploring the wreck.

**123 Franziska** 58 28.30N; 02 27.40W. This iron steam-driven collier of 669 net tons was on her way to Vlissingen, her holds brimming full of Welsh coal, which had been loaded at Cardiff. All was well until, off Portland, on 24 February 1889, disaster struck in the form of a violent collision with the barque *Honour*. The *Franziska*, already weighed down by her cargo, quickly filled with water and sank into the raging waters.

The wreck lies just south of the most turbulent area, but still in the Portland Race, almost 3 miles off The Bill. She is at a sea bed depth of 55m. Her mainly intact hull stands 4m high. Most of her decking has now disappeared, exposing her two-cylinder compound engine. *Boats: Weymouth 10 miles.*

**124 SS Barmston** 50 32.74N; 02 27.30W. This Norwegian steamship of 1,451 tons – sometimes referred to as the *Madelaine* – was carrying a cargo of coal when she stranded herself beneath the high cliffs of Blacknor Point on 3 March, 1918. She was built in 1888, and at the time of her sinking was sailing from Swansea to Rouen. Her crew of 20 were all saved. Today the *Barmston* lies 20yds or so to the south of the wreck of the *James Fennell*. She consists mostly of a mass of flattened steel plates, although her keel, propeller shaft and forward end (standing 4m high) are quite readily identified. The wreck lies on bedrock and gravel at a depth of 16m. She is not marked on the chart. *Launching: Chesil Cove 1 mile. Boats: Weymouth 11 miles.*

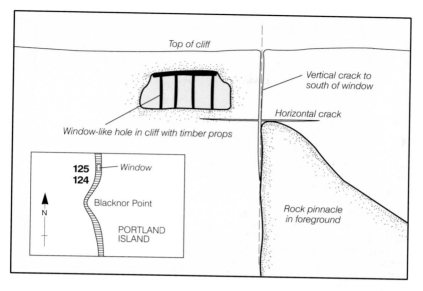

*Transit marks for the Barmston (Site 124) and the James Fennell (Site 125), just north of Blacknor Point. To locate the James Fennell, line up the left hand top corner of the rock pinnacle so that it is exactly in line with the vertical crack in the cliff face behind it. At the same time the top edge of the pinnacle must just touch the horizontal crack. You are now over the wreck. The Barmston lies 20yds to the south.*

**125 James Fennell** 50 32.75N; 02 27.30W. This steam trawler was built in 1918 by Fullerton & Company at Paisley. She was built specially for the Admiralty as one of the Strath class of auxiliary patrol vessels. She was 215 gross tons and measured 123ft long with a beam of 22ft, was fitted out with a triple-expansion engine and was armed with a 12 pounder gun. Disaster happened on 16 January, 1920, when the ship drove straight onto the rocks below the high cliffs just north of Blacknor Point, in thick fog. All her crew came safely ashore by means of a rope strung from the stem of the ship to a large rock by local fishermen. A few days later an attempt was made to tow the *James Fennell* off the rocks, but she immediately sank.

Today the wreck lies at a depth of 15m and makes a fine dive. Her stern is still complete and stands almost 5m high above a large propeller. Amidships is her engine and boiler. Her forward end is badly smashed with her bow section detached and twisted, but still in contact with her hull. She faces away from the shore to the west. The wreck lies in Halleluja Bay, between Tar Rocks and Blacknor Point. Diving can be carried out at any state of the tide, but it is best to avoid the 3 hour period before high water at Portland when a fairly strong current flows southwards in the area. Outwards, offshore from the wreck the sea bed immediately slopes to a depth of 24m. This area of Portland is best avoided if the

*The British steam trawler James Fennell (Site 125), a victim of fog, lies grounded on rocks at Blacknor Point in January 1920. An attempted re-floating caused her to sink in deep water.* Photo: Weymouth and Portland Museum

wind is much above Force 3 from the south or west. It is however, extremely sheltered and ideal when an easterly or northerly is blowing. Visibility can be up to 13m in settled periods. *Launching: Chesil Cove 1 mile. Boats: Weymouth 11 miles.*

**126 Myrtledene** 50 32.20N; 02 27.30W. The *Myrtledene,* a steamer of 2,500 gross tons, ran onto the boulders of the western shore line of Portland on 25 March, 1912. She carried a very heavy cargo of iron ore, and irretrievably tore her plates on those unforgiving rocks. She lies at a depth of 8m at the bottom of the shoreline boulder slope, south of Blacknor Point, at a place called Mutton Cove. Although now broken, she is still recognisable as a ship, and the area between where she lies and Blacknor Point is worth diving in its own right with rocky ground and usually good visibility, little current and lots of marine life. *Launch: Chesil Cove, 2 miles. Boats: Weymouth 9 miles.*

**127 SS Thames** 50 33.15N; 02 27.15W. On 2 January, 1891, a vessel badly holed herself on Tar Rocks, ½ mile out from Chesil Cove. She was the steamer *Thames,* and she became a total loss. Today her position, just off the southern point of Tar Rocks, is marked by her boiler and scattered steel plates. She lies at a depth of 10m and is an ideal beginner's wreck. Currents are weak and visibility is usually good. *Launching: Chesil Cove, ½ mile.*

*The Gertrude (Site 128) ran onto the western shore of Portland in thick fog.*
Photo: Weymouth and Portland Museum.

**128 Gertrude** 50 32.79N; 02 27.10W. Like the *James Fennell*, which lies not far to the south-west, the *Gertrude* was a victim of thick fog. She drove ashore on 26 August, 1894, in the small bay just south of Tar Rocks. The ship is still partially on the slope of boulders down which she slipped and is still pointing upwards, towards the shore. For the diver searching among rocks and kelp, her boiler, which has fallen out to the starboard side and now lies 4m away from the ship's side, is probably the easiest item to recognise.

Her bows are on the kelp line at a depth of 6m. To be found around her stern – at 14m – are masses of steel plate and a rudder with a blade of her propeller sticking out of the sea bed. The ship's anchor lies a short distance away, off the port side. This is an excellent beginner's wreck, with rocks and fish in abundance. Currents are non-existent and the visibility is usually extremely good. The wreck lies near the boulder strewn shore. *Launching: Chesil Cove, ¾ mile.*

**129 Sea Vixen (Portland Harbour)** 50 34.74N; 02 26.96W. Substantially intact, but with its wings missing, this Naval aeroplane stands 3m off a silty harbour bed, at a depth of 9m. It makes an unusual dive and, being towards the Chesil shore of the harbour, is not too badly affected by blows from any direction. This is an excellent beginner's dive, but care should be taken not to fin madly around kicking up the bottom and changing a pleasant location into a nil visibility dive. There are no current problems and the site is easily picked out on an echo sounder once you are over it. *Launching: any site in Portland Harbour, 1 mile.*

105

**130 Britannia** 50 20.35N; 02 26.58W. Although known as *Britannia* when sunk, her name at her launch in 1889 was the *Earl of Aberdeen*. She became a victim of a torpedo fired by the German submarine *UC-75*, when on a voyage from Middlesbrough to St Malo on 19 October, 1917. She carried a cargo of pig iron, which must still be intact in her holds. The gross registered tonnage was 765, and her sinking cost the lives of 22 men, including her Captain. She lies upright on a fine sandy sea bed into which much of her bulk has sunk – now standing only 3 to 4m, her two boilers are the highest point. She is not frequently dived. Probably because of its low profile, the wreck has never been charted. Although the helm has been recovered, her bell is believed to still be within the wreck. Depth 57m. *Boats: Weymouth, 17 miles.*

**131 Himalaya** 50 34.70N; 02 26.50W. Infrequently dived, and lying on the sea bed in Portland Harbour at the above position, can be found a substantial amount of wreckage distributed over a wide area. It consists mainly of wrought iron plates and beams, with traces of teak decking and tons of coal scattered everywhere. A careful observer will also note the presence of pulley blocks and wires and parts of what were derricks. Nowhere more than 2m proud, the wreckage is in a surrounding depth of 13m. Built for P&O and christened the *Himalaya*, she created much excitement and interest for the attending crowds and nobility at her launching from the Blackwall yards of C.J. Mare & Company on 25 May, 1853.

*The screw steam ship Himalaya simply oozed luxury, but this only added to the sadness of her becoming a coal hulk in Portland Harbour. This beautiful model is in the Science Museum, London, and is illustrated with their kind permission.*

This was just 8 years after the completion of the *Great Britain*, a ship with which the *Himalaya* shared many common features. By the time of her completion she was equipped with masts, sails and rigging, but her main method of propulsion was a single screw, driven by a massive steam engine.

With a length of 372ft 2in, a beam of 44ft 4in and a gross tonnage of 3,438 she was, at the time of her launch, probably the largest ship ever built. At the outbreak of the Crimean War, the Government chartered her as a troop ship and her accommodation was increased from 200 berths to a less luxurious 1850. Later, the Government purchased her outright and she continued as a very popular troop ship, but sadly she was eventually converted to a coaling hulk and re-christened HM *Hulk C60*. It was during an air raid on Portland on 5 June, 1940, that her career finally came to an end. A Junkers Ju 88 dropped a stick of bombs across her, and despite her originally much vaunted six bulkheads, the "Old Warhorse" sank by the stern to the sea bed on her moorings.

Even as a hulk, her size must have been an impressive sight. It certainly must have impressed the pilot in the Ju 88, for after his return to base a German propaganda radio broadcast claimed the Luftwaffe had sunk the aircraft carrier *Ark Royal*.

In 1947 the remains were blown up and largely removed. Lying at a depth of 12m, the wreck lies ½ mile out in the harbour, directly in line with the longer sides of the Mulberry units at Castletown. A good transit to the south from the wreck is the middle of the north end of the Mulberries directly under the lift shaft of the large military block behind and above, on the hill. Transits at right angles to this are difficult to see, but by moving along this south transit until the chequered fort, situated to the east (at the north end of the outer breakwater at the south side of the east ship channel entrance) is at 70° magnetic the wreckage can be located by echo sounder. *Launching: any site around the harbour – 1 mile.*

**132 Submarine UB-62** 50 24.70N; 02 26.00W. Lying north to south, with bows to south, this World War One submarine is almost certainly the German *UB-62*. She was attacked and sunk in October 1917 by a torpedo dropped from a flying boat that caught her on the surface. She lies on the sea bed at 45° over onto her starboard side and is shown on the chart 6 miles south of Portland Bill. There is a split in the conning tower and a hole in the hull, just forward of the tower. Depth to sea bed is 49m. *Boats: Weymouth, 15 miles.*

**133 Landing Craft (Portland Harbour)** 50 35.58N; 02 25.78W. The position given is on the inside of the north-eastern breakwater, approximately 150yds south of the North Ship channel entrance. Here, on the harbour bed at a depth of 15m and no more than 20ft apart, are two small World War Two landing craft. Weymouth diver Chris Hovard is an expert on this area and advises that with their hinge-down ramps and still complete with engines, both craft are easily recognisable. Both lie with their bows up onto the bottom rocks of the breakwater.

To find these two wrecks, move from the north ship channel along the Harbour side of the breakwater, in a southerly direction. On top of the breakwater wall there is first a conglomeration of small buildings and a look out tower, then a long grey concrete wall with patches of red brick, at the southern end of which is

*The wrecks of the landing craft (Site 133) are at the base of the harbour breakwater opposite the centre of the building with two doors and three windows. Photo: Author*

a building. The wrecks are exactly opposite this building at the base of the wall (see photograph above). There is a slight current towards the North ship channel entrance on the ebb – be careful not to be carried into the prohibited area of the harbour entrance. *Launching: Castletown, Ferrybridge or Sandsfoot Castle Cove, all within 1 mile.*

**134 Sudon** 50 30.97N; 02 25.60W. This wreck, believed to be that of a steam-driven Swedish coaster, lies just over a mile east of Portland Bill. The name may be incorrect, or may be a local derivative of the correct one. She lies on the sea bed of mussel-covered rock at a depth of 15m. The whole area is made up of rock ledges and is teeming with crustaceans. She is not shown on the chart but the wreckage is of a substantial vessel.

Large winches, a boiler, a propeller shaft and an iron propeller still lie beside the rather-flattened main structure, which is broken and well spread. The highest part is the boiler, which stands 3m high. The marks for this wreck are accurate and enable divers in small boats to find it reasonably easily. However, for most of the 12-hour tide cycle a very heavy current flows across this site. It is variable in direction, and can swiftly take a diver or a small boat with engine trouble into The Portland Race.

The best and safest way to visit this site is therefore by charter boat from Castletown or Weymouth. This site is reasonably sheltered from the north and west, but currents and rip tides can produce rough seas anywhere in this area. *Boats: Castletown 7 miles, Weymouth 8 miles.*

**135 Landing Craft (Portland Harbour)** 50 34.99N; 02 25.59W. This rarely visited wreck is ½ mile due west of the east ship channel entrance, a small intact landing craft sitting on a rather silty and shell covered bed. Depth 15m. *Launching: Any site around the harbour, 1 mile.*

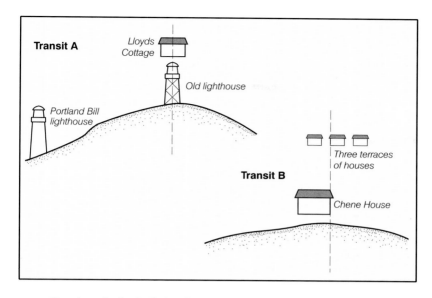

*Transit marks for the Sudon (Site 134). All the features shown are on Portland, at Weston, or near the Bill and can be identified on the Ordnance Survey map. For Transit A line up the centre of Lloyd's Cottage behind the old lighthouse (which is now a bird observatory). For Transit B line up the left-hand end of the centre terrace with the right-hand side of Chene House.*

**136 Hartlepool** 50 36.49N; 02 25.47W. Just over ½ mile off the Nothe, near the entrance to Weymouth Harbour, rest the remains of the 5,500 ton merchant ship *Hartlepool*. She was the victim of a torpedo fired on 5 July, 1940, in a daring attack by a German E-boat. Although she was partly removed, her remains were dispersed by heavy explosive charges and now lie in two areas. The main area is the position given; the other is just to the south at 50 36.43N; 02 25.85W. Being sheltered from the south-west it is often possible to dive here when it is too rough to go elsewhere. Watch out for sea traffic though – large ships entering or leaving the harbour usually pass directly over the wreck. *Launching: Weymouth Harbour.*

**137 Unidentified dredger** 50 34.03N; 02 25.45W. This wreck, unmarked on the chart, lies on the outside slope of the inner breakwater of Portland Harbour, in the area known as Balaclava Bay. The small dredger is well broken and lies at 10m almost at the foot of the breakwater. The wreck is easily found, being almost opposite (but 25yds to the right of) the large crane mounted on the quay, on the harbour side of the breakwater. Also here on the sea bed, approximately 50yds outside the dredger, is a Lada car! This is an extremely sheltered site except from the east and south-east. Currents are nil; visibility is normally good. *Launching: Castletown 1 mile, or any other launch-site in the harbour.*

**138 Black Hawk** 50 26.17N; 02 25.30W. Situated 4½ miles south of Portland Bill, this wreck lies at 48m, the stern section of a huge ship. The wreck is on its starboard side and rises 12m off the bottom, with a large gun mounted on a platform on the top deck. The location of the other half of the ship was a mystery until markings on a recovered telegraph proved the wreck to be the *Black Hawk* – the stern section was blown off when she was torpedoed on 29 December, 1944. Her forward half remained afloat and was towed into Worbarrow Bay (Site **193**). The massive propeller of this wreck was taken off and landed at Weymouth many years ago. This is still an extremely exciting dive, and in the area subject to the influence of the Portland Race. *Boats: Weymouth 12 miles.*

**139 Motor Fishing Vessel** 50 35.25N; 02 25.28W. At the above position, 10m away from the foot of the inside of the north-eastern breakwater and roughly 300yds north-west of the wreck of the *Countess of Erne* (Site **141**), lie the remains of a 30ft wooden fishing vessel (see photograph on page 113). Weymouth registered and based at Castletown, the boat sank in a storm in about 1986 and is now reduced to a pile of wreckage. But there is still, plain to see, an inboard three-cylinder diesel engine, upright and bolted to the timber frame. Other items include hydraulic steering components and the rudder. Depth 14m. *Launching: Any site around the harbour 1 mile.*

*The late Andy Smith, perched on a small fortune of phosphor bronze that he had just salvaged from the stern of the Black Hawk (Site 138).*
Photo: A. Smith collection

**140  HMS Hood** 50 34.10N; 02 25.22W. A battleship of the old Sovereign class, she was sunk on 4 November, 1914, as a blockship across the south ship channel at the entrance to Portland Harbour. With a length of 380ft and a beam of 75ft, she almost completely sealed the entrance. She effectively eliminated any clandestine entry of submarines, besides preventing torpedoes being fired at ships in the harbour. At the last moment, after her cocks were opened and she was flooded, she very suddenly and unexpectedly turned over and so is on the sea bed upside down.

Her broad kelp-covered bottom is less than 2m from the surface at low water, and prevents the entrance of any craft much larger than an inflatable. Small boats can squeeze through at either end of the ship, particularly at the eastern end. Divers should be aware of the possibility of this traffic when diving. There is a wire slung across the entrance above the water. The wreck is to the south of this wire. The *Hood* is swarming with fish and makes an exciting and very convenient dive. The wreck is completely sheltered from most winds, including south-westerly gales. The best period to dive is from 3 hours before high water at Portland to 1 hour after high water at Portland. Another period, at low water, when currents are weak is from 6 hours before high water at Portland to 5 hours before high water at Portland. Sea bed depth 18m. *Launching: Castletown or Ferrybridge.*

WARNING  Because the *Hood* lies across the harbour entrance, it is often subjected to a very fierce current – especially on the ebb, when the falling level of water in the harbour and the Fleet rushes over, around, under and through her. These times should, particularly on spring tides, be carefully avoided. In places she is starting to break up, with plates missing on her side. Do not be tempted to enter the wreck through these holes. Her heavy fittings and machinery may come crashing down on you if dislodged.

*HMS Hood is still on duty as an underwater blockship across the southern entrance to Portland Harbour. Photo: Authors' collection*

**141 Countess of Erne (Portland Harbour)** 50 35.18N; 02 25.18W. An old paddle steamer, this 830 gross ton 241ft long iron vessel, was used as a coal hulk in Portland Harbour from around 1890 until, in a gale in September, 1935, she broke her moorings. After drifting across the harbour, she hit the inner wall of the north-eastern breakwater, was badly holed and sank. She still lies exactly as she sank, upright with her hull mainly intact, but, like most of the wrecks here, rather silty.

She lies at the foot of the breakwater wall and almost parallel to it with her bows towards the east ship channel entrance, approximately 100yds to the south. Her exact position is opposite a small grey concrete building on top of the breakwater, which has "No. 84" marked on it (see photograph below). Her iron decks are clear and flat and there are three holds, which are easily entered. The wreck stands some 7m high. Depth to the deck is 6m. About 25yds forward of her bow is part of a bombardon unit, lying on the harbour bed. Bombardon units were one of the more weird inventions of World War Two. They were made of a series of metal tanks or pontoons fastened together in the form of a long snake. They were to be used to try to break up waves prior to invasion landings, but were not a success.

*Anchor opposite this easily identified building on the harbour breakwater to be over the Countess of Erne.*
*Photo: Authors*

There are usually many small fish around the Countess of Erne. It makes a good beginner's wreck dive, and an ideal site when conditions are rough outside the harbour. It is sheltered from the east, but can be affected by choppy waves during a blow from the west. The visibility in calm periods – even in winter – can be up to 8m until the first diver fins around in the silt, reducing it to nil. Currents are virtually non-existent. *Launching: any slip or shore around the harbour.*

**142 Balaclava Bay Reef (north end)** 50 33.50N; 02 25.00W. This site is on the eastern shore line of Portland. It is a 6m ledge, which forms a drop off in the island's foundations. It starts as a steep slope at its northern end from

*300 yards north west, along the harbour breakwater from the wreck of the Countess of Erne, directly opposite this pattern of rocks, lie the remains of an MFV (Site 139).*

Photo: Authors

approximately ½ mile south of the *Hood* (Site **140**) and extends roughly parallel to and never more than 100yds from the shoreline to beyond Grove Point. An easy way to find its northern end is to be opposite a point just south of the very large square building above the shoreline.

The reef is very steep in places, in others it forms a less steep slope of smaller ledges and boulders. At the bottom, at a depth of 14m, there is a sandy sea bed with scattered rock patches. Farther south, nearer Grove Point, the depths at the base of the reef, are down to 22m. The current for 9 hours out of 12 is always flowing southwards, towards Grove Point, and usually allows a good drift dive. At times, this flow of water accelerates into a race at Grove Point, making it very difficult for boats to pick up surfacing divers. However, if divers do surface in this race they are soon out into calmer, safer conditions to the south.

Marine life is prolific. This is an excellent, sheltered site when the wind is from anywhere between south-west, west and north-west. It is however, open and subject to disturbance with an easterly blow. Visibility in summer can be up to 10m. Dive here at any time, but watch out for the current at Grove Point, especially in the 3 hours between 5 hours after high water at Portland to 4 hours before high water at Portland. *Launching: Portland Harbour, 1 mile.*

**143  Earl of Abergavenny** 50 36.15N; 02 24.95W. Built in 1796, this fine ship of the English East India Company was on its way from London to the Far East with 400 passengers and crew living in cramped conditions below decks. A pilot taken on at Weymouth sailed her straight onto the Shambles Bank and badly holed her bottom. She finally sank in 15m at 11pm on 5 February, 1805, in Weymouth Bay. Despite the many hours between stranding and sinking, and the presence of rescue craft, as many as 350 people perished.

Salvage was carried out at various times during the months after her sinking, and by 1807 all her treasure of silver pillar dollars in sealed chests had been removed. The sea bed is soft and silty, which has prompted lengthy investigation

*A brass syndicate seal and a brass
uniform cap badge or pouch badge of
the Honourable East India Company,
both excavated from the wreck site of
the Earl of Abergavenny (Site 143).*
Photos: Richard Larn

of the wreck since 1979 by a group of divers. Their underwater investigation continues, and hundreds of precious artefacts may be seen displayed in several British shipwreck and maritime museums, including the Deep Sea Adventure Shipwreck Museum at Weymouth.

The wreck is not protected and is open for any interested diver to visit. It is often possible, after periods of work by the archaeological group, to find gun flints scattered across the site. However, project leader Ed Cumming (tel. 01908 313751) asks divers to contact him before diving here. The site is sheltered from the south-west and west and can be dived when sites farther offshore are badly affected by south-westerly winds. Currents are mostly weak. Visibility can be good, but is easily reduced to nil by careless finning around. *Launching: any site in Portland Harbour. Boats: Weymouth 2 miles.*

**144 Bombardon Unit (Portland Harbour)** 50 34.33N; 02 24.91W. Plainly marked on Chart 2255, this wreckage rests on the slope of the harbour wall on the inside of the outer breakwater at a depth of 11m (see photograph opposite). Being mainly on the rocks, it tends to be much less silty than some of the other wrecks in this area. It is easily located, just north of the bend in the breakwater, 20m north of a position marked by a 3m metal pole on the summit of the wall. *Launching: any site around the harbour (all under 1 mile).*

**145 Landing Craft (Portland Harbour)** 50 34.37N; 02 24.90W. This wreck is located on the harbour bed, 70yds north of Site **144**, and can be successfully visited as part of a dive on the latter. The landing craft is in good condition sitting upright with its decks complete, and two large diesel engines can be seen. *Launch: Any site around the harbour, all between ½ and 1 mile.*

*At a point inside the outer breakwater, just north of the bend and 20 yards north of a 9ft high metal pole, lies a Bombardon unit on the rocks above the sea bed (Site 144).* Photo: Authors

**146 Enecuri** 50 34.86N; 02 24.85W. This wreck, better known to those who have dived her as *The Spaniard*, is situated in Portland Harbour at the foot of the inner side of the outer breakwater. She is clearly marked on Admiralty Chart 2255 as an obstruction. She was a Spanish steamship, which drifted on to the breakwater on 29 December, 1900. At the time of her sinking her crew of 26 were all saved, but her captain was later drowned after returning to his ship.

The *Enecuri* is badly broken, with only her bow really recognisable. The depth to the top of the wreck is 7m (sea bed 14m). This is a good beginner's dive and is sheltered from the east and south. The visibility is usually good, but the silt soon stirs with divers around. There is no tidal current. The position can be

*The Enecuri (Site 146) lies inside the harbour at the foot of the outer breakwater at a position directly opposite where the level of the wall lowers to the north and the number "83" is painted in red.* Photo: Authors

easily found; there is a long, low wall along the top of the breakwater and the wreck is directly opposite the position where the wall's level changes by a drop to the north – "83" is marked in large red letters on the wall at this point (see photograph on page 115). A short distance to the north is a look out tower with "99" on it. The wreckage extends almost 50yds to the south, where a high section – probably the bow – is located. The wreck was almost certainly violently disturbed by the Russian oil rig that broke loose from its moorings in a Force 10 gale on 28 October, 1996, and crashed its way northwards along the rocks of the breakwater at this point. *Launching: Castletown or any site around the harbour ½ to 1 mile.*

**147  Unidentified barge (Portland Harbour)** 50 34.93N; 02 24.84W. This unidentified wreck lies about 70m north of the wreck of the *Enecuri* (Site **146**). The vessel is sitting on the sloping breakwater wall almost at its base. She is a whole vessel complete with propeller. Depth to the deck is 11m. It is possible to enter her holds. Her position is fairly easy to find as there is a large number "86" on the wall, 10yds to the north. *Launching: Any site around the harbour, between ½ and 1 mile.*

**148  Sea Otter** 50 35.04N; 02 24.80W. At the northern end of the Portland outer breakwater is the Chequered Fort. On the harbour side of the fort is an almost secret, tiny harbour, enclosed on three sides and very sheltered. In the middle of the harbour at 7m lies the *Sea Otter*, an 18ft fishing vessel that sank here in about 1993. Special permission is required to dive here. *Launch: Any site around the harbour 1 mile.*

*The very sheltered and almost secret harbour at the chequered fort contains the wreck of the Sea Otter.*
Photo: Authors

**149  Two Steel Tanks** 50 35.00N; 02 24.75W. At this position below and outside the Portland Harbour outer breakwater, approximately 100yds south of the chequered fort, are two huge steel tanks measuring approximately 40 by 10ft and standing up 4m. Depth is 13m. This is a very sheltered area when westerly gales blow and there is lots of life along the rocks of the wall here with good visibility and weak currents. *Launch from any site around the harbour, 1½ miles.*

**150 Unidentified wreck** 50 34.87N; 02 24.72W. This wreck is badly broken and consists mainly of plates and steel sections. It lies at a depth of 19m and is the same distance out from the base of the outside face of the outer breakwater. *Launching: Any site around Portland Harbour 1½ miles.*

**151 Dumb Lighter C19** 50 27.70N; 02 24.60W. This vessel sank while under tow, some time prior to 1956. The wreck is at a depth of 40m, some 2 miles or more south of the western end of the Shambles Bank. *Boats: Weymouth 10 miles.*

**152 Valdes** 50 23.68N; 02 24.42W. Lying 7½ miles south of Portland Bill, this British steamship of 2,233 gross tons was another victim of a torpedo fired by the *U-84*, on 17 February, 1917. The *Valdes* had set out down the ship canal from Manchester and was on her way to Cherbourg – so what was she doing off Portland? – with a cargo of hay and flour. Eleven of her crew were lost, but her Captain was among the survivors. She measured 265ft long with a 40ft beam and she was only 3 years old. Today she lies at a sea bed depth of 49m, from which her highest point stands up 5m. She lies east to west. *Boats: Weymouth 15 miles.*

**153 Bombardon Unit** 50 37.63N; 02 24.20W. This site is on a line of 165° magnetic, travelling out from Redcliffe Point. The unit that sank here is plainly marked on the Admiralty chart. Another section is marked separately 150yds to the south-east at 50 34 48N; 02 24 09W. The wreck consists of large metal tanks with a few single metal sheets. The sea bed, at a depth of 12m, tends to be rather soft and silty. The wreck is up to 3m high, but averages a flatter 1m. A good, safe dive with hardly any currents. Visibility: up to 10m in calm periods. *Launching: Bowleaze Cove, 1 mile.*

**154 Domed Reef** 50 37.80N; 02 24.05W. This peculiar feature is a strange geological aberration, just under ½ mile due south-east of Redcliffe Point. From a sea bed of flat, rippled sand at 11m rises a circular mountain of large, loose-looking stones. The whole structure is dome-shaped, rising at an angle of 40° at its steepest point to within 5m of the surface. The upper parts of the reef are covered in delicate varieties of seaweed. Currents are weak. *Launching: Bowleaze Cove, ¾ mile.*

**155 Shambles Fishing Grounds** 50 30.50N; 02 22.50W. If, in late March or early April, you stand on the cliff top at Portland Bill on any fine, calm Saturday or Sunday you will see a fleet of small boats over the Shambles Bank. They are there for one reason only – fishing for plaice. During late March fully grown plaice of well over 3lb in weight begin to arrive in the area. The area around the Shambles Bank is smothered with mussels, but the top of the banks themselves and their slopes are clean sand and gravel. For some odd reason, on arrival, the plaice ignore their feeding grounds of the vast mussel beds and settle in a thick carpet on the sand banks, perhaps attracted by the plentiful sand eels. Gradually, over the next few weeks the majority of the plaice begin to move into the surrounding deeper water to feed on the young mussels and remain there in thousands throughout the summer months. In late summer, they tend to spread into surrounding areas and sometimes by September can be found in quantity as far inshore as the sand fringes off Chesil Cove. Local divers are also well acquainted with this huge sustainable food source and to prove it, there is many a full freezer in Weymouth by the end of the summer.

However, diving the Shambles Bank is not a simple matter: it is an area of very strong currents and there are areas of very deep water. The easiest and safest way is to use the services of the local charter boats from Weymouth. All the skippers are experts in this area and besides knowing the intricacies of the tidal cycle will also know where the main concentrations of fish are located. Depth 6 to 43m. *Boats: Weymouth 8 miles.*

**156 Unidentified wreck** 50 29.30N; 02 21.38W. In 1992, Weymouth diver Peter Knight dived to retrieve a local fishing boat's trawl nets. At a depth of 45m, in good visibility, he was surprised to find a vessel with three propellers. Apparently upside down, the wreck is probably that of a U.S. landing craft. The wreck stands 2m high and measures approximately 60ft long with a beam of 20ft. Both ends are square, the top is flat, and there are holes where the hull is rusting away. At least one engine is plainly visible. *Boats: Weymouth 10 miles.*

WARNING Beware of strong currents in this area.

**157 Saratogo** 50 36.02N; 02 21.20W. This converted wooden motor vessel sank here while under tow in the autumn of 1981. Very little remains of her on the sea bed of silty sand at 23m. The patch of higher ground shown on the chart – just north of the wreck – looks even more interesting. *Boats: Weymouth 4 miles.*

**158 Ethel** 50 28.37N; 02 20.87W. A British steamship of 2,336 gross tons, the *Ethel* was hit by a torpedo fired by the German submarine *UB-104* on 16 September, 1918, and so was one of the last casualties of World War One. She did not sink immediately, but did so later, when under tow. She had been returning in ballast from Rouen to Barry Roads, to collect a cargo of coal. Her owners were Brudick & Sons of London, and she had been built in 1899 at Stockton on Tees. She measured 290ft long with a beam of 42ft.

She is situated two miles off the back of the Shambles Bank, and is a popular dive with Weymouth boats – especially *Channel Chieftain* and *Tiger Lily*, which run evening trips out to her in summer. Sea bed depth is 36m, in an area of good visibility. The bows are detached and lying on the western side of the main body of the ship. She lies within an area of extensive mussel beds, which attract shoals of large feeding plaice into the area. *Boats and launching: Portland Harbour 9 miles, Weymouth 9 miles.*

**159 Elena R** 50 30.19N; 02 20.66W. This 4,576 gross ton Greek steamship was mined and sunk on 22 November, 1939, while on a voyage from Rosario to Antwerp. The *Elena R* had been built in 1917 and was 370ft long with a beam of 53ft 2in. She was equipped with a three-cylinder triple-expansion engine, and had originally sailed under the name of *Munindies*. The ship has been well salvaged and broken open and lies at a depth of 27m, with some parts standing 7m high. She tends to be well sanded over on her lower parts and is surrounded by loose, shifting sand banks.

Timing a dive here is critical. There are strong currents at most times along and over the nearby Shambles Bank. The best period to dive is between 2 and 3 hours before high water at Portland. *Boats: Weymouth 8 miles, Castletown 7 miles.*

**160 Landing Craft** 50 35.66N; 02 20.44W. Almost two miles south-west of the high chalk cliff of White Nothe, at a depth of 21m, is the complete wreck of a World War Two landing craft. Difficult to find and lying on a rather muddy sea bed, this wreck is only occasionally visited by divers. Tidal currents on this site are mainly weak. *Launching: Ringstead 2½ miles. Boats: Weymouth 4½ miles.*

**161 Binnendyk** 50 32.11N; 02 20.01W. This 400ft Dutch steamship of almost 7,000 tons was sunk by a mine on 8 October, 1939. The *Binnendyk* now rests on the sea bed, badly broken up as a result of heavy salvaging. Within the wreck's lower parts there is coarse white sand. But strangely, at a depth of 27m, the sea bed around the wreck consists only of clean, rough stones and rocks. In places the wreck rises as much as 8m high. This is a good, easy dive, but it is only possible to undertake it at slack water. *Boats: Weymouth or Castletown, 7 miles.*

*Cathedral Cavern at Stairhole leads out to an adventurous snorkel expedition or shore dive.* Photo: Authors

# Purbeck and Swanage Bay

The section covered in this chapter lies between White Nothe headland in the west and the Old Harry Rocks, north-east of Swanage, in the east. Except at Swanage, access to the sea is by narrow lanes leading from the main A352, which runs parallel to the coastline. The section includes Durdle Door and Lulworth Cove – two of the best known and perhaps most photographed spots on the British coast. In the western part of the area the shore sites are particularly suitable for beginners, with gently sloping sea beds descending to 8m or so. Central to the area are the almost deserted high cliffs of the Isle of Purbeck. For almost 10 miles, between Kimmeridge and Anvil Point, there are no roads to the sea. With such a shoreline, a boat is essential.

Offshore, many exciting wrecks, the majority only recently discovered, and many almost undived reefs are waiting to be explored. Directly off St Aldhelm's Head (also known as St Albans Head) is St Aldhelm's Race with its precipitous underwater rock walls descending almost vertically to a depth of nearly 60m, within only ½ mile of the shoreline. Visibility is generally excellent, but the shore sites can be adversely affected when strong winds blow from the southern half. Offshore, especially in summer, only a major storm will make much difference to the underwater conditions. On windy days Swanage Bay gives shelter from the south-westerlies, while Worbarrow Bay is sheltered from the east. Lulworth Cove is sheltered from all but a southerly wind.

Tidal slacks generally occur 1 hour before high water at Dover and 6 hours later. There are however, considerable variations near the shore. For instance, the high water Swanage Bay slack at Peveril Point is 3 hours 2 minutes before Dover.

---

**PARKING AT LULWORTH COVE AND DURDLE DOOR**

The large car parks at these sites are owned and managed by the Weld Estate. Season tickets are available, valid at either park, and offer a considerable saving if you intend visiting the area frequently. They can be obtained at the car park office or at the Weld Estate office.

---

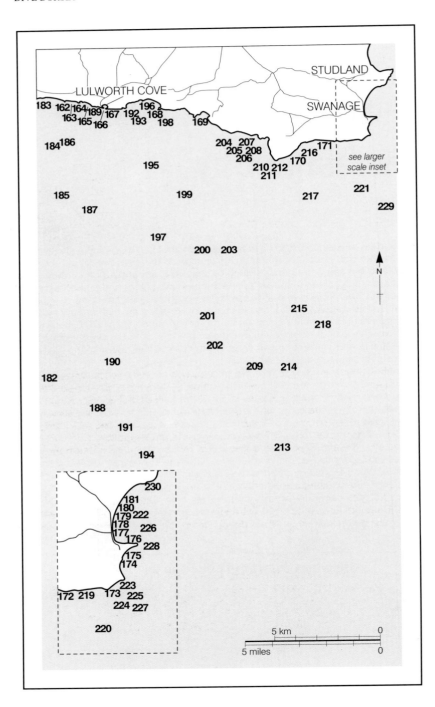

# Army gunnery ranges

The Lulworth Gunnery Ranges (see map on page 127) are situated in the centre of this part of the coast. An area of sea extending from just east of Lulworth Cove almost to St Aldhelm's Head and up to 6 miles offshore is affected when firing on the ranges is taking place at the RAC Gunnery School. Although firing at weekends happens only about six times a year, the ranges are well used on weekdays. During firing the whole sea area, apart from a narrow inshore corridor into Kimmeridge, is closed. Range safety boats patrol the extremities of the danger area and will intercept any mariner careless enough to enter it. Certain coastal roads are also closed when firing takes place.

Details of each week's firing are published in the *Dorset Evening Echo* on Thursdays. Firing times are also broadcast by BBC Radio Solent on weekdays during the shipping and weather news at approximately 5.35, 6.35 and 7.45am and, for the following day, at 5.35pm. The firing programme can also be obtained from the guardroom at Bindon Abbey (tel. 01929 462721 ext 4824). The range control listens out on VHF Channel 8 when firing is taking place. Do not enter the range before first ascertaining that firing is not taking place.

WARNING  Throughout the sea area of the ranges (and particularly in the area of Worbarrow Bay), the sea bed is littered with all manner of shell heads and projectiles. Never touch these objects, let alone bring any of them to the surface. Many are unexploded and can be lethal if handled.

# Shore dive and snorkel sites

**162  Middle Bottom Beach**  SY 785 806. *Snorkel and aqualung.* Middle Bottom Beach is one of the most glorious beaches in Dorset but cannot be reached by land (the most convenient point for launching is Lulworth Cove). It extends almost from White Nothe Head in the west to Bats Head in the east, a distance of 2 miles and it is unusual to find more than a handful of people on it. Towards the eastern end there is an underwater reef within easy snorkelling distance of the beach. The site is suitable for any grade of diver but it must be borne in mind that there is no telephone here.

**163  Durdle Door Beach**  SY 806 803. *Snorkel and aqualung.* To arrive at this site leave the A352 Wool to Dorchester road at the Red Lion Inn, near Winfrith Newburgh. Follow the road south through the village and onwards for a distance of approximately 2½ miles. At Newlands Farm, the entrance to the Durdle Door

**Opposite: Dive sites in Area 3, Purbeck and Swanage Bay. This area is covered by Admiralty charts 2610 (Bill of Portland to Anvil Point), 2172 (Swanage and Studland Bays plus local anchorage), 2615 (Bill of Portland to the Needles); Ordnance Survey maps: Pathfinder sheet numbers: 1332, 1334, however Outdoor Leisure Map sheet number 15 covers this whole section.**

Caravan and Camping Park will be seen. Drive through this to the cliff top car park situated above Durdle Door. From the car park the beach is approached by a ½-mile public footpath with flights of steps over the last 75yds. From the car park to the beach is a descent of almost 350ft. While it is possible to carry a full set of equipment to the sea, it is hard work, especially when struggling back up at the end of the day. If an inflatable is available, it is a good alternative plan for one or two members of the diving party to use it to transport the heavy equipment from Lulworth Cove.

The beach at Durdle Door extends westwards for a distance of almost 1 mile from the only access at its eastern end. The beach is fairly steep and composed of fine, sandy gravel. Parts of the beach are still accessible at high water. Behind it are high unscalable cliffs of white chalk. The famous rock arch of Durdle Door is the main feature of the eastern end of the beach. At the western end is another small headland known as Bats Head. Here, another chalk arch is appropriately called Bats Hole.

An underwater reef, which dries out in places, extends about 100yds offshore along almost the entire length of the beach. Between the beach and reef depths do not exceed 7m. Outside the reef a drop-off with broken stones and rocks occurs to depths of about 14m. Diving here is excellent, especially for the snorkeller, who does not have to carry heavy gear to the beach. Kelp occurs on

*Durdle Door, Lulworth Cove and the nearby sites. There are many opportunities for the snorkeller in this area.*

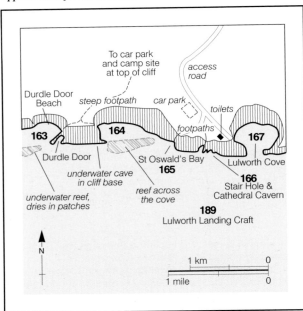

the reef, but only in isolated patches between the reef and the beach. The reef itself can give several hours of very interesting underwater exploration. Although there is no obvious wreckage on the reef, the laws of chance dictate that wrecks must have occurred here. The traces are probably hidden beneath the sea bed. Life on the reef is prolific with the usual species of wrasse in the shallower kelp. Somewhat deeper, lobsters and large crabs are to be found.

This site is exposed to southerly and south-westerly winds, but the reef acts as an underwater breakwater causing swells to break so there is usually an area of relatively calm water between the reef and the beach. This site is usually diveable up to a Force 5 or 6 wind. There are no currents inside the reef and only slight east or west tidal currents immediately outside it. Apart from the onerous distance to carry gear, this site is ideal for the beginner, and provides more than adequate interest for the experienced diver.

There is neither a telephone nor toilets at this site. The nearest telephone is a public kiosk near the café and store in the Durdle Door Caravan Park. Toilets are also there. However, on most fine days during the summer season a small mobile snack bar is towed by tractor down the path to within 100yds of the beach. The proprietors usually have with them a private mobile telephone, which would be available in an emergency.

*An unusual view of Durdle Door from the sea.* Photo: Roy Smallpage

**164 Manowar Cove** SY 807 803. *Snorkel and aqualung.* Access to this site is by public footpath from the car park at Durdle Door Caravan and Camping Park (*see* Site 163). Manowar Cove is just east of Durdle Door. After following the path from the summit of the cliffs, head for a flight of steps cut out of the cliff slope which approaches the beach. Like the previous site, the carrying of diving gear from the car park is possible, but is a very onerous task. An easier way is to launch an inflatable at Lulworth Cove and transport the heavier equipment by sea.

Access to the water is from the gently shelving beach composed of small pebbles. The cove is small and shallow and is almost divided from the open sea by the Manowar Reef. Although this name suggests that a ship of the line was wrecked here in the distant past, there is no record of such an event. It is, however, doubtful if a proper underwater survey of this reef and adjacent sea bed has ever been carried out. At the rear of the curving beach are high cliffs. It is a good idea not to sit directly beneath them as the approach footpath is very near the rim. With lots of people walking to and fro in summer there is always a chance of stones being dislodged. The cove is very well sheltered from all rough seas by its surrounding reefs. It is a sun-trap on a clear day.

Underwater there is a great diversity of interest. The lagoon has depths to about 5m. Here, the bottom is not flat, but rocky with deep and shallow patches. There are many different types of seaweed and a multitude of small fish, which dart in and out of the rocks as divers glide by. The lagoon is ideal for beginners and is safe for families to swim or practise snorkelling. Outside the reef there is some excellent diving. A few yards to the west of the small gap that forms the entrance, the cliff shelves down to depths of 8m. Here, almost 5m below the surface, there is a beautiful cave, large enough to accommodate a diver. The cave has a blow-hole through which beams of light stream down to illuminate the interior. The whole of the cliff between Manowar cove and the arch of Durdle Door can be explored. Aqualung divers and snorkellers will find plenty to see here. Only a very slight east or west tidal current occurs immediately outside the reef. The sea near the outer walls of the reef can get very choppy if a wind is blowing from any direction other than north. For facilities *see* Site **163**.

**165 St Oswald's Bay** SY 815 800. *Snorkel site only.* To reach this site park in the Lulworth Cove car park, and on foot take the private road at its south-east corner. Follow the road to its end at the summit of the hill, then continue west by a footpath that descends steeply to the beach. Even at low water the beach is rather narrow, and is backed by soft chalk cliffs towering to over 300ft. High water is approximately as for Portland. The snorkel diver will enjoy the shallow areas interspersed with many deeper crevices containing small fish. At the outer extremities of the rocky areas, after a reef has been crossed, the sea bed falls away to depths of 6 to 7m. There is plenty of kelp around the outer parts of the site.

The bay is exposed to wind and swell from the south and west. The experienced snorkel diver may try a long-distance expedition from this site along the base of the cliffs, through the rock-studded area to Stairhole (Site **166**), or even to Lulworth Cove (Site **167**). There is a gentle east-flowing current to aid this swim starting 3 hours before high water Portland and continuing for 5 hours. The nearest public telephone is outside the car park at Lulworth Cove. For other facilities, *see* Site **167**.

**166 Stairhole and Cathedral Cavern** SY 822 798. *Snorkel and aqualung.* Leave the Lulworth Cove car park by its south-east corner. Cross the private road and enter the grassy area beyond, continuing for 40yds towards the cliff top. Stairhole will then be seen to the landward side of the cliff, down a steep slope. The sea has broken through the cliff here; a large gap and two separate arches lead out to the open sea. The footpath to this beach changes constantly and needs to be reconnoitred carefully before leaving the summit of the slope, especially when carrying heavy gear. Unless there has been a good dry spell, it can be dangerously slippery.

Once in the water, which is shallow and boulder-filled, a swim of only 12yds will take you into the archway or caves and then into the open sea. The larger of the two archways provides the easiest route. Beyond it the depth increases fairly rapidly to 8m and the sea bed then slopes gently away from the land. Although it is an extremely pretty dive, it is not suitable for beginners. From the outer entrance of the archway a band of thick kelp on large boulders thins out and ceases as the depth increases. To the left and right the scenery is also outstanding, with isolated

*The marine wildlife reserve at Kimmeridge and the Army firing range. The map shows Stairhole and Cathedral Cavern (Site 166), Lulworth Cove Beach (Site 167), Worbarrow Bay and Pondfield (both marked as Site 168) and Kimmeridge (Site 169).*

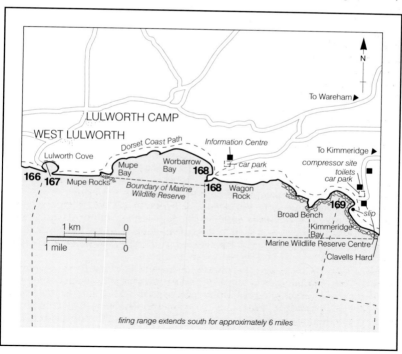

boulders set in clean gravel. Different varieties of weed grow at different depths, and many highly colourful cuckoo wrasse live around the boulders. About 100yds from the cliff, depths of 10 to 12m are encountered. Here there are huge blocks of fallen cliff standing up to 7m high on the sea bed. Each has its own small kelp forest on its upper surface together with its own colony of territorial fish swimming around its walls.

A dive must not be attempted here if the state of the sea in the archways means you could be injured by being thrown against the rocks. Entry is difficult from the boulder beach at these times. If a swell is breaking against the cliff, diving is very uncomfortable, even at depth, and the excellent visibility is marred. The current along the face of the cliff is rarely anything but gentle. Experienced snorkel divers can swim eastwards along the cliff and into Lulworth Cove (Site 167). The nearest public telephone is outside the car park at Lulworth Cove.

WARNING At Stairhole there is a nasty hazard to be avoided. At the base of the cliff, towards the cove entrance, there is an outfall discharging raw sewage into the sea – divers should keep well clear.

**167 Lulworth Cove Beach** SY 824 799. *Snorkel, aqualung, free launching.* The main route to Lulworth Cove is from Wool, which is on the A352 Wareham–Dorchester road. Take the B3071 and continue through West Lulworth to the cove. From the large car park there it is about 400yds to the sea; access to the water is down a few wide steps or a narrow concrete slope, then across 10yds of pebble beach. Lulworth Cove is a small, circular bay roughly ½ mile across and enclosed by cliffs with a narrow entrance to the open sea. Skirting most of it is a narrow pebble beach. When a storm brings in a swell, the waves at high tide reach the foot of the cliffs. At the eastern side of the cove are grassy areas, but these are quite a long walk from the access point.

Underwater, depths run down to 6m, the deepest areas being in the centre and the eastern side of the entrance. The sea bed near the shore consists of loose stones and rocks covered in a variety of weeds. The central area is of clean, rippled, yellow sand. Many small fish live in the weed areas, and some small plaice and an occasional flounder can be seen on the sand. While the cove is sheltered from most winds, the visibility can be adversely affected by a swell which, on rough days, can enter and break on the shore. Otherwise, visibility can be up to 10m in summer. There are no currents.

The natural features of this site make it ideal for the beginner, whether aqualung diving or snorkelling, but there are several snags. The popularity of the site with holidaymakers and divers makes for heavy congestion on the beach around its entrance point, especially on bank holidays. Diving groups should therefore gather farther along the beach, away from this area.

Boat traffic in the cove, particularly between the western shore and the entrance, can be quite heavy. Aqualung divers must use large surface markers and, if possible, snorkel cover. Do not dive in the traffic lane in the eastern half of the cove entrance. From May to October there are by-laws in force: one restricts all pleasure boats to a speed of 8 knots; another states that boats must be manoeuvred with care and with "reasonable consideration for other persons."

*Lulworth Cove. The section of the beach below the boatyard is easy to launch from and is favoured by diving groups (Site 167).* Photo: By kind permission of John Hinde (UK) Ltd.

The 400yds of access road between the car park and the beach is narrow and fairly steep, with no turning area at the beach end. It is subject to the following restrictions: no vehicles 10am to 6pm, 15 May to 30 September; no waiting 8am to 8pm all year round. This means that after 10am boats and gear can only be manhandled on trailers, or carried down from the car park to the sea. Immediately east of Lulworth Cove are the Army gunnery ranges (*see* page 127).

Beside the road between the car park and the cove are shops, public toilets, a café, a pub and two hotels. There is a public telephone kiosk on the road near the car park. There is also an emergency telephone mounted on the outside wall of the fishermen's store building, 30yds up the road from the beach.

WARNING Around Lulworth, including the cove itself, the cliffs are very unstable. Do not attempt to climb them. On fine summer days hundreds of people risk their safety by sitting beneath the cliffs. Do not be tempted to join them – keep well clear.

## 168 Worbarrow Bay, Pondfield and the South of Ireland SY 870 794.

*Snorkel and aqualung.* Worbarrow Bay, the site of a former fishing settlement, is now deserted and lies at the heart of the gunnery ranges. To find this beautiful, isolated bay take the A351 by-pass around Wareham, following road signs for Swanage. Leave the A351 by turning right into a country lane (signposted Creech and Kimmeridge) 1 mile beyond the road island where the A352 divides off for Weymouth. Keep straight on for almost 3 miles to the summit of the Purbeck Hills, from where there are fantastic views. Keep straight ahead – signposted to Tyneham and Lulworth via the army ranges – for a short distance until you reach the outer perimeter of the range, which is marked by a military gate and sentry box. This is as far as you will get if firing is taking place (see page 123).

If the road is open, drive straight on, and after ½ mile fork left through a second military gate. Continue until you reach the ruined village of Tyneham, where there is a large grass and gravel parking area; from here it is a 1 mile walk to the beach on a wide track with a smooth, gravel surface. Vehicles are barred by a locked gate; pedestrians must pass through a narrow gap.

Divers who regularly visit Worbarrow overcome the problem of carrying heavy gear by bringing prams, pushchairs or wheelbarrows to transport it to the beach. Apart from the last 100yds, the track descends towards the sea very gently. There are two other ways of transporting heavy gear. One is to send half the diving party to Kimmeridge (Site **169**), and ferry the gear round to Worbarrow by inflatable. The alternative is to enquire politely whether one of the Range

*Diving and snorkelling around Worbarrow Bay and Pondfield. The track behind the beach offers good, level access from the car park at Tynham, 1300yds away.*

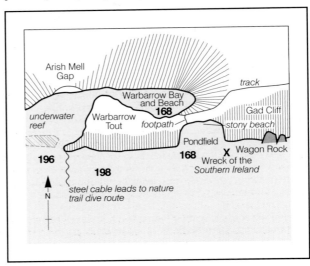

Wardens will transport heavy gear to the beach by Land Rover (an unofficial arrangement and not one of the Warden's duties).

The shore at Worbarrow – especially to the east – is sheltered by the high land to the north, and is flanked to the south by the high mass of Worbarrow Tout. This gives a natural sun trap, which is affected only by south-westerly or westerly winds. The beach is of fine shingle and coarse sand. Underwater, the scenery is enchanting: the sea bed slopes gently away from the beach to depths of 7 or 8m within 100yds of the shore. Near the rocky shoreline of the Tout there are reefs covered in many varieties of weed, but depths are more shallow here. Diving along these reefs is just like being in an aquarium containing many varieties of fish, large and small. A lucky diver may see a John Dory on this site. On calm sunny summer days the visibility can be around 15m. Currents near the shore are non-existent, making this an ideal shore dive site for any grade of aqualung or snorkel diver.

On the other side of the Tout is another, almost secret little bay squashed between cliffs. This is Pondfield, a mere 70yds from Worbarrow Beach. The beach here is composed of flat pebbles at high water mark, but at low water there are many weed-covered rocks and boulders to be negotiated (entry for the aqualung diver is awkward at low water even if the sea is calm; it should not be attempted if any swell is breaking on the rocks). Pondfield offers tremendous diving possibilities. Depths are greater than in Worbarrow, and the underwater scenery is much more rugged.

At the foot of Gad Cliff, just a short distance to the east of Pondfield, at a depth of 10m, there are rocks as big as houses, with a wide variety of life around them. Between the rocks, sand and gravel reflect the sun and floodlight the whole scene, but there is more excitement here, for in the shallower rocks, near the base of the cliff, just 100yds east of Pondfield are the flattened plates of a very old shipwreck. For it was here that on Christmas morning in 1883 the Great Western Railway Company's Weymouth to Cherbourg ferry, the 502 gross ton paddle steamer *South of Ireland* drove ashore at top speed in thick fog and became a total loss. This is an infrequently dived wreck.

Another good dive plan is to enter the water at Pondfield and follow the underwater rock wall of the Tout around into Worbarrow – a distance of ½ mile. This gives depths of up to 15m, but there can be a fairly strong current and underwater swell on the outer tip of the rocky promontory. This swim should therefore only be attempted in very good conditions by experienced divers. While crossing the tip of the promontory, look out for a wire cable descending over the rocks and heading off south into deep water – this is the start of the Kimmeridge Underwater Nature Trail (*see* Site **198**). Worbarrow Bay and Pondfield are part of the Purbeck Marine Wildlife Reserve (*see* Site **169**) and the sea around Pondfield forms part of the reserve's study area. *Please do not disturb anything – look but do not touch.* There are no facilities at Worbarrow. In emergency contact the Range Warden, who in the summer months is on duty from 8am to 8pm and in radio contact with the Coastguard.

The old telephone kiosk near the church at Tyneham is part of the exhibition, and does not contain a working telephone. The nearest public telephone is 3½ miles away, ½ mile beyond the bottom of Creech Hill on the Wareham Road. There are toilets at the Tyneham car park, clearly signposted near the start of the track to the sea.

**169 Kimmeridge** SY 909 787. *Snorkel, aqualung, free launching.* This has always been a popular site, and in recent years it has gradually become more and more heavily dived. But the owners, the Smedmore Estate, have taken an enlightened approach and have created a large car park 100yds inland of the slipway. Inland from the car park there is a small, well signposted area reserved for compressors. However, Kimmeridge has become so popular that it is worth considering alternative launching venues on fine Sundays during the summer months. On these days, especially on neap tides, the immediate area of the slipway can become congested, with many other users besides diving groups attempting to launch.

To find this site, follow the directions for Site **168** until you reach the summit of the Purbeck Hills. Then turn left, and continue for 1 mile to a signpost on the right for Kimmeridge village; the shore is nearly 1 mile beyond the village along a private estate road for which a toll is charged (extra for trailers and boats). However, launching is free and there is plenty of car park space. The slipway is built of concrete and rough cobblestones; vehicles can reverse trailers into the sea, but at low water there are only a few inches of water at the bottom of the slip covering the flat, shale bottom. At such times it is a good idea to row well away from the slip before starting engines, as clumps of rock stand off the shallow bottom for up to 45yds out. At low water on springs, it is almost impossible to launch or recover a hard boat or RIB. After launching, vehicles and trailers must be returned to the parking area. Boat users are particularly requested not to leave boats anchored or tied up alongside the quay wall just out from the slip.

*Kimmeridge Bay (Site 169) is one of the traditional nurseries of British diving. The wide slipway allows boat access to many exciting offshore sites.* Photo: Authors

For tidal information refer to the Portland and Weymouth tables; there is little difference for Kimmeridge. Range is approximately 0.7m on neaps with just over 2m on springs. The low tide times quoted refer to the first low, this is followed by a slight flood for approximately 1 hour, then ebbing to a second low 3½ hours after the first. The second low is usually lower than the first. There then follows a rapid flood for the next 3 hours. Kimmeridge Bay is wide and shallow with reefs of black shale running out from the shore. It is ideal and safe for the snorkeller. There are lots of weeds and fish on the ledges. Depths run down to 7m, but these are found only well out in the bay. Currents in the bay are negligible, but outside fairly strong flows may be encountered running parallel to the coast. For a serious aqualung dive a boat is required to reach deeper water. Outside the bay, the sea bed is generally of flat black shale broken every so often by 1m high ledges running north–south. This is skate ground. West of the bay the sea bed becomes much more gravelly, with other types of rock strata to be seen. Here scallops and crabs are found. Depths within ¾ mile of the shore run down to 25m, but a very shallow aqualung shore dive can always be enjoyed on the ledges just east of the bay, especially at high water. Here, the best place to enter the water is from the base of the cliff beyond the ruins of the old quay.

Kimmeridge is fairly sheltered, except from the south. Visibility can be excellent, but the bay can become black when storms stir up the shale. There is an emergency telephone on the outside of the Coastguard store near the slipway. Toilets can be found in the parking area. In the village the post office shop provides hot drinks and snacks and nearby is a telephone kiosk. Sites for camping are sometimes available in the village.

Above the slipway at Kimmeridge is a large hut housing displays of photographs and fish in tanks. It is open most days in the summer months. Guide books to the reserve and the underwater nature trail at Worbarrow Tout can be obtained here. On duty in the hut is a warden, who is pleased to meet with visiting divers. Together with providing information, the warden is keen to receive information – reports of sightings and observations will be most welcome. There are a number of other things to be aware of before diving at Kimmeridge:

● There is a line of yellow markers across the mouth of the bay – inside these there is a speed limit of 5 knots (May to September). It is possible to encounter swimmers or snorkellers anywhere in this area.

● Particularly if you dive here during the week, check whether firing is taking place on the nearby army ranges; if firing is taking place, boats may leave the bay only by a narrow inshore corridor to the east. There is a notice at the entrance to the quay that gives details of the firing programme.

● A large sea and shore area to the west of Kimmeridge Bay forms the site of the Purbeck Marine Wildlife Reserve. This reserve was created by voluntary agreement of owners and regular users. It is sponsored by the Dorset Trust for Nature Conservation. The Trust's Marine Committee is responsible for the management of the reserve. In an advisory capacity is the Purbeck Marine Wildlife Reserve Sub-committee, on which the BSAC is represented. The reserve has no legal status but relies on the co-operation of all users. Underwater swimming is encouraged, but in keeping with the spirit of the reserve divers are asked to observe the policy of *look but do not touch* throughout the area.

133

**170 Winspit** SY 977 761. *Snorkel site only.* Winspit is accessible only by a public footpath of over 1 mile in length. To find it, take the A351 Swanage road from Wareham. After passing through the village of Corfe Castle turn right for Kingston. When this elevated village is reached, turn left towards Langton Matravers. After 1 mile turn right for Worth Matravers. Just as the road enters this village a visitors' car park will be seen in a small paddock on the right-hand side. From here, walk down into the village centre, past the Square and Compass Inn, and past the grassy area and pond until you come to a well signposted footpath to Winspit.

Winspit not only makes an excellent snorkel dive for beginners, but is also interesting for the more experienced snorkeller. When the tidal current is favourable an advanced snorkel diver can explore along the base of the cliff eastwards for ¾ mile to Seacombe (Site **171**) – passing the wreck site of the *Halsewell* (Site **216**) – then quite easily walk back along the cliff-top path. The nearest facilities are at Worth Matravers.

**171 Seacombe** SY 984 766. *Snorkel only.* Situated in a break in the Purbeck cliffs, Seacombe is well known for its underground caves quarried out over hundreds of years for the valuable building stone and for the horrendous wrecking of the East Indiaman *Halsewell* (Site **216**). Nowadays, with quarrying long ceased and the only access being a public footpath from the nearest road 1 mile away at Worth Matravers, all is tranquil at Seacombe. Access to the water is from a sloping path that leads through a narrow gap in the low cliff to rock ledges.

**172 Dancing Ledge** SY 998 769. *Snorkel only.* From Langton Matravers, at a point a short distance west of the church on the B3069, a road named Durnford Drove starts towards the sea to the south. Drive along this road and finally up a rough narrow lane to a small National Trust car park; from here you need to walk for ¾ mile over public footpaths via Spyway Barn Farm. Access to the sea is by climbing down low, rocky walls on to the main ledge, from which it is easy to enter the sea direct into depths of 7m – a good beginners' snorkel dive, but with no facilities.

**173 Anvil Point** SZ 031 769. *Snorkel and aqualung.* This site is just over 1½ miles along the coast from Swanage. It is a remote area of high cliffs, grassy slopes and wheeling sea birds and lies within Durlston Country Park. To reach it, drive from the town centre towards the pier. Just before the pier entrance take the right hand turning up the hill. Near the top, where there is a sign for the country park, turn left into Durlston Road. Carry straight on until the road terminates in a U-bend within a landscaped car park. Park as near to the bend as possible to pick up the start of a gently descending grassy footpath to the cliff top. Gear has to be carried down this path to the cliff top and then down a very steep descent into a deep valley. It is easy to climb down a series of rock ledges onto a rock platform at sea level, though it may be handy to have a rope to lower heavy cylinders down the rock ledges to the platform. The distance from the car park to the sea is approximately 500yds. Access to the sea is by rolling off the rock platform into water 3m deep. At some states of the tide it can be a little difficult to climb back out of the sea on to the platform; a rope held by a buddy ashore is a great help.

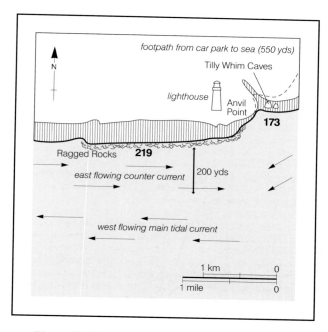

*The snorkel diver can harness the power of the counter-current off Anvil Point. By moving nearer to or farther from the cliff it is possible, for a period of four hours, to be carried either east or west along two miles of coast.*

Anvil Point is particularly rugged, with wild, open scenery, and the sea bed is equally rugged. Giant blocks of rock lie around the base of the cliff. From the point of entry, the bottom quickly slopes away over kelp covered rocks to a depth of 7 or 8m. The boulders do not extend far from the base of the cliff, but soon there is a change to a flatter rock bottom with small gravel patches. This site is a little sheltered, being in a slight cove in the cliff. Nevertheless, even the slightest swell makes entry and exit extremely dangerous for divers. A calm period or one in which the wind is blowing from the northern half is most suitable. South or south-west winds soon bring waves battering across the entry platform.

The visibility is usually excellent, but divers must keep well within the narrow strip of water along the base of the cliff bounded by a line drawn from Anvil Point to Durlston Head to avoid very strong counter currents. When more than 200yds offshore there is a simple 6 hour tide: the slack period occurs 1 hour before high water at Dover and 5 hours after high water at Dover. But from Anvil Point westwards inshore for almost 2 miles along the cliff a strange tidal aberration occurs. After ebbing westwards normally for 2 hours with the main tide after high water, a counter current starts to flow strongly eastwards along the cliff. This continues to flow until eventually it is reinforced by the next flood tide. The width of this reverse current is up to 200yds out from the base of the cliff. The effect of all this is that during the 4 hours when the counter current is running, the adventurous snorkel diver can choose whether to be carried east or west by swimming farther from or nearer to the cliff.

There is an emergency telephone by the gate at the western side of Anvil Point lighthouse. Near the car park there is a payphone in the foyer of the Durlston Castle pub, and above the car park there are toilets at the park information shop. In emergency only, a vehicle can be driven from the car park down the private road to the cliff top at the Anvil Point lighthouse, but this is still 140yds of steep path away from the sea.

**174 Durlston Bay** SZ 035 781. *Snorkel and aqualung.* To reach Durlston Bay, follow the directions for Site **173** but shortly after the top of the hill out of Swanage, turn left off Durlston Road into Bellevue Road. Drive along it to its most seaward point and park here – there are no yellow lines and not many other motorists. Between two blocks of flats, down a few steps, runs the coastal footpath; follow this for 50yds until, on the left, you see a short length of spike-topped iron railings. Immediately at these railings an unsigned path winds down through a wooded break in the cliff to the beach.

The beach is composed of loose rock slabs that have been shifted around by the action of the waves to form a natural crazy paving. Access across the beach into the sea is easy, but at low tide a jumble of weedy rocks has to be carefully negotiated. The sea bed slopes gently away from the beach. Within the bay, depths of 8m can be encountered. At this depth there are areas of rock covered

*Durlston Bay, particularly when a westerly or northerly wind blows, provides a sheltered shore dive.* Photo: Roy Smallpage.

in kelp with, between them, extensive patches of light-coloured gravel and coarse sand ridged in places by the waves. There are many forms of life here. Shoals of fry swim near the surface in summer in translucent clouds. Crabs and lobsters are in evidence. Pollack swim over the kelp. Bass are to be seen, particularly near the southern end of the bay. The visibility in this bay can be excellent but can be spoiled by a strong southerly or easterly wind, which will soon bring a swell from out at sea. The bay is very sheltered from the west and north.

WARNING  Currents within the bay are negligible, but outside a line drawn from Peveril Point to Durlston Head there is almost always a strong current, particularly when the tide is ebbing. This is particularly so at Durlston Head, where a strong rip tide rushes along the base of the cliff on the point. *Keep clear on the ebb.*

**175  Peveril Point** SZ 039 785. *Snorkel and aqualung.* To get to this beach from the centre of Swanage drive to the Broad Road car park on the hill opposite the pier. Continue through the car park and follow the narrow road past the boat park to Peveril Point, a distance of 200yds. There is turning space here but no parking, so after unloading your gear, cars must be taken back to the car park. At the very end of the point a path leads to the beach. Do not enter the water here: walk along the rocky beach westwards towards Durlston Head for approximately 75yds to a place where a steep path descends the cliff. Access to the water is easy over a few flat ledges and rocks.

   The depths here are shallow. Deeper water can be reached by swimming towards Durlston Head – soon 7m and an interesting bottom of rocky patches will be found. Near and certainly outside a line drawn from Peveril Point to Durlston Head there is a strong current, especially when the tide is ebbing.

---

### SPEED LIMIT IN SWANAGE BAY

A large part of Swanage Bay, including Sites **176** to **181** and **222**, is subject to a 5 knot speed limit. This applies in an area extending outwards for about 400yds from the beaches, starting near Peveril Point and finishing well to the north of the built up area at the other side of the bay. The boundary of this restricted area is marked by yellow buoys.

---

**176  Peveril Boat Park and Launching Ramp (Swanage)** SZ 038 786. *Launching point only.* To find this site, drive south from the centre of Swanage, turning right just before the pier, and then left into Broad Road car park. Drive straight along through the car park, and at its southern end follow the lane for 100yds until a large boat park is found on the left. The way to the launching ramp is through this boat park. The ramp is a very wide concrete platform, sloping into a sandy sea bed. Two jetties run out into deep water, one on either side of the ramp. The ramp is usable at all states of the tide, but the water is very shallow on low water, especially on springs.

   Boats can be launched from trailers here; the trailers can be parked in the boat park but cars must be taken back to the car park. Conditions on the ramp can become rough if a strong wind is blowing from the eastern quarter, otherwise

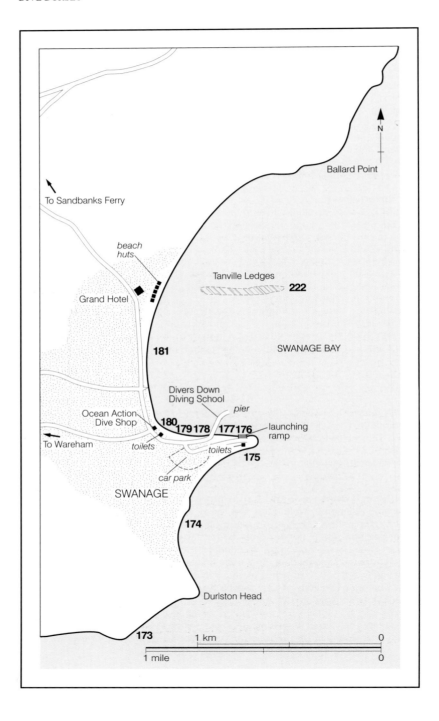

this is a sheltered site. For notes on the dangers of Peveril Race *see* Site **228**. Toilets can be found just south of the boat park entrance, where there is also a National Coast Watch lookout post (not always staffed). There is a telephone in the lifeboat station immediately beside the launching ramp and an emergency telephone on the outside of the National Coast Watch building.

**177  Buckshore (Swanage)**  SZ 036 787. *Snorkel and aqualung.* From the centre of Swanage follow the road south to the pier. Car parking is available on the pier itself, or in Broad Road car park on the hill above the pier. From the pier entrance walk south for about 60yds, then fork left along a public footpath to a secluded beach of pebbles and sand behind Swanage Pier and the sailing club buildings.

The sea bed slopes gently away from the beach. To the south is a large area of weed-covered rocks; to the north is the derelict old pier and beyond it the modern pier. In this area the sea bed is sandy with patches of rock and weed. Straight out from the shore, just beyond the ends of the piers, depths of 7m can be found. Quite large flatfish venture on to this sandy bottom, to be fed by the anglers who use the pier. In the immediate area are moorings and some boat traffic, so be sure to use a surface marker or appropriate surface cover. This area is extremely sheltered from the south-west and can be dived quite safely when strong winds from that direction have stopped diving offshore. A wind from the eastern quarter, however, will soon upset the visibility and bring a choppy swell on to the beach. In quiet spells visibility of up to 10m can be expected here.

Tidal currents inside Swanage Bay can be fairly strong, especially on the ebb. When the tide is flooding, a steady drift develops off this site parallel to the shore and runs toward Peveril Point a couple of hundred yards to the south. This site is ideal for the beginner, whether using snorkel or aqualung. Inflatables can safely be used off this beach after launching elsewhere (*see* Sites **176** and **179**). There is a telephone, which could be used in an emergency, in the sailing club premises at the rear of the beach.

**178  Swanage Pier and Monkey Beach**  SZ 034 786. *Snorkel and aqualung, launching.* Thousands of divers have done their snorkel tests and their first open water dives around Swanage Pier. Experienced divers can be seen on most summer Sundays, shepherding groups of trainees around the framework of the pier. Here, many a diver has become overly excited at their first face-to-face confrontation with a wrasse, albeit only 3in long!

There are several factors that make this site such a good one for beginners. Access to the water is extremely easy, down stone steps from the pier. Near the pier entrance, opposite the Pierhead Café, there is a small beach where the sea bed is level and sandy. This is Monkey Beach, where small inflatables can be carried into the sea directly from the road. A whole day parking ticket allows parking on the pier and includes launching of inflatables down the stone steps. Other car parking is available near the pier. Depths around the pier are fairly

*Opposite: Swanage and Durlston Head, showing Anvil Point (Site 173), Durlston Bay (Site 174), Peveril Point (Site 175), Peveril Boat Park (Site 176), Buckshore (Site 177), Swanage Pier and Monkey Beach (Site 178), Swanage Quay (Site 179), Swanage Parish Slip (Site 180), Ocean Bay Beach (Site 181) and Tanville Ledges (Site 222).*

*Swanage Pier is home to the Divers Down shop and diving school. Many divers carry out their first open water dive here.* Photo: Roy Smallpage.

shallow, but 7m can be found off the seaward end except at low water. The sea bed is generally sandy, with stony patches covered in short weed. The tidal range here is only about 2m on springs with a double high water, which tends to keep beaches narrower and depths deeper for longer periods than if there were a normal 6 hour tide. Currents are weak around the pier. Plaice and flounders are frequently found here, and turbot can sometimes be seen.

Swanage Bay is extremely sheltered on its southern side, being affected only by winds from the easterly quarter; it is only when there are winds above Force 6 from that direction that this site becomes undiveable. Visibility in settled periods can be as good as 10m. This site is therefore highly recommended for beginners. You just need to be careful of the small motor boats on hire near the pier during the summer months. Holidaymakers, including children, buzz around in these boats quite unaware of the damage their propeller could do to a diver. Your A-flag surface marker will be of not the slightest use in warding off this danger, and will probably attract attention. In theory, these boats are restricted to the town side of the pier within a line drawn north-west from the end of the pier across the bay. This means that the safest place to dive is under the pier and in the area of water between the pier and the derelict pier. There are toilets on the pier. Divers Down diving school, gear shop and air station is situated on the pier. There is a telephone for emergency use in the shop.

**179 Swanage Quay** SZ 033 787. *Free launching only.* Swanage Quay is an old stone platform built out from the promenade with a short flight of rather narrow stone steps leading down to the water. Small boats that can be easily carried can be launched here or can be taken across the sandy beach next to the quay.

At low water, especially on springs, the stony bottom dries at the foot of the steps so it is safer to use the beach where the bottom is sandy. The main snag at this site is the lack of parking; double yellow lines run along both sides of the road near the quay.

This site is not recommended as a launching site during the period May to September when the quay is let to commercial hire craft and the adjacent beach and promenade is the pitch of other local boat hirers.

**180 Swanage Parish Slip** SZ 032 787. *Free launching only.* To find this slip drive through Swanage towards the pier. As soon as you are clear of the one-way system turn left into The Parade – this road leads to the sea wall where there is a wide slip. Although the ramp is capable of taking large boats on trailers, this site is recommended only for launching small boats that can be easily carried. The slip is subject to a breaking swell if the wind is more than Force 5 from the east or south. It is very sheltered from all other winds.

**181 Ocean Bay Beach (Swanage)** SZ 031 796. *Snorkel site, launching.* Ocean Bay Beach lies north of Swanage town centre at the point where the road swings away from the sea front. Access to the beach is via a private slip down which boats of up to 14ft can be wheeled to the sea. Although it is permitted to reverse trailers down the ramp, the beach itself is too soft for all but four wheel drive vehicles. There is a small charge for launching. There is also a footpath access to this beach by the side of the Grand Hotel, down Burlington Chine. Diving parties are welcome on this private beach, but although trailers can be stored at the rear of the beach, car parking is a problem. The nearest car park is the North Beach car park, 400yds away. Launching from the beach is easy. The sea bed at low water is of flat sand that slopes gently away from the beach. This site is fairly sheltered, but a swell can start to break on to the beach if a wind from the southern quarter blows much above Force 4.

Just east of this launching point, under the cliff-top Grand Hotel, is the shore end of the main Swanage Bay reef, which dries in places near the shore on low water springs. A short distance farther north is a smaller reef that also stretches out at right angles to the beach. Both reefs are shallow near the shore and ideal for the snorkeller, who can follow them by swimming out into progressively deeper water. Tidal currents, although weak near the beach, can be quite strong farther out, especially on the ebb when the sea flows in a northerly direction towards Ballard Point. There is a telephone kiosk on the promenade and public toilets are situated just off the promenade, a short distance towards the town.

# Offshore boat diving and wrecks

**182 Unidentified wreck** 50 25.00N; 02 19.00W (position approximate). This wreck was discovered in 1994 by John, Steve and Mike Ballett, three professional scallop divers from Poole. From their observations then and since, the brothers think that the wreck is that of the 1,342 gross ton steam collier *Spiral*, which was sailing from the Tyne to Bordeaux with a cargo of coal. She was scuttled by a boarding party from the German submarine *UB-18* on 4 August, 1916; the reported sinking position was 6 miles south-east of the co-ordinates given. The Germans forced the English crew into the ship's boats at gunpoint and not only confiscated the ship's papers but took time to do a bit of looting before detonating the scuttling charges.

Owned and registered at West Hartlepool and built in 1906, this ship was fitted with a three-cylinder triple-expansion engine. The wreck lies upside down on the sea bed, with the stern and bows broken away. The two factors that point to this being the *Spiral* are the coal found encrusting all the recovered items and the great gash in the upside down hull, which allows a "brilliant" view into the midships-positioned engine room. If this gash is evidence of those German scuttling charges so long ago, this almost certainly is the *Spiral*, though a recovered bell bore no name. The sea bed depth is 47m with the upside down section standing 6m proud, with the gash in a position 4m above the sea bed. *Boats: Weymouth 13 miles.*

**183  Offshore from Middle Bottom Beach**  50 37.20N; 02 18.90W. Just under ½ mile offshore between White Nothe Head and Bats Head there is a line of shallow gullies on the sea bed. Depths are about 14 to 16m and the gullies lie between low ledges of outcropping rocks. Particularly during the months of May and June, these gullies seem to be the favourite haunts of large plaice. A scattering of scallops is also present. A little farther offshore, before the sea bed starts to rise on to the Lulworth Banks, depths of 24m can be encountered with a sea bed varying from sand to perfectly clean, broken stones. *Launching: Ringstead 1½ miles, Lulworth Cove 2½ miles.*

**184  British Inventor**  50 35.40N; 02 18.37W. This wreck, situated on the western end of the Lulworth Banks, is difficult to locate by virtue of the fact that it now consists mainly of flattened steel plates and no part stands much more than 1½m high. The *British Inventor*, a steam-driven oil-tanker, hit a mine on 13 June, 1940, while sailing to Britain from Abadan. Only the bow half of the 7,000 ton ship lies on the sea bed, for the rest of the vessel did not sink. It was towed to Southampton and eventually repaired. The sea bed around the wreck is of gravel and sand, with low rock outcrops. Scallops are present in considerable numbers. Depth: 17m. *Launching: Ringstead 3 miles, Lulworth Cove 3½ miles.*

**185  Golden Sunset**  50 33.18N; 02 17.80W. This wreck has never been definitely identified but this 856-ton wooden steam drifter was a victim of a collision on 4 January, 1918, in the area of the Adamant Shoal. She was Government chartered and on Government business when sunk. She measured 84ft long with a 19ft beam. She had been equipped with a 6-pounder gun after she was hired in 1915. Wreckage in the position given consists of a boiler and other debris. Depths 24m. *Boats: Weymouth 7 miles.*

**186  Lulworth Banks**  50 35.70N; 02 17.30W and the surrounding area. Lulworth Banks, with their prolific life and over 4 square miles of rugged underwater scenery, have much to offer any diver. The area is some 2 miles away from the shore and the banks are particularly famous for scallops. Between the high rock peaks and plateaux are many gravelly, sandy patches where mature scallops occur in commercial quantities. Divers have been successfully harvesting this food resource for many years. There are, however, several other attractions in this large offshore area. An exploring diver will see underwater drop-offs and high rock bluffs with rocky pinnacles, around which swim huge shoals of pollack and pouting. Large, brightly coloured cuckoo wrasse are also common. In some areas the sea bed is composed of horizontal rock strata, so clean, smooth and level that they run like a table top for over 100yds before breaking abruptly. Crabs and lobsters are present in large numbers and the area is quite heavily potted by Weymouth and Lulworth boats. Depths on the Lulworth Banks vary from 9m on top of some of the higher peaks to 21m on the lower gravel beds.

Another exciting feature of the area is the many large brass shell cases that are regularly recovered. In the 1950s there was a naval gunnery range here and many hundreds of 5in diameter shell cases appear to have been lost overboard from the firing vessels. Discovering these items seems to be a matter of pure luck. No single area of the banks seems to offer a better chance than any other.

Tides are quite strong at times, but rarely unmanageable. Slack periods of over 1 hour can be expected, particularly on neaps. The westerly flowing ebb current is usually stronger than the easterly flood. Times of slack here are approximately 3¼ hours before high water at Portland and 2¼ hours after. The visibility throughout the area in the summer months is usually excellent. *Launching: Ringstead, 2½ miles, Lulworth, 2 miles. Boats: Weymouth or Castletown, 6 miles.*

**187 Alex van Opstal** 50 32.48N; 02 16.03W. This Belgian passenger liner of 5,965 tons was the first of a series of large ships to be sunk by mines near the Shambles Bank at the start of World War Two. The *Alex van Opstal* was only two years old and sailing from New York to Antwerp when she met her end on 15 September, 1939. She is a large wreck, and measured 420ft with a 57ft beam. Her forward end is still intact and stands almost 7m off the sea bed. Towards the stern the ship is increasingly damaged, and salvage work has left her rear end

*The splendid Belgian cargo ship and passenger liner Alex van Opstal (Site 187) was only two years old when she was torpedoed. Photo: Steve Shovlar collection*

143

a tangled mass of girders. Her stern section is broken off and located approximately 100yds to the south-west at 50 32.43N; 02 16.05W. Depth around the wreck is about 27m. Currents are strong in this area and slack water is essential for diving. The bottom is composed of shifting sand and gravel. Visibility in the area can be affected by the strong current during periods of spring tides. The wreck lies south-west to north-east with her bows towards the north-east *Boats: Weymouth or Castletown, 7 miles.*

**188 Unidentified wreckage** 50 23.67N; 02 15.40W. A rectangular object standing high off the sea bed was discovered by scallop divers in 1995. The object is said to stand up no less than 9m from the 58m sea bed, but it is only 50ft long. This may be a World War Two Mulberry unit. Although deep, it may well be worth a dive onto its summit. *Boats: Weymouth 15 miles.*

**189 Lulworth Landing Craft** 50 36.93N; 02 15.05W. This small wreck, although quite easily recognised for what it is, is quite badly broken. It lies just over 150yds out from the cliff and is opposite Cathedral Cavern at Stairhole (Site **166**). The wreck lies on a rocky sea bed with patches of gravel. Here and there huge sections of rock topped with kelp forest stand up to 4m proud of the sea bed. The general depth is 12m. Currents do not prevent diving at any time but can be quite strong on springs. During choppy spells this whole area off Lulworth is affected by a wave reaction off the face of the cliff. This can make conditions uncomfortable for at least 200yds out from the shore.

This site lies on the route of the large pleasure boat *Smoothtalker* from Lulworth Cove, which, during the summer, is constantly in and out of the cove on short trips along the shoreline. So before you dive it is a good idea to advise the skipper of your plans and location. Certainly a large SMB should be used and an attending boat should fly an easily seen A-flag. If these precautions are taken, this makes an excellent dive for beginners. *Launching: Lulworth Cove ¼ mile.*

**190 Trial Oil Well** 50 25.90N; 02 14.37W. On behalf of British Gas, the jack-up rig *Britannia* established an exploratory well (now capped off) at this position 11 miles due south of Lulworth Cove, during March and April 1996. Depth 45m.

**191 Evertsen** 50 22.89N; 02 13.61W. The Dutch coaster *Evertsen*, a 392 gross ton oil-driven motor vessel and formerly the *Flying Scotsman*, was built in 1930 in the Netherlands, measuring 154ft long with a beam of 25ft. She was on her way home from Par, with her holds full of china clay, when, in thick fog on 24 June, 1961, she had an almost head-on collision with another Dutch coaster – the *Favoriet*. There was no loss of life, because almost 2 hours elapsed before the *Evertsen* sank enabling the less severely damaged *Favoriet* to rescue the crew and passengers. The wreck lies on a sandy sea bed at a depth of 49m, rising up 8m at the highest point and is still more or less undamaged. *Boats: Weymouth 17 miles.*

**192 Mupe Rocks** 50 36.92N; 02 13.30W. This is a delightful place to dive, especially on a bright day when the sun is reflecting off the light gravel bottom. Several rocks rise out of the sea to a height of 10m. Around the rocks, depths are about 7m. Although no record exists of shipwrecks in this locality, some ancient sailing vessels must surely have perished on these rocks, their remains still lying

*The Evertsen (Site 191) was a victim of a collision in 1961.*
Photo: Adrian Ponchaud collection.

undiscovered. On calm days, or when a northerly wind blows, visibility can be excellent. This is an ideal site for the less experienced diver, but is still interesting for any diver who likes exploring underwater cliffs. Keep clear if the sea is at all rough, especially if waves are surging between the rocks. *Launching: Lulworth Cove 1 mile.*

**193 Black Hawk** 50 36.68N; 02 12.43W. If ever a ship refused to sink into oblivion it was this United States liberty steamship of 7,191 tons. She was hit by a torpedo some way off Portland Bill on 29 December, 1944. The whole of her stern, including a large mounted gun and her very large bronze propeller, went to the bottom (*see* Site **138**). The rest of her miraculously refused to sink. On 30 December she was towed in and run aground in Worbarrow Bay and by 2 January 1945 was reported to be partly submerged. She was finally declared a total loss on 2 April, 1945.

Liberty ships were mass produced prefabricated cargo ships, built by the Americans between 1941 and 1945 to replace tonnage sunk by German submarines. They had a speed of 11 knots and in all an amazing number of 2,770 were built. So great was the effort and efficiency put into their production that the record time for building a complete ship was just 4½ days, but this did not mean that durability was compromised. For many years the superstructure of the *Black Hawk* showed well above the water, and despite being open to the storms from the south and south-west that sweep into Worbarrow Bay, she refused to break up. Eventually, because she was considered a navigational hazard, the Navy blew her up. That should have been the end of her, but years later she was again blown up to clear a path for the discharge pipeline from the Winfrith Atomic Energy Research Establishment, which leaves the land through the nearby Arish Mell Gap. This is why today the wreck in Worbarrow Bay is in two halves.

145

At a depth of 12m there are masses of steel sections and plates up to 3m high. The bow section can be identified by the heavy anchor chain that runs almost 75m south to a 3-ton Danforth anchor. The sea bed around the wreck is mainly gravel ridges. Near the wreck, to the south, is an outcropping rock ledge, one of a series that cross the bay from Worbarrow Tout in the east to Mupe Rocks in the west. The wreck is within the area of the Purbeck Marine Wildlife Reserve (*see* Site **169**) and within the Army firing ranges (see page 123). Currents can be quite strong at times, but never preclude diving. *Launching: Lulworth Cove 2 miles, Kimmeridge 3 miles.*

**194 HMS Warrior II** 50 21.56N; 02 12.23W. Besides being requisitioned by the Navy in both world wars, she had a number of private owners in her peacetime capacity as a private yacht. Built in 1904, she measured 298ft long with a beam of 32ft. Her end came while carrying out her naval duties on 11 July, 1940 when, during an air attack a German aircraft scored a direct hit with a bomb and sent her 1,166 gross tons straight to the sea bed. One of her crew was killed.

The ship (previously called the *Goizeko Izarra, Wayfarer* and *Warrior*) lies upright in an area where, because of a shingle, pebble sea bed, the visibility can be exceptionally good. The ship is well broken open with all of her decks and much of her superstructure gone or collapsed. Her hull is chiefly broken down, but some features are recognisable. The high quality of the specification to which she was built is still apparent in her superb brass fittings, some of which are still to be seen – of particular interest are the square brass portholes. Pipe work around the engines points to where her high quality oil boxes must have been fitted. Her identify was originally verified by the recovery of her bell by a group diving from the Weymouth charter boat *Skin Deep*. Sea bed depth is 54m with wreck standing up 3m at her highest point. *Boats: Weymouth 19 miles.*

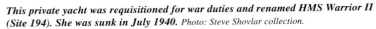

*This private yacht was requisitioned for war duties and renamed HMS Warrior II (Site 194). She was sunk in July 1940. Photo: Steve Shovlar collection.*

**195  Railway Line Wreck** 50 34.52N; 02 11.85W. This wreck is a mystery, lying 3¼ miles south-west of Kimmeridge Bay. Very few people have dived her and no one seems to know her name or when she sank; she does not figure in any wreck list. This vessel lies on a sandy sea bed at a depth of 25m. Her main feature is the cargo – a large pile of pieces of railway line, which give the wreck its name. Information on the length, size and condition of the hull is scanty, and there is a suggestion that this may have been a wooden boat. No doubt the clues of her identity are there for an inquiring group to find. *Launching: Kimmeridge 3½ miles. Boats: Weymouth 9 miles.*

**196  Worbarrow Bay Ledges** 50 36.80N; 02 11.45W. A glorious reef drift dive is possible at this approximate position, across the outer area of Worbarrow Bay. A series of high reefs start just west of Worbarrow Tout, extend westwards right across the bay and can be traced along the sea bed until well west of Lulworth Cove, passing its entrance ½ mile out to sea.

The easiest way to locate and dive them is to commence a dive 200yds south-west, out from the end of the Tout, then swim along the sea bed in a due north direction (into the bay). Soon, the outer and highest reef will be located, intersected at right angles to its length; this is the position given. By turning west along it, a dive with excellent scenery will certainly be enjoyed. There are other reefs running parallel, farther to the north.

The tide runs parallel to the reefs, so that on a west-going stream it is possible to "fly" along the top of the ridge, surveying the landscape on either side at the base of the steep rock walls. Somewhere along or just off the highest and southernmost reef are the remains of a four-engine World War Two bomber. The wreck of the *Black Hawk* (Site **193**) is also near. General depth of sea bed is 14m. The top of the reef is 10m. *Launch: Kimmeridge Bay, 2 miles, Lulworth Cove, 2 miles.*

**197  A3 Submarine** 50 31.41N; 02 11.25W. Like most submarine wrecks, the *A3* is sitting upright on the sea bed. She measures 105ft 5in long with a beam of 12ft 9in and had a displacement of 207 tons when submerged. The sea bed depth is 38m and the top of her conning tower is at 32m. She is in an area that usually affords good visibility. Janine Gould of The Old Harbour Dive Centre at Weymouth describes the sea bed around the submarine as being of clean, smooth, flat rock and geologically interesting in its own right. In the vicinity, probably to the north-west, is believed to be a high rock ledge. The submarine is complete and undamaged except that the outer conning tower hatch has been removed and is displayed in the Deep Sea Adventure Centre on the Quay at Weymouth. There is a layer of silt within the conning tower which points to the inner hatch being closed. It is a small target and difficult to locate on an echo sounder, especially when the tide is flowing.

The A class submarines were in service well before the start of World War One, but not without tragedy. The *A1* was run down by a steamer while exercising in the Solent with the loss of her crew. Also in the Solent, on 2 February 1912, HMS *Hazard*, the escort to the submarine flotilla, accidentally rammed the *A3* and she sank with a full loss of crew. She was eventually recovered and taken out of service. Later, in 1912, she was towed to her present position and sunk as an ASDIC target. She lay there, eventually disused and forgotten until Simon

*The diminutive A3 (Site 197), here photographed at speed before her sad loss.*
Photo: Authors' collection

Bird, then skipper of *Autumn Dream*, was returning to Weymouth one day in 1989 from a dive on the *Aeolean Sky* (Site **200**) when he spotted a blip on his echo sounder. He was lucky to be able to relocate the position and luckier still to have divers aboard with diving time left! It did not take long for a shot to be flung overboard and a diver to investigate – the *A3* was rediscovered. *Boats: Weymouth 11 miles, Swanage 13 miles.*

**198 Kimmeridge Underwater Nature Trail** 50 36.85N; 02 11.19W. On the very tip of the remote rocky promontory of the Tout at Worbarrow Bay (at SY 868 794) is the start of a Nature Trail, which is within the Purbeck Marine Wildlife Reserve. Almost at the end of the rocks, when observed from the south, is one prominent black rock. At the west side of this rock, in a crack, will be seen a steel cable descending into the sea. The cable leads to a sinker in a rocky gully. From here, a white rope guides the visitor westwards through a terrain of rock gullies and boulder slopes within which there is an astonishing array of underwater life. Numbered tags have been set up along the way.

The numbers correspond to a description of the trail and its species clearly laid out in a guide booklet obtainable from the display hut at Kimmeridge or from the head office of the Dorset Trust for Nature Conservation (tel. 01202 554241). It is strongly recommended that visiting divers obtain a copy, seal it in plastic and take it down the trail in order to be able to identify the many plants and animals that will be seen. There is even a wreck down there.

The trail leads a distance of 150yds and then visitors are encouraged to deviate and find their own personal route back to the start. Do however remember you are in a reserve: the strict rule is *look but do not touch*. At times, especially on springs, there can be a fairly strong current flowing around the Tout, but this is usually manageable. Depths are down to 15m.

The one hazard is if the sea is rough – usually caused by south or south-west winds – when any swell is magnified as it crashes onto the rock wall of the Tout. At these times it is essential to descend to the sea bed without approaching the rock wall on the surface. *Launching: Kimmeridge 2½ miles, Lulworth Cove 2½ miles.*

As this book went to press, what appears to be the wreck of the 227 ton trawler *Arfon* was discovered, 7 miles south of Worbarrow Tout and just over a mile south-east of the *A3* submarine (Site **197**) at 50 29.81N; 02 10.37W. She sank rapidly on 30 April, 1917, after hitting a mine, and nine of her crew perished. The wreck is at 35m, and faces south-west.

**199 Pin Wreck** 50 33.16N; 02 09.57W. There is a considerable mystery and not a small amount of speculation as to the history and use, and exactly what type of vessel this was. At first sight the wreck appears to be that of a large wooden working barge with a four point mooring system. The wood has virtually rotted or been eaten away, leaving a crop of hundreds of phosphor bronze pins or rivets littered around over the entire site, some still attached to baulks of timber, but others lying loose. Each rivet is about 1in thick and up to 2ft in length. They are being avidly collected by visiting divers, who have come to know the wreck by the above name.

*Bob Harris of Runnymede Dive recovered these bronze pins from the unidentified vessel known as the Pin Wreck (Site 199).* Photo: *Authors*

Martin Foley, diver, potting fisherman and owner of the charter dive boat *Catharine* at Weymouth, found the wreck when his pots got hitched up in it in 1990, but did not put his diving group onto it until 12 months later. He states that the wreck had certainly not been dived before. A survey of the wreck led to the realisation that there was something different about it, though only a few small items were removed for identification purposes. Since that time Martin has been engaged in an intensive programme of research and has discovered that the vessel is of military origin. An important clue was the crow's foot military stamp on one end of the pins; another was the brass military tunic buttons from the best uniforms of what today we describe as Royal Marines. His investigations lead Martin to suggest that the date of loss was between 1880 and 1890 and that stores aboard were probably loaded at Portsmouth, but no record of the vessel or her loss has so far been uncovered. Within the area of the wreck are four large anchors and piles of associated chains. A donkey boiler is plain to see, as is a steam-driven capstan winch. Other machinery looks like a pump of some description – its use so far unknown.

The wreck became generally known to other diving groups from 1993 onwards. With a depth of 27m, it makes an excellent dive, and like all wrecks, this site is an island of life with fish above and crustacea living in and under the wooden beams. A serious search of the site may yet turn up a clue to the wreck's identity. Any information about such discoveries should be passed on to Martin Foley (tel. 01305 779691). *Launching: Kimmeridge 3½ miles. Boats: Weymouth 12 miles.*

**200 Aeolian Sky** 50 30.55N; 02 08.33W. This was a large ship of some 16,000 tons that sank 5 miles off St Aldhelm's Head on 4 November, 1979, with her holds stuffed solid with general cargo and more piled high on her decks. She stood within 9m of the surface after sinking, and although she has now been

*The Aeolian Sky (Site 200) is now on the sea bed, her four cavernous holds still full of cargo.* Photo: Adrian Ponchaud collection

cleared by explosives to a depth of 18m, most of her hull is still intact with the holds still full of cargo. She lies on her port side with the decks facing east and her bows to the south. The bows themselves have been blown off the ship and lie some 4m away from the main hull.

The sea bed around the *Aeolian Sky* is of chalk or limestone rock, and here and there can still be found items of cargo. The wreck is in the care of the Salvage Association. Some salvage was carried out soon after her sinking, but most of her cargo remains inside her holds, a large proportion of it within unopened containers. The commercial divers who carried out the salvage warn that in times of bad visibility it is easy to get lost inside the wreck before you realise you have entered it. Slack water on the wreck is 2½ hours before and 3½ hours after high water at Portland. On neaps there is up to almost 1½ hours of slack water on low water slack, with slightly less time on the high water slack. This is reduced to only 30 minutes on big springs. Currents outside the slack water periods are strong. In good periods in summer the visibility can be in excess of 15m. *Boats: Weymouth or Castletown 12 miles.*

**201 Iolanthe** 50 27.64N; 02 07.96W. This position is 9 miles offshore, south of Kimmeridge Bay. Here is a large and virtually undived wreck, only very recently discovered by the Ballett brothers of Poole, who confirmed the identification by recovering her bell. The *Iolanthe* was sunk on 4 January, 1918, by a torpedo from the German submarine *UB-75*. Records tell us that she was on a voyage from the Clyde to St Helens roads with a cargo of hay and trucks. She was reportedly sunk 10 miles south-east by east from Portland Bill, within a couple of miles of where she has now been found. She was a British steam driven, armed merchantman of 3,081 tons gross, measuring 325ft long with a 49ft beam and was built in 1904. The owners were the London Marine Steam Ship Company. She is now well broken, but certainly worth a dive. Depths in the vicinity are in excess of 40m. *Boats: Weymouth 15 miles, Poole 22 miles.*

**202 Unidentified wreck** 50 26.29N; 02 07.53W. On the sea bed in this position is a steel barge or lighter, 4m proud of a 43m sea bed. Not much detail is available, but the wreck is scattered with a white substance (which could be an explosive). The Poole scallop divers John, Steven and Mike Ballett came across it in 1993, but did not take much time examining the wreck. *Boats: Weymouth 16 miles.*

**203 Hartburn** 50 30.74N; 02 06.42W. In the above position lies a large wreck. Charter boats *Tiger Lily* and *Channel Chieftain* of Weymouth have both had success in finding the wreck and putting diving groups onto it. After a successful dive here, Janine Gould of the Old Harbour Dive Centre at Weymouth reported a sandy sea bed at a depth of 39m and a large wreck with at least two very large boilers. The position is 1 mile north-east of the *Aeolian Sky* (Site **200**) and 1 mile west of what used to be thought the position of the *Start*. It is possible this is the wreck of the 2,367 gross ton merchantman *Hartburn*, reported sunk by a mine laid by German submarine *UB-62* on 15 October, 1917, about 10 miles south of Anvil Point. Other reports stated she was torpedoed. The *Hartburn* had started her voyage from Manchester with a cargo of hay and trucks so a search of her holds might help to confirm her identity. *Boats: Weymouth 15 miles, Poole 20 miles.*

*The Hartburn (Site 203) is here seen in the River Avon.*
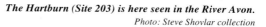
Photo: Steve Shovlar collection

**204 Hildegarde** 50 35.30N; 02 06.10W. Many diving groups will have driven their inflatables out of Kimmeridge and turned east to various dive sites. Their coxswains are usually careful to run well out to sea before turning east to avoid the shallow ground of the Kimmeridge Ledges – to be really clear of these ledges, the route has to be a surprisingly long way out. To strike the ledges with a light inflatable is usually of minor consequence, but it is a different matter when a large steamship loaded with iron ore drives straight on to them at 7½ knots.

Just such a fate befell the 1,886 gross ton, 262ft long British steamship *Hildegarde,* while on the last leg of her journey from Almeria to the Tyne on the misty, drizzly evening of 12 November, 1900. She had been built at Jarrow in 1882, but even the best of British shipbuilding could never survive such a collision with unyielding rock. Her bottom torn and firmly impaled on the ledge, she quickly flooded and became a total loss. Her remains still lie where she struck, but now somewhat broken and scattered at a depth of only 7m, amid a waving kelp forest. Little known, and little dived, somewhat difficult to find among the ledges, she is certainly worth a visit, if only to find any interesting items turned up by the booming surf that runs over this area in winter storms. *Launching: Kimmeridge 2 miles. Boats: Weymouth 14 miles.*

**205 Palala** 50 35.23N; 02 05.61W. If you enjoy a struggle through a dense kelp bed while rummaging through the equivalent of an extremely scattered scrap heap, at the mere depth of 4m, being subjected to every pull and push of the waves above, then this could turn out to be your favourite wreck site. The *Palala,* a 1,760 gross ton cargo and passenger liner, made the mistake of not keeping far enough offshore and steamed right up onto the Kimmeridge Ledges, on 6 May, 1886. As it was a fine, calm evening the crew and passengers at first thought there was no reason for concern and that the ship could either reverse or be towed off the ledge with no harm done. Reports state that the passenger's tea was delayed for only a short time while the Captain had the engine running at top speed astern for half an hour. Later, tea was served in the cabins.

This calm state of affairs did not last long. Deteriorating weather caused the ship to bounce, grind and pivot amidships. First it was discovered that the foremast had lifted by 2ft, then the boiler had shifted, splitting the pipes and releasing high pressure steam into the engine room. The next day, the passengers and their belongings were taken off. The almost brand new ship became a total loss. The parts of the ship the salvors could not take away now lie broken and scattered by the sea. *Launch: Kimmeridge, 2½ miles. Boats: Weymouth 14 miles.*

**206 Sea Bed Caves** 50 35.06N; 02 05.04W. This is a unique dive: the position given, 1 mile south-west of Chapman's Pool, is the rim of a reef that forms a major drop-off seawards and the abrupt end of the dense kelp forest that extends out from the shore ¾ mile away. The rim runs north-west to south-east for hundreds of yards either way; if you descend to the sea bed and find yourself in the kelp forest you must move to the south-west until you find the rim. The drop-off extends from 8 to 14m at an angle of 30° or less, depending on the area. The whole slope is covered with thousands of rectangular, smooth, kelp-free rocks, all perfectly arranged in straight lines, like huge stone coffins. Each monolith is divided from its neighbour by a gap 1m deep but only a few inches wide, but in some places the gaps are large enough to drop into, and some of the monoliths are undercut, enabling a diver to wriggle through and emerge at another point on the sea bed. The gaps in the rocks are a perfect habitat for crabs, lobsters, conger eels and other fish.

However, these extraordinary monoliths are not the most sensational feature. All along, below the strata of undisturbed rock that form the rim of the reef are deep caves and what is even more exciting (or frightening) is the nature of the entrances. Each consists of a long horizontal slot several metres in length in a vertical rock face, wide enough at only one end for a diver to wriggle – or in some cases swim – through but reducing down to only a few inches at the other end. A diver can see out all along the subterranean room but must return to the original entry point to get back to the surface of the sea bed and rejoin fellow divers. Once inside a cave, time should be allowed for the eyes to become accustomed to the gloom; a torch is essential for exploring the innermost recesses. The interiors are mostly clean with little silt. Some of the caves are large enough to accommodate several divers. It is possible that deeper caves exist farther along the reef to the south-east.

Although diving here is possible at all states of the tidal cycle, one of the better times is 3 hours after high water at Portland. At this time a strong west-flowing current ceases and a slack occurs, after which a gentle easterly flow runs for at least the next 4 hours. The authors would be pleased to receive further information about this interesting site. The remains of the *Treveal* (Site **208**) lie approximately 100yds to the north-east. *Launching: Kimmeridge 3 miles.*

**207 Glenmore**  50 35.17N; 02 04.90W. The *Glenmore* was a British 65 gross ton steam-driven tug carrying out salvage work on the partially submerged wreck of the *Treveal* (Site **208**). While manoeuvring close to the *Treveal*, the tug was carried over a submerged part of the wreckage, and in the trough of a wave settled onto parts of the hidden steelwork. Speared through her bottom, she flooded and sank on 24 March, 1922. Her boiler can be found at the above position, just north of the *Treveal*. Depth is 6m, with a rock sea bed and kelp forest. *Launching: Kimmeridge 2 miles.*

**208 Treveal**  50 35.15N; 02 04.90W. The *Treveal*, a 3,226 ton cargo steamer, was returning from Calcutta to Dundee on her maiden voyage with a cargo of jute and manganese when she sank on 10 January, 1920, after ploughing into the Kimmeridge Ledges. In all, 36 of her 43 crew died in the disaster. Today her remains still lie where she struck just north of the edge of the ledge and in a kelpy hollow.

Depths are around 5 to 8m and the currents are mainly weak. Visibility in this shallow area can be excellent so long as breaking waves are not stirring up the black shale along the shoreline. The *Treveal* caused two other wrecks: a drifter being used to salvage her cargo of jute and, in 1922, the *Glenmore* (Site **207**). *Launching: Kimmeridge 2 miles.*

**209 French Chasseur**  50 25.46N; 02 04.84W. This wreck is either Chasseur No. 6 or Chasseur No. 7. Both were completed in early 1940, and were sunk together by German gunfire on 12 October, 1940. The second has yet to be found but the wreck at the above position was located in 1992 by Steve Ballett. The wreck, upright and completely untouched for 50 years, was littered with high quality brass fittings. She is almost an exact copy of the *Carantan* (Site **255**), except that she is not loaded with ammunition and is much more broken up. This must be partially due to damage inflicted at her sinking. Like the *Carantan*, her midships engine room contains twin diesel engines with a narrow walkway between with lots of gauges, brass pipes and valves. Steve Ballett recovered the large beautiful brass compass binnacle, and when cleaned up the compass was found to be still working perfectly. Sea bed depth 40m, wreck rises 3m. *Boats: Weymouth 19 miles, Poole 20 miles.*

**210  Licence to Kill**  50 34.40N; 02 03.83W. This is a 32ft British sloop, which sank on 27 July, 1981, after catching fire. It was reported that she broke up and sank in this position, about 1 mile outside Chapman's Pool, towards St Aldhelm's Race. *Boats: Swanage 6 miles, Weymouth 15 miles.*

**211  St Aldhelm's Race**  50 34.05N; 02 03.52W. St Aldhelm's Ledge is a terrifying place to be at the wrong time. Look carefully at the chart: there are warnings of "overfalls" on the east- and west-flowing streams. Even on a flat, calm day this is an area to keep well away from when the tidal currents are in full movement. The ledge stretches out to sea from St Aldhelm's Head for a distance of almost 5 miles. The 20m contour line on the chart forms a shape like a giant bony finger pointing to the safe route that ships must take out to sea. On the flood, all along its line a 40m deep mass of water meets an almost vertical 20m underwater cliff. High-speed currents occur, streaming vertically up the rock faces. So fast is the acceleration of this immense volume of water that the surface rises in a series of violent waves.

Remarkably, there is a highly adventurous dive site in the race, right in the very roughest part. Just ½ mile offshore is a gully 55m deep, bounded on its eastern side by an underwater cliff of almost 40m in height. Those who have successfully dived this spot speak of cliff faces covered with anemones and large lobsters. To take advantage of the total length of time the currents are slack it is best to start a dive on this cliff with the tide still slightly ebbing. Below the cliff rim the water will be still, but the chief difficulty at such times is being dragged off by your SMB in the moving water above. Obviously the timing of such a dive in relation to the tide is of paramount importance. The times of slack water in the area are 1 hour before high water at Dover and 6 hours later. An expedition into this area must choose a neap tide. *Launching: Kimmeridge 4 miles, Swanage 6 miles.*

**212  Montanes**  50 34.56N; 02 03.35W. Perhaps over millions of years, the sea has pounded St Aldhelm's Head. Huge boulders have gradually split off and have fallen from the high cliffs above to form one of the most inhospitable shores in the British Isles. It was during a period of thick fog, not unusual for the time of year, that the Spanish steamer *Montanes* drove straight onto these rocks on 23 November, 1906. What the collision had started was soon completed by the rise and fall of a heavy swell which caused the rocks to buckle and pierce the plates of her bottom. She was sailing from Seville to London with a mixed cargo of 1,300 tons of ores and food. Her remains can be found at the most south-western tip of the headland, still there among the boulders. She now consists of bent and buckled plates, both around and under the rocks.

*The wreck of the Montanes (Site 212) at St Aldhelm's Head in November 1906.*
*Photo: Steve Shovlar collection*

Diving author Steve Shovlar found the wreck in the early 1980s still bearing a number of portholes. Depths are from 6 to 12m. Diving is best carried out on the ebb tide, when currents are much gentler than during the flood. The immediate area is brilliant for diving in its own right. Attempt diving here only in calm weather and when there is little swell on the sea. *Launching: Kimmeridge 4 miles. Boats: Swanage 6 miles.*

**213 Unidentified wreck** 50 21.78N; 02 02.92W. The large wreck at the above position is seldom dived, though Andy Smith put divers on this wreck several times and dived there himself. He reported a very old steamer with the hull still standing high off the sea bed. One possible identification is the *Saxmundham*, a 2,537 gross ton British steamship carrying a cargo of coal and coke and lost in a collision on 4 November, 1888. Sea bed 53 metres. *Boats: Weymouth 21 miles, Poole 22 miles.*

**214 Safari** 50 25.34N; 02 02.54W. Those who have dived this big, fat, 750-ton British S class submarine say that she makes a splendid dive, with lots of interesting things to see, and that this is probably the best submarine dive in the Dorset area. She lies in line with the tide on a hard sea bed of boulders, small rocks and gravel with her bows facing south-south-east – upright but leaning at 40° to port. The sea bed depth is 42m with the main deck at 38m. The conning tower has been removed, exposing access to her interior, but such an excursion could prove exceptionally hazardous because of the narrow entrance and the large number of conger eels.

*The submarine Safari (Site 214) is now permanently infested with conger eels.*
Photo: Steve Shovlar collection

The wreck is owned by Dave Saywell, owner of the Poole charter boat *James Alexander*. Divers from his boat originally discovered the submarine while investigating a snagged fisherman's net. After the discovery, Dave and a colleague carried out two years of research, eventually identifying the wreck and successfully tracing her owners – from whom Dave managed to purchase her. She had been one of the Royal Navy's most successful World War Two submarines and her exploits are well documented. It was after the completion of her active service, while being towed to a breaker's yard with no crew aboard, that the tow snapped and she sank in her present position. *Boats: Weymouth 20 miles, Poole 20 miles.*

**215 Dagmar** 50 28.00N; 02 01.85W. The Dagmar, previously called the *Leonora*, was built in 1922 and at the outbreak of war was requisitioned and well armed by the Government. This collier, of 844 gross tons and measuring 213ft long with a beam of 31ft, was fully loaded with Welsh coal and endeavouring to deliver it to Poole. On 9 June, 1941 the Luftwaffe raked her with machine gun fire and then dropped a bomb into her bunkers – within the hour she was on the sea bed, and there she stayed – untouched and uncharted for almost 50 years. That was until she was rediscovered in 1988 by divers from the Poole Charter Boat *James Alexander*. The big surprise for skipper Dave Saywell was the pottery the divers recovered – it proved that this wreck was the *Dagmar*, a wreck he had purchased 5 years earlier.

Today the wreck remains largely untouched and although she is well broken and mixed up, makes an interesting dive. Plain to be seen are her boiler, three-cylinder triple-expansion engine and shaft with propeller. The bows are twisted over but rise well off the gravel sea bed while the hull tends to be laid out flat. Although her telegraph has been recovered, there remain many other artefacts yet to be found. Depth 42m. *Boats: Weymouth 19 miles, Poole 18 miles.*

**216 Halsewell** 50 34.10N; 02 01.75W. The 785-ton *Halsewell* was one of the finest ships in the service of the East India Company. She was sailing from the Thames to the Far East with 240 passengers and crew and a valuable cargo when she was wrecked against the cliffs of the Isle of Purbeck on 6 January, 1786. The position of her sinking was not, as popularly thought, at the mouth of the large, shallow cave 50yds or so west of Seacombe. Her remains lie much nearer Winspit, at a spot 400yds to the east of there, and just east of the last of a series of quarried caves (which can easily be seen on a terrace halfway up the cliff face).

Dennis and Bob Wright, working with Bob Campbell of Swanage, first located this wreck site in the 1960s and presented a series of recovered artefacts to the Dorset County Museum, where they form a permanent display. Garry Nuthall, a Swanage diver, is an expert with an underwater metal detector and has been quietly and patiently panning backwards and forwards with his detector doing long dives, just off local beaches, never deeper than 3 to 4m. He is now the owner of a large and fascinating collection of artefacts. Together with his diving colleague Colin Hobbs, he decided to devote several seasons to the *Halsewell* site. Some of the results can be seen in the Swanage Tythe Barn Museum. Finds include beautiful Spanish American silver coins of 8 reales ("pieces of eight"), silver spoons, wedding jewellery and three diamonds. The 1997 season produced the superb find of a quantity of gold George III guineas in very fine condition. Apparently the majority of remains are around and under the rocks at the base of the cliff.

Diving conditions on this site are good in calm weather, the only current being a fairly weak west-flowing one on the ebb. The area is sheltered except from the south and east. The sea bed is very variable, with high rocks beneath the cliff, but away from the cliff are gravel and sand patches with areas of bedrock showing. *Launching: Swanage 5 miles.*

*A pair of George III gold guineas and a 1780 Spanish American 8 reales piece of 8 pillar dollar, recovered from the Halsewell wreck site by Garry Nuthal. (Actual size silver coin 1½ inches diameter.)* Photo: Authors

**217 Kaylena** 50 33.00N; 02 01.00W. The yacht *Kaylena* was sunk in 1970. No other information on her exists except that she had been dismantled. Usually known as "The Old Yacht", she is plainly marked on the chart as an unsurveyed wreck. Depth to sea bed, 30m. *Launching: Swanage 5 miles.*

**218 Derna** 50 27.24N; 02 00.30W. This wreck threw up an interesting discovery when a party of divers visited her in the early 1990s. On and around the wreck they found lead ingots, tied with rope in bundles of four. Each ingot weighed around 200lb. Subsequent inspection of the cast numbers on the ingots proved that they were part of the cargo of the wreck of the *Fanny* (Site **226**), which had been salvaged at Swanage in 1980. How many more of the bundles remain to be discovered is unknown, but given their widely separated locations, it seems unlikely they were all found.

The *Derna* (the former *Girgenti* and *Danby*) was built at Stockton on Tees in 1890, but had Italian owners when lost in a collision with HMS *Centurion*, a King George V battleship, on 10 December, 1912. The collision occurred before dawn – the *Derna* sank almost immediately and lost her entire crew of 36 men. She had been sailing in ballast to Port Talbot. Her weight was 2,210 gross tons and she measured 272ft long with a beam of 39ft. Her midships triple-expansion engine was powered by two boilers.

The wreck makes an exciting dive. She sits upright on the sea bed at 41m, is beginning to collapse with age, but still rises up at her highest point to 5m. She is parallel and only 2 to 3m from a 2m high vertical rock ledge that stretches all along one side of the wreck. *Boats: Weymouth 20 miles, Poole 17 miles.*

**219 Alexandrovna** 50 35.43N; 01 58.00W. This wreck lies at the very base of the high Purbeck cliff, just under ½ mile west of the Anvil Point lighthouse. On the cliff above this site is a pitch particularly favoured by rock climbers, who sometimes leave code words painted on the cliff. Directly below this pitch, at a depth of 7m, is a startling array of artefacts. On the rocky sea bed is a seam of typical shipwreck black crud. Firmly cemented into this are a number of cannonballs each measuring about 6in across. There is also a sheet of lead measuring some 12in by 15in, and a large number of what look like pig iron ingots.

The *Alexandrovna*, a 1,250 ton sailing ship, crashed into the cliff on 28 April, 1882, during a hurricane. The ship was badly smashed, and within 10 minutes she became a total loss. There were no survivors from her crew, believed to number 18. In 1882 a ship of this type would be very unlikely to be carrying cannon, so were the cannonballs being carried as ballast along with the pig iron? Or is this a far older wreck site? This is an ideal dive for beginners. Tidal aberrations occur (*see* Site **173**). *Launching: Swanage 2½ miles.*

**220 Barcarolle** 50 34.35N; 01 57.65W. The *Barcarolle*, a 43ft long unregistered yacht No. 3035, was on passage from Bursledon to Plymouth on 1 December, 1990. She struck an unknown object and was holed. The Swanage lifeboat responded to her distress call, located her and took her in tow, but she sank at the position given, approximately 1 mile south-west of the wreck of the *Kyarra* (Site **224**). To date there is no record of her being dived. Depth 30m. *Boats: Swanage 3 miles, Poole 10 miles.*

**221 Fuel Barge** 50 33.51N; 01 57.47W. This wreck was first located by Poole charter boat skippers Dave Saywell and Jim Scott on 2 April, 1981, while carrying out a search of the area using a hired magnetometer. The wreck measures 75ft in length, with a beam of approximately 23ft. The once upright boiler is hanging over the side, almost out of the vessel. Sitting 2m high on a gravel and rock sea bed at a depth of 36m, bows to the south-east, the wreck is heavily infested with conger eels. *Launching and boats: Swanage 3 miles, Poole 14 miles.*

**222 Swanage Bay and Tanville Ledges** 50 37.05N; 01 56.80W. Draw a line from the Mowlem Theatre on the promenade at Swanage, across the bay in a north-easterly direction to the high cliffs of Ballard Point. Motor out on this line until a point is reached opposite the Grand Hotel (the large building on the hill at the northern end of Swanage) at approximately the position given. A dive anywhere here and towards Ballard Point will reveal some extremely pretty scenery. Extending out from the shoreline in the area beneath the Grand Hotel is a series of rocky reefs or ledges, the two largest of which are known as the Tanville Ledges. Depths are in the region of 7m, with a drop off the piled rocks of the reefs to about 10m. Within several hundred yards are a number of smaller reefs running parallel to the main two. Between the reefs are areas of brightly coloured sand with small rocks and stones.

The main reefs are covered in kelp on their higher surfaces, and shoals of brightly coloured small fish can be seen in summer. Tidal currents exist in this area and are impossible to swim against during the ebb period; the direction of flow crosses the reefs at right angles. The tidal stream in the bay, except for the last half hour before first high and low, is in a counter direction to the main tidal stream out at sea. There is a slack at the time of high and low water at Swanage. The second high produces neither a slack nor a change of flow direction in the bay. Times of the Swanage tides are included in the Poole tide table and are on sale at Ocean and Action, 11 The Square, Swanage.

Swanage Bay is an ideal dive when winds are strong from the north, west or south-west. At such times, it is possible to dive in the bay even with winds up to around Force 6, but the bay is badly affected by winds from the south or east. This is a great area for a beginner's first open water dive or an outing for a more experienced diver. Conditions are excellent for underwater photography, with good visibility in summer complemented by the bright sunlight that reflects from the light-coloured sea bed. Also of interest in this area are the cannonballs that are regularly discovered by divers. These were fired long ago from a battery on Peveril Point at a practice target anchored in the bay. They measure some 6in in diameter, but often come in lumps of irregularly shaped crud up to 14in across. *Launching: Sites 176, 178, 179, 180 and 181.*

**223 Durlston Head** 50 35.60N; 01 56.70W. The area off Durlston Head makes an excellent diving ground, with depths generally between 7 and 12m. Extending out from the headland is a rocky ledge with an interesting drop-off and a number of shallow broken gullies running a short distance to the south-west. Currents around the head can be strong, and at these times the area is ideal for a drift dive. Under the cliff of the headland directly beneath the stone globe at Durlston Castle an unusual phenomenon occurs. About 200yds out from the cliff natural gas can be seen bubbling out of fissures in the rock of the sea bed. On a calm day the bubbles can be seen breaking the surface. Large pollack seem to favour this area. There is good, adventurous diving here but beware, particularly on rough days of the swell which can kick up every so quickly when once the sea has started to flow westwards on the ebb. *Launching and boats: Swanage 1 mile, Poole 12 miles.*

**224 Kyarra** 50 34.90N; 01 56.59W. The *Kyarra* is and always will be an exciting and advanced dive. She is without doubt Dorset's most popular wreck; on a fine, sunny weekend it is not unusual to find up to a hundred divers on this huge vessel. She lies at a depth of 30m at a point ¾ mile offshore from the Anvil Point lighthouse and rises 18m from the sea bed in some of Dorset's most inhospitable waters. The current can run at over 3 knots at times, making it virtually impossible to reach the wreck except during the slack periods that occur every 6 hours.

The ship itself is exciting. She was built on the Clyde in 1903 by W. Denny Brothers, measured 415ft by 52ft and weighed 4,383 tons. One of her main features was the huge number of brass fittings used in her construction. Not only was she covered from stem to stern in heavy brass portholes, but the interior fittings were also made of solid brass wherever possible. The *Kyarra* (the name is Aboriginal for a small fillet of opossum fur) traded between England and Australia under the flag of the Australasian United Steam Navigation Company Ltd of London, but for a period during World War One she was requisitioned and used as a hospital ship bringing home thousands of casualties from the battlefields of Flanders. Released from this humanitarian mission later in the war, she went back to her normal trading duties and had just left Southampton on a voyage from London to Sydney laden with a mixed cargo when she was torpedoed by the German submarine *UB-57* off Purbeck on 5 May, 1918.

*Roger Wagstaff's collection of gold watches recovered from the Kyarra (Site 224) in 1995.*
Photo: Authors

Although local fishermen had an idea where the *Kyarra* lay, she was not discovered by divers until the late 1960s when a member of a London club bumped into her. She was later bought by a group of members of the club. The level of cargo in her holds is now somewhat lower after thousands of visiting divers have taken away small items. Nonetheless she is still yielding a seemingly never ending supply of perfume, champagne, stout, red wine, sealing wax, medical supplies, very ornate and large vinegar bottles – year by year more exciting and extraordinary items are found. The 1994 season produced exquisite silver purses in extremely good condition; 1995 produced even greater surprises, from one of the more gloomy corners of her forward hold came a continuing supply of large gentlemen's pocket watches and exquisite ladies' gold wrist watches. No wonder it is the burning ambition of most divers who know of the *Kyarra* to dive and explore her.

Even the ground around the wreck is exciting. There are rocky reefs with dips and drop-offs that give a feeling of potential discovery at every turn. The slack water times for the *Kyarra* are 1 hour before high water at Dover and 6 hours later. Slacks on neaps can be as long as ¾ hour, but are much less on springs. Visibility on the site can be as much as 15m on the neap tides in summer, with high water slack always the clearest time. Choose a period of calm weather: winds above Force 3 from the southern half (especially the south-west) can soon make surface conditions dangerous for small boats. Be warned, a change of tide from one flowing with the wind to one flowing against it can lead in minutes to a very rough sea with large breaking swells.

There are good marks for the wreck. The flagpole on Peveril Point National Coast Watch lookout should line up with the second white patch at the western

*The Kyarra may be the most dived wreck in the English Channel but is by no means dived out. She is still stuffed full of the general cargo that should have been unloaded in Australia.* Photo: Authors' collection

end of Ballard Cliff (where the cliff line descends and the background changes to a field pattern). The other mark is the more lofty of a pair of white mile posts to the east of the Anvil Point lighthouse. When the correct position is reached, this should lie under the western end of a long group of bushes shaped like a shark's fin on the skyline above it. But by far the easiest way to find and dive the *Kyarra* is to take advantage of the shuttle services provided from Swanage pier by the boat *Sidewinder,* operated by Richard Titchener. *Launching and boats: Swanage 1½ miles, Poole 10 miles.*

**225 Carantan** 50 34.95N; 01 56.18W. After the fall of France in 1940 the French submarine chaser *Carantan* (Chasseur No. 5) was seized by the British and later handed over to the Free French, who operated in conjunction with the Royal Navy from a base at Brixham. She measured 120ft long with a narrow beam of only 20ft, and weighed 400 tons. At the time of her sinking, she was operating as an escort and support vessel to the incoming British submarine HMS *Rorqual.* She capsized and sank on 21 December, 1943 in a fierce south-westerly storm. Only 6 of her crew of 23 were saved.

Besides the horrific seas that can occur where she sank – especially when the west going ebb is meeting rollers driven eastwards by such a storm – another possible cause of instability might have been the large heavy Boer War gun bolted to her deck just forward of the bridge. Nor did the heavy brass plating from which her bridge was constructed help. Adding even more top heavy weight were two Browning machine guns, mounted on heavy steel pedestals, one either side, just forward of the bridge. Along her rails and on the aft deck, just clear of the engine room entrance were even more armaments. There was at least one quick-firing automatic gun and several other mounted guns of various types.

*This is a Chasseur class submarine chaser identical to the Carantan (Site 225); the latter lies on the sea bed off Anvil Point. Although sunk in 1943 she still has a large quantity of live ammunition aboard. Photo: Imperial War Museum*

Author John Hinchcliffe was the first to find and dive this wreck in 1984. The visibility was brilliant at the time. At a depth of 32m he saw an object in the distance. As he swam towards it, across a rock and sand sea bed, it quickly turned into a wreck lying over on its port side. As he approached from the starboard he saw nothing at first but the rounded shape of a hull. Swimming upwards he soon rose 3m to the highest part of the wreck and surveyed the incredible sight of an untouched wreck with its contents scattered out onto the sea bed – in front of him were detached portholes, brass fittings of all descriptions, full brass ammunition boxes, a huge gun, a large cast brass ship's whistle, and large lobsters hanging out of seemingly every crevice.

Everywhere there was ammunition; every space on the wreck was crammed with boxes of it. There were wooden boxes broken open with streams of small bullets cast around like pebbles. Inside the engine room entrance were further lockers and spaces filled with more live ammunition. On the rear deck, rolled to one side, was a pile of depth charges; over the stern was another large pile of depth charges on the sea bed. Co-author Vicki Hinchcliffe, who was in charge of the boat, had decided to drop anchor – John was alarmed to see that this anchor was bouncing up and down in the pile of depth charges!

The wreck is now a little more broken, but still makes a good dive with lots to see. She is owned by the well known Swanage skipper Eddie Bennet, who had purchased the wreck from the French long before she was found. The huge gun has been removed from the foredeck and is in the care of its owner. Watch out for tidal currents: even on neaps the wreck can only be dived at slack water, which is 1 hour before high water at Dover water and 6 hours later. *Boats: Swanage 1½ miles, Poole 10 miles.*

**226 Fanny** 50 36.58N; 01 56.11W. This wooden sailing vessel lay completely undisturbed at a depth of 18m from the day she sank in 1780 until a search was mounted in 1975 and 1976. The fact that she had not been found earlier was remarkable, for her resting place was a mere ½ mile from the end of Swanage Pier. Even more remarkable was her valuable cargo of no less than 600 lead ingots, which was recovered intact. Only the heavy wooden keel and lower part of the flattened hull remain. The *Fanny* lies in an area of rather muddy gravel, roughly half-way between Evans Rock and the Peveril Race buoy. The diving is good in this area, but only when the tide is slack; otherwise, watch out for the Peveril Race. *Launching: Swanage ¾ mile.*

*Local diver Dave Wickens with some of the Fanny's 600 lead ingots he had helped recover to the deck of the ship Gold Beach off Swanage, August 1979.*

Photo: Authors

**227 Castle Reagh** 50 34.82N; 01 56.10W. This wreck was discovered by diver Dave Weightman in 1967 and was positively identified when he later recovered the bell, engraved with the ship's former name *Firth Fisher*. On 25 February, 1925, this sturdy little 168ft cargo steamer had been transporting a consignment of coal along the South Coast when she was reported lost after being last sighted off Prawle Point in South Devon. On 1 March the bodies of the cook and second engineer were washed up at Freshwater on the Isle of Wight, but it had always been assumed that the vessel had sunk somewhere off the Devon coast.

The wreck lies at a depth of 37m and is just over ¼ mile roughly south-east of the *Kyarra*. When discovered, she was complete with her above-deck accommodation. This has now gone, but the ship is still fairly intact with some of her cargo still in the hold. Her bows stand 6m off the bottom, but her stern is rather more broken. Around the wreck the sea bed consists of rocky ground with reefs and small drop-offs which give a wide variation of depth on an echo sounder, making the wreck difficult to spot. This is an advanced dive – *see* Site **224** for tidal details. *Launching: Swanage 1½ miles. Boats: Poole 12 miles.*

**228 Peveril Ledge** 50 36.38N; 01 56.00W. Located at the extreme southern end of Swanage Bay, Peveril Ledge extends outwards from the end of Peveril Point for a distance of well over ½ mile. The reef consists of several parallel walls of rock that thrust out of the otherwise level sea bed. The upright faces of rock, in places many metres high, form a vertical barrier across the flow of the tidal currents. Especially when the tide is ebbing, this rock wall forces vast amounts of water to rise and accelerate over the top of it. The result is often a roaring barrier of standing waves on the surface – small boats innocently rowed or motored out of the nearby Swanage Bay can be quickly sucked into this maelstrom. There have been many fatalities, though these have not included divers.

*The Castle Reagh (Site 227) rests on the sea bed off Durlston Head. Here she is sailing up the River Avon.* Photo: Adrian Ponchaud collection

During periods of slack water the reef makes a brilliant and adventurous dive. This is particularly true of the area around and outward of the large red navigation buoy that marks the point along the reef's length where it is considered that decreasing depths over the reef's fangs make it unsafe for large vessels to pass on the shoreward side. Between the vertical sections of rock are sheltered hollows where crabs, lobsters and fish shelter. The rock faces are covered in highly coloured sponges, their growth encouraged by the generous flood of nutrients carried by the currents.

Depths in this area vary from 10 to 23m. Visibility can be excellent, reaching 13m at times in summer. The best visibility is on high water slack. Tide times are distorted by the peculiar double tide of Poole Bay and Swanage Bay. High water slack at Peveril Point is 3 hours 2 minutes before high water at Dover, but this gets a little later the farther offshore the position. The shoreward end of the reef is not so good for diving as it is near the outlet of the main Swanage sewer. *Launching: Swanage ¾ mile.*

WARNING Particularly on springs after the high water slack the ebb current can pick up very quickly in this area.

**229 Stella M** 50 32.40N; 01 55.60W. On 19 August, 1987, this 30ft fishing boat, owned by William Crabtree of Poole, sprang a leak and foundered in this approximate position, 3 miles south of the wreck of the *Kyarra*. Her crew were picked up from the life raft. To date she has not been found. Depth in the area is 34m. *Boats: Swanage 5 miles, Poole 11 miles.*

**230 Ballard Point to Handfast Point** 50 38.25N; 01 55.30W. There is an excellent diving area stretching between Handfast Point (Old Harry Rocks) and Ballard Point. It extends about 300yds out from the base of the cliff, and with depths down to 10m there is much life to be discovered on the rocky ground. Shallow gullies extending away from the base of the cliff dissect the sea bed, which is coated with short weed in places. Thick kelp grows in the shallows directly under the cliffs. There was an aircraft gunnery range at the northern end of this area during World War Two and a lucky diver can occasionally still find a spent 20mm brass shell-case in good condition. There are also the remains of a Hawker Typhoon aircraft that crashed here.

The best time to dive here is when the tidal current is ebbing strongly out of Poole Bay. The current is deflected out to sea by Handfast Point and an area of still water can be found all along this site. Farther out from the cliff the depth increases to about 13m. The ground here is less interesting, and heavy currents can be encountered. This site is sheltered from west and northerly winds. This is an excellent area to take a beginner. *Launching: Swanage 1½ miles, Studland 1 mile.*

*The range finder unit from the conning tower of the mystery German U-boat (Site 292) is on display in the Blue Boar Inn at Poole.* Photo: Authors

# Poole Bay and Poole Harbour

This area covers the Dorset Coast between Handfast Point in the west and the Hampshire boundary at Chewton Bunny, just east of Highcliffe. Access to this area of the coastline is good – Bournemouth, Poole and Christchurch are served by good connections from the A31.

Outside the bay, farther offshore, the area has a large number of exciting deep water wrecks. Many are losses of the two world wars, including victims of the massive air assault on southern England that started on 8 August, 1940. On the first day, Allied shipping in the Bournemouth and Isle of Wight area was targeted; this was the opening action of what was to become known as the Battle of Britain.

At Poole, such boats as the *James Alexander* and *Poole Angler* spearhead a fleet of charter boats with experienced skippers who are also fully trained divers. Despite this, the area has largely lacked the patient wreck investigation and surveys that have taken place farther west and led to the positive identification of many wrecks. Instead, many wrecks remain only tentatively identified and the uncertainties have been compounded by the discovery of many deeper wrecks. However, one fact on which most experienced commentators agree is that there are other wrecks of large ships lying still undiscovered in this area. For instance, where is the real wreck of the *Hazelwood*? Where are the wrecks of the *Ajax* and the larger *Coquetdale* – both victims of the German attack of 8 August, 1940? In the past, all three were claimed to have been discovered, but now it seems they were wrongly identified.

## Shore dive and snorkel sites

**231  Studland Bay**  SZ 035 834. *Launching only*. To reach this launch site take the ferry across the mouth of Poole Harbour from the tip of the Sandbanks peninsula. After disembarking at South Haven Point, drive towards Studland village. After 2½ miles there is a well signposted entrance to a large car park at the rear of the beach. This is Knoll car park; launching and parking fees are charged. There are areas for cars only and other large sections for cars with boats and

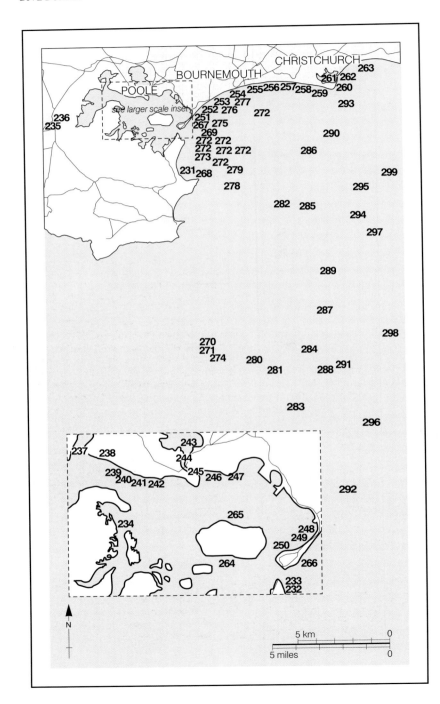

trailers. An alternative route to this site is via Wareham and Corfe Castle. The concrete launching ramp is situated at the extreme southern end of the boat trailer parking area. The short ramp leads onto a firm sand beach. Launching is still possible at low water, but care should be taken to avoid vehicles sinking into the softer lower levels of the beach. The boat park and launching area is closed from the end of October to Easter to allow the grass to rejuvenate. During this period, boats would need to be carried to the beach via the café area.

The whole of the beach and hinterland is owned by the National Trust. There is a large National Trust Shop and café; nearby is a public toilet. There is a payphone in the shop. Although beautiful and unspoiled, with a splendid beach, Studland Bay is of little use to a diver. The whole bay beneath the sea is composed of a sandy, featureless bottom, which is so shallow that two or three areas well out from the shore dry on low water springs. This is not a recommended shore dive. The bay is sheltered from the south and west, but catches the full force of a blow from the east. At such times, launching can be difficult. Local by-laws forbid any boat to exceed a speed of 5 knots anywhere off this beach within an area marked by a line of yellow buoys. There are two other National Trust car parks in Studland village from which it is possible (with difficulty) to carry or wheel small boats to the beach.

**232 Shell Bay** SZ 037 866. *Snorkel and launching.* This bay is best reached using the ferry that crosses the mouth of Poole Harbour from the end of the Sandbanks peninsula. There is a car park on the east side of the road immediately after the ferry toll booth. From here to the beach is a distance of 100yds over a marshy area on a wide wooden footbridge. Small boats can be launched here if they can be carried. For the lightly-loaded snorkel diver who is able to walk to the southern end of the bay there is an excellent chance of an exciting offshore snorkel dive along the training bank (an artificial rock bank), which joins the shore here. It is frequented by wrasse, pollack, bass, mullet, crabs and many other smaller species. Flatfish swim on the sands nearby. The bank runs obliquely from the shore for ¾ mile out to sea. At low water the uppermost sections dry, exposing rocks and kelp. It is marked by red stakes with beacons on top. No matter what the wind direction there is usually some sheltered water on one side or other of the bank, especially near the shore.

An easterly or south-easterly wind tends to stir up the sand and reduce the visibility, which, in quiet periods, can be up to 8m. Although a fairly strong current flows on the ebb on the outer side of the bank, there is always plenty of still water on the inside. This enables snorkellers to drift with the current in one direction, then, by crossing the bank, swim back in still water. This site is not suitable for the absolute beginner unless accompanied by a more experienced snorkeller. The nearest telephone is on the road near the ferry at South Haven Point, where a café and toilets may also be found.


**Opposite: Dive sites in Area 4, Poole Bay and Poole Harbour. This area is covered by Admiralty charts 2611 (Poole Harbour and approaches), 2175 (Poole Bay), 2172 (Swanage and Studland Bays plus local anchorages), 2615 (Bill of Portland to the Needles); Ordnance Survey maps: Pathfinder sheet number 1301, and Outdoor Leisure Map sheet numbers 15 and 22.**

---

## DIVING IN POOLE HARBOUR AND POOLE BAY

Parts of Poole Harbour can be a good second choice for a dive if gales are blowing out at sea. There are no special rules for diving in the harbour apart from the obvious ones of keeping well away from fairways and busy areas and making sure an "A" flag is used at all times. Poole Bay has many interesting patches of rock and regularly produces surprise discoveries, but with its shallow sandy shore line (you can walk out 50yds and still only be chest deep), it is not much good for the shore diver.

Within Poole Bay and Poole Harbour there is a large tidal aberration. A second high water occurs between 4 to 6 hours after the first high. Between the two highs only a minor fall-off occurs. This gives very weak currents throughout the area during this phase of the tidal cycle. Once well outside the confines of Poole Bay, the tide reverts to a normal 6 hour ebb-and-flow cycle. In the outer areas, slacks occur shortly after 1 hour before high water at Dover and 6 hours later. The former always provides better visibility. Strong currents occur at certain stages of the tidal cycle around Handfast Point, at the Haven entrance to Poole Harbour and across Christchurch Ledge.

There is a speed limit in Poole Harbour of 8 knots.

---

**233 Shell Bay Marine and Watersports Centre** SZ 035 865. *Snorkel and launching.* This boatyard and slip is situated at South Haven Point on the Poole Harbour shore side. From the Sandbanks ferry, after passing through the toll booth, turn immediately right around a small road island and right again into a sandy road, which doubles back, parallel to the ferry approach. After 75yds the boatyard gate will be seen on the left. There is limited parking in the yard for cars and trailers, but the Shell Bay car park is also available nearby. The Shell Bay Marine slip is of concrete but soon gives way to a flat area of pebbly sand, and is not usable anywhere near low water. Boats launched here can easily be taken out into Poole Bay through the nearby harbour entrance or are conveniently placed for diving in the southern half of the harbour.

The south-east corner of the harbour is a popular snorkelling area; it is an advanced snorkel dive and beginners should always be accompanied by an experienced buddy, preferably one with local knowledge. Diving is not recommended during the months of July and August when boat traffic in the harbour is very heavy. Adjacent to Shell Bay Marine are a café and public toilets. There is a telephone kiosk on the other side of the road.

WARNING Before attempting to snorkel in this area, study Chart 2611 and the local tide tables. Do not dive in Poole Harbour when the tide is ebbing after the second high tide. At this time extremely strong currents flow towards the harbour mouth and out into Poole Bay. The best time to dive is in the 4 to 5 hour period from just before the first high water through to second high water, when weak currents can sometimes be harnessed for carrying divers backwards and forwards along the channels. Be out of the water before the main – and very swift – ebb takes place after the second high.

**234 Shipstal Point** SY 984 884. *Snorkel only.* This site is on the tip of the Arne Peninsula. To reach it from Wareham town centre, drive south over the river bridge and along the Corfe Castle Road for ½ mile to Stoborough, before taking the only turning left. Keep straight on to the small village of Arne, a distance of almost 4 miles. Just before it there is a car park on the right; parking is not possible beyond here. Continue by walking along the road to where, opposite the church, a well signposted sandy track leads to the shore at Shipstal Point ¾ mile away.

The main snag at Shipstal Point is the visibility. Rain or wind reduce it to ½m and even in a dry, still period it is unlikely to be better than 2m. Currents are weak. The site is sheltered from most winds, but is vulnerable to north-easterlies. The upper fringe of the beach is sheltered and pleasant, with white sand. To the rear of the beach is part of the Arne Nature Reserve, an area of outstanding natural beauty and a Site of Special Scientific Interest. There are no facilities and no telephone at this site, but there are toilets, in the wood, back at the car park.

**235 Redcliffe Farm** SY 932 867. *Launching only.* Redcliffe Farm is a pleasant camping and caravan site on the River Frome, ½ mile downstream from Wareham. It is a quiet spot and the large concrete launching ramp on the site is never very busy. Here, boats on trailers can be launched at any state of the tide except dead low on springs. To find this site drive south from Wareham town centre over the river bridge on the Corfe Castle road. After about ½ mile, take the first turn left in the village of Stoborough. Proceed down this lane for ½ mile, again take the first turn left, then another left after 200yds into a private road that slopes steeply to the river. Permission to launch and further information can be obtained from the owner, Nigel Barnes (tel. 01929 552225).

**236 Wareham Bridge** SY 923 871. *Snorkel, aqualung, launching.* This is a river site located where the main street crosses the River Frome at the southern side of Wareham. There is easy access to the water on the town side of the bridge, and the upstream side in the area of Abbots Quay is specifically recommended. There is a concrete public launching ramp capable of taking boats of 6m or so. The river is tidal and is subject to the same double-high sequence as Poole Bay. Diving is best done between first and second high waters when currents are weak or non-existent. Tide times are just over an hour later than at Poole; all relevant information is given in the Poole tide table. Around the buttresses of the bridge old coins can sometimes be found. Like all bridges in the Dorset area there is, on the river bed, a scattering of live small arms ammunition. Resist any temptation to collect these items. Old bottles can be found 100yds above the bridge, where tree roots and earth form the underwater bank at the north side of the river. This is a good winter site when storms make diving in the open sea impractical. On the town quay on the lower side of the bridge there are restaurants, toilets and a car parking area. There is a telephone 100yds away, towards the town centre.

**237 Rockley Point** SY 972 911. *Launching only.* Rockley Point is at the western extremity of the vast Rockley Park holiday estate on the Hamworthy shore of Poole Harbour. There is an excellent launching facility in the form of a gently

*The slipway at Wareham Bridge.* Photo: Roy Smallpage

sloping concrete ramp 14yds wide, down which boats on trailers can be reversed by vehicle and launched at any state of the tide. Inflatables can either be launched here or carried across the beach to the water.

To find this site, cross the bridge at the western end of Poole Quay and follow the A350 for almost a mile until the Red Lion pub is seen on the right. Take a left-hand turning opposite this pub. This is Lake Road. Proceed down this road for about ½ mile, then turn right into Lake Drive at the Yachtsman pub. Keep straight on along Napier Drive. The route now enters the holiday estate. Keep straight on over the hill and down to the beach. There are toilets and a payphone at the offices of Rockley Boat Services in the boat park behind the beach.

**238 Hamworthy Lake** SY 982 908. *Snorkel and aqualung.* This site is included as a training site, and is particularly useful in the winter when bad weather can prevent sea diving. To find it, drive through the Rockley Park Holiday Estate and take the first road on the left. The lake is an old clay pit, deepest at its western end where 8m can be encountered. In winter, the water is very cold, and although the surface warms rapidly in summer, a definite thermocline can be encountered on descent. Visibility can be up to 10m, but a diver finning near the silty clay bottom can soon reduce it to nil. The lake lies within Ham Common, a nature reserve and Site of Special Scientific Interest situated between Rockley Park and the shore of Poole Harbour. Anyone wishing to use the lake must arrange this with Diving Leisure Unlimited at Rockley Park (tel. 01202 680898). Divers may use only one access point into the water, where a small landing stage has been constructed to avoid eroding the soft clay bank of the lake.

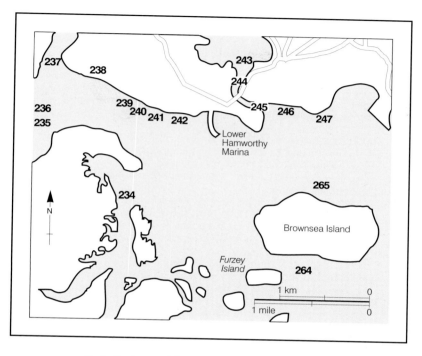

Poole Harbour and Brownsea Island, showing Shipstal Point (Site 234),
Rockley Point (Site 237), Hamworthy Lake (Site 238), Rockley Pier (Site 239),
Lake Road (Site 240), Branksea Avenue (Site 241), Hamworthy Park
(Site 242), Slip Way (Site 243), Wilkins Way Slip (Site 244), Poole Quay (Site
245), Fisherman's Dock (Site 246), Baiter (Site 247), Blood Alley (Site 264)
and Wych Channel (Site 265).

**239 Rockley Pier** SY 983 905. *Snorkel site, free launching.* Rockley Pier is an
old wooden structure, once used for refuelling Sunderland flying boats. It protrudes
from a beach that is pleasantly sandy in its upper reaches, but composed of
rather muddy gravel at lower tide levels. Inflatables can be launched across the
beach so long as they can be lifted over the low stakes bordering the car park.
During the period of ebb between second high and low water a very strong
current sets in to the east running parallel to the shore at and beyond the end of
the pier.

To find this site, follow the directions for Site **237** until you reach Napier Drive.
Then take the first left at a mini road island into Lake Drive. After a short distance
a sign on the right points down a narrow road to the beach and car park. There are
toilets in the car park. The nearest telephone is a kiosk back on the junction with
Napier Drive at the mini road island.

**240 Lake Road** SY 989 902. *Launching only (free).* To find this site, follow the directions given for Site **237** until you reach Lake Road. Drive straight along it for almost ½ mile, forking right for a short distance to where the road finishes on the beach.

A concrete ramp leads to the high water line. Boats can be launched by vehicles and trailers at any state of the tide, across the compact sand and gravel beach, though their size is limited by a barrier. There is a size-restricting barrier to the beach with an access measuring 6ft 9in wide by 6ft 9in high.

**241 Branksea Avenue** SY 992 901. *Snorkel site, free launching.* To find this pleasant stretch of sandy beach, cross the bridge from the western end of Poole Quay and follow the A350 for about 400yds to a set of traffic lights. Turn left into Ashmore Avenue, right into Lulworth Avenue and left into Purbeck Avenue. At the far end is Branksea Avenue.

At this junction a public footpath leads between large detached houses to the beach, a distance of 75yds. This path is level and wide enough for an inflatable to be wheeled or carried, though at the beach there is a 1ft drop down a step. Beware of a fairly strong current flowing east along the shoreline between the second high water and low water.

**242 Hamworthy Park** SY 995 901. *Snorkel site, free launching.* To find this pleasant beach site, cross the harbour bridge from the western end of Poole Quay and follow the A350 for about 400yds to a set of traffic lights. Turn left into Ashmore Avenue; the entrance to Hamworthy Park is at the far end and from the parking area it is only 50yds to the shore. Inflatables can be launched here, but only if they are capable of being lifted over a knee-high fence and down a 3ft sea wall. Between second high water and low water a fast ebb takes place here, giving a fairly strong current flowing east along the shore. There are toilets and a café in the park.

**243 Slip Way** SZ 008 908. *Launching point only (free).* From the large traffic island outside Poole's Dolphin Shopping Centre, take the road leading over Towngate Bridge to a second large traffic island. Leave this island by the fourth exit and follow West Quay Road for about 300yds. Directly opposite the headquarters of the Royal National Lifeboat Institution is a short road leading to the water's edge. The name of the road is Slip Way as it once led to a small slipway on the shore, but now you have to climb down three 1ft concrete steps to reach the water of Holes Bay. Small boats that can be lifted down the steps can be launched here at all states of the tide except dead low. There is usually room nearby to park.

**244 Wilkins Way Slip** SZ 006 906. *Launching only (free).* Wilkins Way is a very narrow lane with a dilapidated surface leading 80yds from West Quay Road to a concrete and cobbled surfaced slope into the Back Water Channel. Although a vehicle can drive to the water's edge, there is no room to turn; any launching trailer has to be reversed in from West Quay Road, and there is nowhere to park. The slip is sheltered from almost all winds, is usable at all stages of the tide and leads straight into deeper water.

Because of the large one-way system, the approach to Wilkins Way has to be made from the direction of Poole Bridge, along the one-way section of West Quay Road. It is the last left hand turning before the road becomes two-way again.

**245  Poole Quay**  SZ 010 902. *Aqualung only.* Particularly during winter months, when bad weather conditions preclude diving elsewhere, Poole Quay is an excellent and convenient place for responsible groups to carry out roped training exercises. Off the quay, depths in excess of 6m can be experienced around high water and the harbour bed is a mixture of mud and stones. Under the quay many items of interest can be found, ranging from coins to the occasional car! Visibility is never good; at best it is only just possible to discern objects 12in away, so low-visibility searches can always be practised. There are many access points in the form of stone steps or iron ladders along the length of the quay. Currents are slight, except on the main ebb between second high water and low water. This period should be avoided.

Permission to dive from Poole Quay must be obtained, at least 24 hours in advance, from the harbourmaster at the harbour office in New Quay Road (tel. 01202 440200). The exact point to be used will depend on traffic movements and must be confirmed on arrival, either at the harbour office in West Quay Road, or the Pilots and Moorings Inspector's Office, a portable cabin at the west end of the quay. The Diver's Code of Conduct must be strictly adhered to, divers must always be roped at this site and a prominent diving flag flown from the quay. There are telephones, toilets, pubs and cafés along the quay, and parking is allowed there.

*Poole Quay, Fisherman's Dock Slip and Baiter, where there is an excellent launching ramp from the car park.*

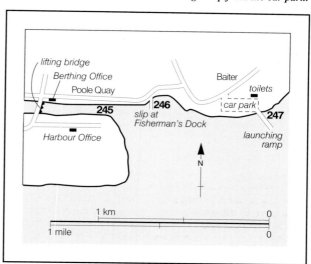

**246 Fisherman's Dock** SZ 014 902. *Launching point only (free)*. At the eastern extremity of Poole Quay is a partly enclosed mooring area used exclusively by fishing boats. Between the end of the quay and the old lifeboat house (now a museum) there is a small, narrow public slip into the dock, which can be used for small boats at any state of the tide. It is an ideal place to launch a large inflatable. Trailers can be wheeled or driven into the water, although the latter is not easy owing to the awkward access to the slip. There is no hardened ramp – the slip is just a short slope of gravel into the water. Adequate parking is available on the road or in the car park at Baiter, 300yds to the east.

**247 Baiter** SZ 021 901. *Launching point only.* This is undoubtedly the best public launching ramp in Poole Harbour. To find it, drive to the eastern end of Poole Quay. Continue east around a small traffic island into Ballard Road. At the end turn right along Green Gardens, which leads to Labrador Drive and a wide area of parkland. Drive through this area until a large car park is seen by the shore. The launching ramp is at the eastern end of this car park.

The ramp has a hardened surface, and stretches out over the rather muddy beach in a gentle slope all the way down to the low water level. Boats on trailers can easily be driven down this ramp. There is ample room in the car park for vehicles and trailers. The car park and ramp are free between 1 October and Good Friday; at other times a charge is levied. No coaches or caravans are permitted. The car park is closed each day at sunset. There are toilets and a telephone kiosk situated on Labrador Drive, 150yds east of the car park entrance.

*Fisherman's Dock (Site 246) with its small, narrow slip in the foreground. Only 400yds to the east is Baiter, where there is a very wide slipway. Photo: Roy Smallpage*

**248 North Haven Lake, Sandbanks.** SZ 046 880. *Launching point only.* To find this site from Poole, follow the B3369 towards the Sandbanks ferry. At the narrowest part of the peninsula the road becomes Banks Road and runs along the shore of Poole Harbour. There is a low sea wall to a narrow sandy beach, where inflatables can easily be lifted down and launched. Cars can be parked on this ½ mile stretch of road on the harbour side, or can be taken to the Sandbanks car park, slightly to the south. The sea bed here is shallow and sandy and is taken up with many moorings. Launching is convenient at most times of the tide except around low water springs. You can reach the open sea from here through the mouth of the harbour one mile to the south. This site is rarely affected by rough water, except when there is a strong north-westerly wind. There is a public telephone at the entrance to the Sandbanks car park. Inside the car park are cafés and toilets.

*Sandbanks and and the western part of Poole Bay, showing Studland Bay (Site 231), Shell Bay (Site 232), Shell Bay Marine and Watersports Centre (Site 233), North Haven Lake (Site 248), Davis's Boat Yard (Site 249), Sandbanks Yacht Company Slip (Site 250), Shore Road (Site 251), The Yards (Site 268), Middle Poole Patch (Site 275) and the locations of the Frenchman (Site 266), the Nibbler III (Site 267), the Antler Wreck (Site 269), the Studland Bay Wreck (Site 273) and the Leny (Site 279). Also shown offshore are the locations of the seven Valentine tanks (all marked as Site 272).*

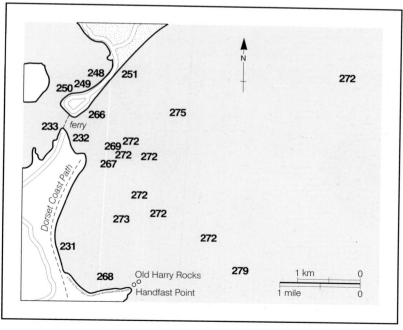

**249 Davis's Boat Yard, Sandbanks** SZ 039 877. *Launching point only.* This site is suitable for small boats, which can be lifted over a 3ft concrete post and carried along a footpath to the beach. To reach it, take the road from Poole to the Sandbanks Ferry, but instead of turning into the ferry embarkation area keep to the one-way system as if returning to Poole along Panorama Road. On the left, by a letter box about ½ mile after the ferry, there is a wide, sandy track to the beach. Launching can be carried out at this site at any time except at low water on springs. At low tide a narrow channel winds through moorings and shallow sandy areas to the harbour entrance ½ mile away. This site is not suitable for diving or snorkelling.

**250 Sandbanks Yacht Company Slip** SZ 040 877. *Launching point only.* This site lies off Panorama Road at Sandbanks just 120yds west of Site **249**. The launching ramp is situated inside the boat yard of the Sandbanks Yacht Company and an all-in fee is charged for use of the ramp and for car and trailer parking inside the yard. This wide and excellent concrete ramp is built across the whole width of the yard and many boats can be launched at the same time. Boats can easily be launched from their trailers into the water either by hand or vehicle. This can take place at any stage of the tide except dead low water on springs.

This is not only the best private launching ramp in Poole harbour, but is certainly the nearest to the harbour entrance, which is only a good ½ mile to the south. To find this yard, drive along to the tip of the Sandbanks peninsula and follow the one-way system along Panorama Road as if returning to Poole. The yacht company's yard lies on the left just over ½ mile after passing the ferry. This site is not suitable for diving or snorkelling.

*The slipway at Sandbanks Yacht Company.* Photo: Roy Smallpage

---

**SPEED LIMIT**

A by-law limits boats to a speed of 8 knots within 100yds of the shore at low water. It covers most of the beach from the Haven Hotel to Branksome Dene Chine, off Sites **251** to **253**.

---

**251 Shore Road** SZ 051 883. *Snorkel, aqualung, launching.* Shore Road, after which this site is named, finishes at the edge of the beach. From Poole or Bournemouth follow the signs for Sandbanks and the ferry. Shore Road is mainly the stretch of the B3369 where the route to Sandbanks first reaches the shore of Poole Harbour. However, instead of following the sandy peninsula, Shore Road branches left 1 mile short of the ferry on to Poole Bay Beach. There is a limited amount of car parking close to the beach and a car park 50yds back from the beach. Launching into the water at this site is by a wide concrete ramp and then across a wide beach of very soft, fine yellow sand. There is a locked gate across the ramp, but during the season 1 April to 31 September, between 8am and 5.30pm, the key is available at the adjacent beach office on the promenade. Otherwise, boats have to be lifted over a 3ft high rail.

Off this site there is an outfall pipe running out to sea for 280yds and marked at the seaward end by a yellow buoy. Kelp and a wide variety of other weeds grow along and over this pipe and because it is the only object in a desert of sand it has become home for a multitude of other marine life. This site is fairly sheltered except from winds from the east or south which will quickly reduce the visibility to a yellow nil. In calm spells when the wind is blowing from the north or west the visibility can be up to 7m. The currents on this site are mainly weak and run parallel to the shore. Next to the beach are toilets and a café. There is a private telephone in the beach office and a public telephone kiosk is situated 100yds back along Shore Road at its junction with Banks Road on the Poole harbour shore side.

**252 Branksome Chine** SZ 066 896. *Launching point only.* To find this site from Bournemouth, drive west following signs for Poole. When you reach the roundabout at Westbourne, where there is an office block called Frizzell House, take the first turn on the left into The Avenue. This leads direct to the sea front. At the Chine (the word means "ravine") there is a fairly large car park, with only the width of the promenade dividing it from the sea. A steep concrete ramp slopes on to the sand. Although small boats can easily be launched, they have to be capable of being lifted over the 3ft concrete posts that divide the car park from the promenade. The sea comes onto the ramp at high tide, but soft sand is exposed at lower stages. This is an extremely busy holiday beach in summer, but shallow and sandy – shore diving is not recommended. There are cafés and toilets here, and a public telephone is situated across the road at the car park entrance.

**253 Branksome Dene Chine** SZ 069 898. *Launching point only.* Follow the route to Branksome Chine (*see* Site **252**). At the Branksome Chine car park entrance turn round, go back up the hill for a few yards and take the first turning

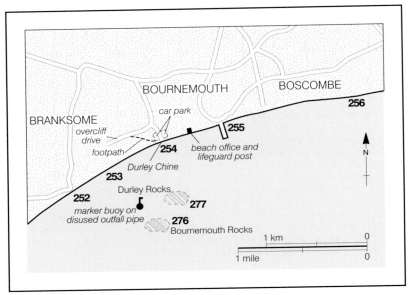

*Branksome and Bournemouth, showing Branksome Chine (Site 252), Branksome Dene Chine (Site 253), Durley Chine (Site 254), Bournemouth Pier (Site 255), Boscombe Pier (Site 256), Bournemouth Rocks (Site 276) and Durley Rocks (Site 277).*

right. The entrance to the site is then the second road on the right. Although clearly signposted, it looks like an entrance to a large private garden and can easily be missed. Drive down the winding, narrow road through pine trees to a secluded car park, from which it is about 50yds to the sea. Boats have to be carried down a couple of flights of wide steps to the promenade, and then down the stepped sea wall onto the beach. This site is shallow and sandy, and shore diving is not recommended. A gate is locked across the road entry to the car park each night at 11pm and not reopened until 6.30am. By the car park are toilets, a café, and a public telephone.

**254 Durley Chine** SZ 079 904. *Launching point only.* This is a good launching site for small boats, provided they can be tipped on their side and carried through a 3ft gap, or lifted over the 3ft rails and concrete posts at the seaward end of the car park, and then carried 50yds across the promenade and down a concrete ramp to the beach. To find this site from Bournemouth Centre, leave The Square to the south along Exeter Road, approximately 200yds along this route, and at a road island, turn right up Priory Road, at the top of the hill it becomes Westcliff Road. After almost a mile, the road descends a fairly steep slope into a dip. The road on the left at the bottom of the dip is Durley Chine Road and leads directly to the promenade. The lower area is a pay-and-display car park. There will probably not be room to leave trailers here in busy periods; they are charged as an extra vehicle and must not overlap their parking bay lines. Free parking is available in nearby Overcliff Drive, which is to the west, at the top of the Chine. From this road there is a shortcut, via a path and zigzag steps, back to the promenade end of Durley Chine.

The beach is of soft sand and can be exceptionally crowded in summer. By-laws restrict boats to 8 knots within 250yds of the beach (this is within a line drawn parallel to the beach from the end of Bournemouth Pier). Shore diving and snorkelling are not recommended owing to the shallow, featureless bottom and poor visibility at this site. There can be quite a swell on this beach if the sea is only slightly rough.

Along the promenade, 100yds to the east, is a lifeguard station and the beach inspector's office (tel. 01202 451771). Divers are welcome at the Chine but groups arriving should call in at the office – which is staffed in the summer from 8.45am to 6.15pm – or telephone to advise of the details of the intended expedition. This enables the lifeguards to be aware divers are out and to keep an eye on what is happening out at sea. The beach inspector requests that diving groups should not monopolise the promenade with gear in busy periods, especially around the seats. Groups arriving during busy summer days could have difficulty carrying their boats across the crowded beach and should take great care when doing so. They should never attempt any refuelling on the beach.

**255 Bournemouth Pier** SZ 088 906. *Snorkel site only.* There is a long-stay car park in Bath Road, on the hill just east of the pier. From here it is a short walk to the sea. Underwater, the sea bed is sandy, but the snorkeller will find much of interest around the supporting piles under the pier, which extends out from the shore for over 250yds. Besides items of lost property and coins, there are usually lots of fish feeding on the weeds around the piles. Mullet is a common species here, and there are lots of highly coloured wrasse. Depths at the end of the pier are about 5m, but keep a watch out for fishing lines dangling from the superstructure above. This area of beach is subject to swell and is popular with surf-boarders whenever the sea is rough. Do not attempt to snorkel here if a swell is running on to the beach. Not only will visibility be hopeless, but you could easily be thrown against the piles and injured. The currents in this area are weak and run parallel to the shore. This site is excellent for beginners. There are telephones, cafés and toilets outside the Pier entrance.

**256 Boscombe Pier** SZ 111 911. *Snorkel site, launching.* To reach Boscombe Pier, leave the square in the centre of Bournemouth by Exeter Road. Drive over the elevated road beside Bournemouth Pier and keep straight ahead up the hill, continuing to the second roundabout at the Lansdowne. Leave this by the fourth exit, Christchurch Road. After almost a mile, the road drops into a dip with traffic lights, after which take the next right turn into Boscombe Spa Road. Then go first right, and keep turning right until you see the pier. Small boats can be carried or wheeled down a concrete slope on the western side of the pier, but this site is not suitable for launching boats using a vehicle. The entry into the sea is across very loose yellow sand.

A southerly or south-westerly wind brings a swell on to this site. Do not swim under the pier if there is a heavy swell running on to the beach: the visibility will be blank yellow and you may be flung against the pier supports and injured.

*Boscombe Pier (Site 256) is a good snorkel site on calm days.* Photo: Roy Smallpage

Watch out also for fishing lines and hooks dropping from the pier, which extends over 200yds from the shore. At its outer end depths of about 5m can be found. Currents are weak and run parallel to the shore; this is an excellent site for the trainee snorkeller, who can make surprise finds of coins or other lost property beneath the pier. If you do launch here, there is a speed limit of 8 knots within a line drawn parallel to the beach extending west and east from the tip of the pier. There are cafés, toilets and public telephone, by the pier.

NOTE There is a by-law restricting boats to 8 knots within 200yds of the beach off Sites **257** and **258**.

### 257 Southbourne, Warren Edge Car Park  SZ 147 910. *Launching point only.*
Warren Edge car park sits on a wide shelf of low cliff at Southbourne next to a vast area of holiday hotels, guest houses and apartments. It therefore becomes very congested during the holiday season. To find this site from the centre of Bournemouth, travel east towards Christchurch as far as Pokesdown, a distance of 3 miles. At the traffic lights turn right along the B3059; continue along this route for 1¼ miles until a wide junction is reached; turn right to reach the top of the cliffs. Now drive ½ mile farther east along the cliff top road. The car park will then be seen between the road and the cliff top.

A short distance along the driveway entrance into the car park, there is a smooth, wide walkway to the beach, 70yds away. Boats can be wheeled or carried down this slope, but at the bottom, adjacent to the promenade, there is a

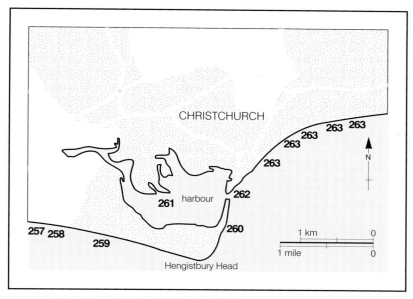

*Hengistbury Head and Christchurch, showing Southbourne Point House Café*
*(Site 258), Solent Beach Car Park (Site 259), Hengistbury Head (Site 260),*
*Christchurch Harbour (Site 261), Mudeford Quay (Site 262) and the access points to*
*the sea between Avon Beach to Highcliffe (all marked as Site 263).*

long section of handrail, splitting the walkway into two narrow halves. Boats
have to be lifted over this length of 3ft high rail and then from the promenade
down a short flight of steps to a beach of soft sand. There are toilets and cafés on
the promenade, and there is a telephone at the beach office. There is also a
telephone kiosk on the road above the car park at its eastern end.

**258  Southbourne Point House Café**  SZ 151 909. *Launching point only.* Proceed
from Bournemouth as for Site **257**, but instead of turning into Warren Edge car
park continue eastwards for just over ½ mile until the Point House Café is seen on
the cliff top on the right. Here, just west of the café, a wide, gently sloping 75yd
walkway leads down to the promenade. Vehicles are not allowed to drive down
here, but small inflatables can be carried or wheeled. There may be a low, locked
barrier at the top of the walkway – a small boat and trailer will have to be lifted
over the barrier or tilted through gaps. On the promenade, a ramp a few yards to
the east leads to a shingle beach. A shorter route to this ramp from the road
above is down a flight of 30 wide concrete steps. These leave the road just east
of the Point House Café, but boats obviously have to be carried down them. This
site is not recommended for shore diving because of poor visibility and a
featureless bottom. There is very little parking space available near this site (but
*see* Site **259**). There is a telephone box outside the Point House Café.

**259 Southbourne – Solent Beach Car Park** SZ 156 909. *Launching point only.* This shingle beach has a pay-and-display car park on the adjacent cliff. To find it from Bournemouth, take the same route as for Site **257** but continue farther east along the southern coast road for a good ¼ mile beyond the Point House Café. The entrance to the car park is clearly signposted, and is in a wide grassy area that stretches for over a mile to Hengistbury Head. Access to the beach is down the low cliff by way of a gravel road 120yds long. Small boats can be wheeled or carried down, but they must first be lifted over a locked gate, or over 5ft wooden posts at the start of this road. The nearest café and telephone are at the Point House Café, ¼ mile to the west. Shore diving is not recommended here because of the poor visibility and lack of underwater features.

**260 Hengistbury Head** SZ 179 904. *Snorkel site only.* Between the western side of the entrance to Christchurch Harbour and the long breakwater on the southern tip of Hengistbury Head is a beach of sand, shingle and rocks. Near and under the headland just east of the long breakwater, the beach and sea bed become very rocky. It is this part that makes an interesting, if shallow, snorkel dive. To reach Hengistbury Head drive from Christchurch to Mudeford Quay (*see* Site **262**). Park on the quay and take the ferry across the harbour mouth. The fare is low and the ferry operates up to 9pm mid-season. From the ferry landing-stage it is a ½ mile walk along the beach or sandy footpath to the most rocky part of the beach.

Hengistbury Head is a scheduled Ancient Monument and a Site of Special Scientific Interest; there was a significant Iron Age settlement here. Many ancient British and Roman gold and silver coins have been found on the beach and also on the headland. It is possible to snorkel here out as far as the Beer Pan rocks, but great caution should always be exercised as an extremely strong current flows westwards round the headland on the ebb tides. This site is sheltered only from the north – a wind from any other direction above Force 3 will bring a short swell on to the rocks. Visibility is low in all but still conditions because of the sediment carried from the nearby sandy beaches in Poole Bay and Christchurch Bay. When the tide is flooding there is an area of still water close inshore to the east of the long breakwater. The nearest telephone is a kiosk among the beach huts, 60yds east of the ferry landing stage. Near the telephone are a café and public toilets.

**261 Christchurch Harbour** *Launching point only.* There are several public launching points in this harbour, and all are free. The distance to the harbour mouth at Mudeford Quay is between ¾ mile and 2 miles. The channel through the harbour is navigable for small boats at all states of the tide and is marked by buoys. However, at low water it is narrow – and too shallow for an outboard motor, which may hit the bottom in several places. There is a speed limit of four knots throughout the harbour and the navigational reach of the River Stour, which forms the upper part of the harbour. The currents are generally not a hazard to navigation. For diving, launching from Mudeford Quay (Site **262**) is probably more convenient than at any other site in the harbour. There are, however, four alternatives to this.

*Wick Lane* slip at SZ 155 921. On the south bank of the river, opposite the old Pontin's Holiday Camp, there is a good gravel launching ramp almost directly

*Mayors Mead slipway at the head of Christchurch Harbour (Site 261) with
the Priory in the background. Photo: Roy Smallpage*

off Wick Lane. There is no parking at the ramp nor on Wick Lane. Cars have to be
taken to a car park farther up the lane to the west. To find this site, leave
Christchurch along Barrack Road. After 400yds turn left into Stour Road. After
crossing the bridge over the river, Wick Lane is the first on the left.

*Mayors Mead* car park and launching ramp (SZ 156 921) lies between the
western end of The Quomps recreation area and the old Pontins Holiday Camp.
The 9yd wide concrete ramp at the river end of the pay-and-display car park
enables boats to be launched by vehicle into the River Stour.

*Christchurch Quay* (SZ 159 923) is suitable for small boats. Provided they can
be carried around the metal posts, it is possible to launch down steps, from a
small ramp, or direct from the quay wall. There is some parking here
(pay-and-display), but the area is largely a yellow-line jungle. There are telephones
and a café nearby.

*Fisherman's Bank* (Argyle Road, Stanpit, SZ 174 920) lies on the eastern side
of the harbour. Its main attributes are that it is very quiet and only ¾ mile from the
sea. Its biggest drawback is the fact that the harbour dries here on low water.
There is a hard, gravelly slip that can be used for launching with a vehicle. To find
this site, leave Christchurch eastwards on the A35. After approximately ½ mile, at
the first road island, turn right, signposted to Mudeford, and keep straight on
over another road island and along the road named Stanpit. After approximately
¾ mile, turn right along Argyle Road, which ends at the slip. There are yellow
lines on Argyle Road, but cars can be parked back along Stanpit. There is a
telephone kiosk on Stanpit near the Argyle Road junction.

**262 Mudeford Quay** SZ 183 916. *Launching point only.* Mudeford Quay lies at the entrance to Christchurch Harbour. Small boats can be launched here at most states of the tide except low water from a public slip, which is free except at popular times. Alongside is a special area for boat trailers, which can be left up to a maximum of 48 hours. At high water even large hard boats can be launched here using a vehicle to reverse the boat trailer down the concrete slip into the water.

To find Mudeford Quay, leave Christchurch eastwards on the A35. After approximately ½ mile, at the first road island turn right. It is signposted to Mudeford. Keep straight on over another road island and along Stanpit. Keep straight ahead for almost 1½ miles, then watch out for a clearly signposted turning on the right into the quay. There is a vast pay-and-display car park at the quay, and its landscaped surrounds are a popular picnic area. The public slip is situated at the north-west corner of this car park, near the pub. Other services on the quay include the inshore lifeboat station, a café, shops, a public telephone and toilets.

Mudeford Quay is situated at the narrow entrance to Christchurch Harbour, through which the rivers Stour and Avon flow out to sea. At the harbour mouth a narrow entrance channel called The Run is marked well out to sea by lines of small buoys – one coloured red, the other green. The red buoys indicate the port side of the channel when approaching *from the sea.* If you have no local knowledge, stand on the quay and watch other boats entering and leaving the harbour before trying it for yourself. This is a tricky entrance, especially in choppy

*This view into Christchurch Harbour at Mudeford Quay clearly shows the deeper channel along the quay and the submerged pebble bank outside the entrance, which dries at low water.* Photo: Peter Bruce

conditions or at low water when a large area of pebble bank outside the mouth dries. Currents through The Run can be dreadful, especially when the water is ebbing out of the harbour. A strong southerly or south-westerly wind will prevent small boats from leaving the harbour. Diving or snorkelling on the sea side of the quay is dangerous. On the harbour side, it is pointless because of the shallow, sandy conditions. There is a speed limit within the harbour of four knots, and an 8 knot limit outside the harbour within 100yds of the shore.

**263 Avon Beach to Highcliffe** Situated between Mudeford Quay and the Dorset–Hampshire boundary at Chewton Bunny, just east of Highcliffe, there are five access points to the sea across pleasant, mainly sandy gravel beaches. These places are all good family beaches with the possibility of some snorkelling when the visibility is good. This usually means when the sea has been calm for several days. Any wind, except from the north, will cause waves to spoil the visibility along the immediate shoreline. The beaches are:

*Avon Beach car park* (SZ 188 922). *Snorkelling and possible launching.* After driving from Christchurch, along Stanpit, do not turn right into Mudeford Quay, but keep straight on to the beach, where the car park will be seen to the east. At the east end of the car park there are cafés, a telephone and a wide concrete path onto a soft beach.

*Avon Run Road – east end* (SZ 192 925). *Snorkelling and possible launching.* A tarmac slope to the beach huts and a short flight of wide steps lead, in only 30yds, onto a sandy beach.

*Friar's Cliff, Steamer Point car park* (SZ 194 297). *Snorkelling and possible launching.* In 100yds, a gravel track leads from the small car park down a gentle slope to a small promenade and a concrete ramp onto the gravel and sand beach. Small boats can easily be carried down the track.

*Highcliffe Castle car park* (SZ 204 930). *Snorkelling only.* The car park is at the cliff top and within the grounds of Highcliffe Castle. A wide gravel path from the eastern end of the parking area leads through the trees in approximately 200yds via a gently inclining zigzag down the cliff to a sandy gravel beach.

*Highcliffe Top car park* (SZ 217 931). *Snorkelling only.* Perched high on the cliff top, which gives the area its name, this car park gives access to a gravel beach via a 200yd steep gravel track. It is not practical to launch here.

# Offshore boat diving and wrecks

**264 Blood Alley (Poole Harbour)** 01 41.12N; 01 58.40W. This shallow channel is ideal ground for the snorkeller. It is situated along the southern shore of Brownsea Island, and is usually just about navigable for an inflatable at low water. But depths are often as little as 0.5m, and on low springs a vast area of mud around this channel dries. The course of the channel is marked by stakes. It is inhabited by large plaice and flounder, as are other nearby locations such as South Deep, Whiteground Lake and Redhorn Lake. It is possible for spear fishing snorkellers to cover the whole of this area from the shore at Shell Bay Marine (*see* Site **233**), but first they must learn to harness the tidal currents by drifting effortlessly westwards with the flood and then catch the swift currents of the ebb to bring them back to the place where their expedition started.

The best time to dive is in the latter part of the flood or between first and second high water. Strong currents occur towards the harbour entrance on the ebb. Visibility during quiet periods can be up to 2m, but it usually drops to nil during the ebb. *Launching: Sandbanks Yacht Company Slip 1 mile (Site 250).*

**265  Wych Channel (Poole Harbour)**  50 41.90N; 01 58.30W. The diving is good all along Wych Channel (clearly marked by stakes) on the northern side of Brownsea Island. The bottom varies from mud to clean gravel or sand. Large plaice and founder are common, and there is also the occasional lobster to be seen. The probability of a fair amount of traffic along this channel, especially on fine weekends, has to be taken into account when planning to dive here. It can, however, make an ideal site when others are "blown out".

Depths in Wych Channel are about 8m at high water. The sides of the channel slope up steeply – almost vertically in places – to the shallower surrounding areas. Visibility can drop dramatically on the ebb, but otherwise 2 to 3m can be expected in average conditions. Very sheltered from south and westerly winds. *Launching: Baiter or Sandbanks Yacht Company slip – both 1 mile.*

**266  Frenchman**  50 40.77N; 01 55.90W. Offshore, just over ½ mile south-east of the Haven Hotel at Sandbanks, in the shallow water on the Hook Sands, are the remains of an unidentified wooden wreck. It has sunk into the sand, and only the traces of her main timbers can be seen at a depth of 3m. She is known to local divers and charter boat skippers as the *Frenchman*. Do not confuse this wreck with the Antler Wreck (Site **269**), which is ½ mile farther offshore, to the south-east. The Hook Sands form the graveyard of many ancient wooden sailing vessels that have come to grief trying to enter or leave Poole Harbour. In several places, in some at only wading depth at low water, the outlines of the timbers of ships can be picked out by the weed that grows up from them in an otherwise sandy desert. This area will doubtless be the focus of some exciting archaeological work in the future. *Launching: Sandbanks Yacht Club slip 1½ miles, Shore Road 1 mile.*

**267  Nibbler III**  50 40.36N; 01 55.78W. On 30 January, 1989, a 52ft Danish gill-netter fishing boat, on passage from Gillingham to Poole, stranded on Hook Sands and became a total wreck. The majority of the vessel has by now disappeared into the sands, but enough still stands up to give shelter for a lobster or two and is worth a dive. Depth is 5m. *Launching: Sandbanks Yacht Company slip or Shore Road 1 mile.*

**268  The Yards**  50 38.60N; 01 55.57W. Off the northern side of Handfast Point is a small area marked *foul* on the chart. The whole area between this and the shore, 200yds distant, is known as The Yards. Several wrecks, including some World War Two casualties, were beached and eventually broken up here. Depths range from 2 to 5m and the sea bed varies from plain sand to small kelp-covered rocks. A patient snorkeller or diver could come up with some interesting artefacts. A practical advantage of this site is that it is very sheltered from westerly and southerly winds, being tucked well behind the point. Visibility can be good at times; and is almost always adequate for a close-up search of the bottom. Currents are generally weak, but rip currents occur nearby at Handfast Point when the tide is ebbing out of Poole Bay. At these times stay well inside the point. *Launching: Studland, 1 mile.*

**269 The Antler Wreck** 50 40.46N; 01 55.42W. This small wooden wreck, possibly an 18th-century stone barge, lies on the eastern edge of Hook Sands at a depth of 7m; most of the lower parts of her hull are still intact. Her cargo, traces of which can still be found, was a rather peculiar mix, consisting of blocks of stone and deer antlers. When she was discovered, the antlers were packed in uncannily tidy bundles. If she was a local stone barge from Swanage her cargo of antlers needs to be explained. Soon after this site was discovered, some preliminary archaeological work was done by local divers in conjunction with Poole Museum. Currents, although fairly strong on the main ebb, are otherwise weak. Visibility on the site is never brilliant: 2 to 3m is average. *Launching: Shore Road, ¾ mile.*

**270 Avanti** 50 29.90N; 01 55.03W. This 2,128 gross ton former Danish steamship, loaded with 3,500 tons of iron ore, was sailing from Bilbao to West Hartlepool when, on 2 February, 1918, the German submarine *UB-55* fired a torpedo into her. The heavily laden ship was reported to have sunk within two minutes of the explosion. Of her crew of 24 only 2 survived. She has not been heavily dived, preference being given to the wreck of the Aparima, only ½ mile to the south. This may have been a mistake, for the Avanti is an exciting dive in her own right. She is a large ship, measuring 272ft long with a beam of 40ft and is well endowed with portholes and other fittings.

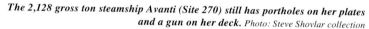

*The 2,128 gross ton steamship Avanti (Site 270) still has portholes on her plates and a gun on her deck.* Photo: Steve Shovlar collection

189

Look out for the large gun on her stern and the rudder stock, which projects upwards, high above the deck. Although twisted, she is mainly upright. Amidships, her bridge and accommodation have collapsed around her two boilers and three-cylinder triple-expansion engine. She is home to many large congers. In about 1988, members of Hurn SAC, diving from the Poole charter boat *Doraydo*, recovered brass letters from her stern making up the word "Avanti". Depth to the rocky sea bed is 42m. Wreck stands up 8m. *Boats: Swanage 8 miles, Poole 14 miles.*

**271  Aparima**  50 29.40N; 01 55.00W. This luxury cargo and passenger liner was built around the end of the 19th century and was owned by the Union Steamship Company of New Zealand. She measured 430ft by 54ft, with a height of nearly 40ft and a gross weight of 5,704 tons. Power was supplied by two triple-expansion steam engines driving two large bronze propellers. On 19 November, 1917, she was torpedoed by a German submarine while sailing from London to Barry. Of her passengers and crew, at least 56 were killed.

Today, the *Aparima* lies at a sea bed depth of 42m, but her bow is only 31m below the surface. The ship must have broken her back, for her centre section is upright but the forward section is listing to 45° to starboard. There is also a definite tilt aft. In about 1970, she was purchased from her original owners by a Swanage man who has worked her for scrap over the years. Despite this, this huge ship is still largely intact, with many of her brass portholes remaining along her hull. The wreck lies with the tide – east to west, with her bows facing west. Visibility on this site, in summer, is excellent and can be, in settled weather, in excess of 18m. *Boats: Poole 14 miles, Swanage 9 miles.*

**272  Valentine Tanks**  A number of Valentine tanks were experimentally fitted in 1942 with canvas screens, which could be raised or lowered pneumatically, to allow them to float in the sea. They were powered by a drive system that enabled the engines to turn large propellers mounted at the rear when the tanks were in the water. Much of the development took place in Poole Bay and it is not surprising that a few succumbed in rough conditions and sank. The screen system was eventually used during the Normandy landings, but on the heavier Sherman tanks.

The positions of these experimental prototype tanks were, for a long time, one of the best kept secrets of the British diving scene. Alas, the retrieval in 1989 of live ammunition by a local diver caused the Royal Navy to pay a visit and clear all other unexploded shells by blowing up each tank with explosives. The remains in Poole Bay lie at around 9m, except for the one due east of Handfast Point – numbered (7) below – which is rather deeper.

They are at the following positions, from west to east:

    (1) 50 40.08N; 01 54.86W  (2) 50 40.23N; 01 54.75W,
    (3) 50 40.48N; 01 54.62W  (4) 50 39.74N; 01 54.19W,
    (5) 50 40.44N; 01 53.91W  (6) 50 39.47N; 01 53.41W,
    (7) 50 41.50N; 01 50.28W

All are situated in flat, sandy terrain and consequently form havens for many fish, conger eels, crabs and lobsters. *Launching: any site in the western half of the bay.*

Top: An experimental Valentine
tank is gingerly launched from
the ramp of a landing craft in
Poole Bay.

Above: A prototype Valentine tank, Type DD (dual drive). It was fitted with a propeller
and the pneumatically raised canvas screen turned it into a boat. The remains of seven
of these tanks can be found in Poole Bay. Photos: The Tank Museum, Bovington

**273 Studland Bay Wreck** 50 39.67N; 01 54.79W. One cold, dark night in January
1984, Poole fisherman Gerry Randle was trawling in Studland Bay and snagged his
nets into an unknown object 40ft below his boat on the sea bed. Puzzled and
somewhat angry to loose his valuable gear in what he had previously considered
to be a clear area, the thought could not possibly have entered his mind that he had
started a chain of events with world-wide implications for the knowledge of ancient
shipwrecks. For he did not know that the ship's timber sticking up out of the sand
and securely holding his nets had laid there, preserved by sand and silt, since
around the first decade of the 16th century. Of equal importance was the fact
that local divers from Hamworthy SAC, called in by Gerry to release his nets,
took the trouble to take into Poole Museum a hand full of brightly coloured pottery
shards that they found amidst the disturbed old timbers. They and Gerry were
astounded when later it was announced that not only had the shards been clearly
identified as Isabela Polychrome, a type of pottery manufactured in Spain around
1510, but that they were the best representative sample of this rare pottery type
ever to be found in the British Isles.

The wreck site, clearly of immense archaeological importance, was quickly

*Diver measuring the late 15th-century timbers of the Studland Bay Wreck, revealed by archaeological excavations of the sea bed.*
Photo: Studland Bay Wreck Project

*Manufactured before 1525, the shards of Isabela Polychrome pottery from the Studland Bay Wreck: the best samples ever found in the British Isles.* Photo: Poole Museum

designated and given legal protection. Under licence and under the direction of archaeological officer Keith Jarvis and diving director Mike Markey, there followed no less than nine years of survey and excavation. Almost 3,000 diver hours were spent under water on the wreck – the work being completed in 1992. The excavation exposed the remains of a three-masted wooden sailing vessel, typical of a Spanish trading ship of around 1510. The complete vessel is estimated to measure 75ft long with a beam of 15ft. Some 750 separate artefacts were recovered and are in various stages of preservation and investigation. Remains of the ship's pump were located, and are of considerable interest as only three others of similar age survive anywhere. A decision was made to leave the ship's timbers safe below the sea bed for any subsequent investigation by future generations. These have been covered with plastic sheeting and heavily protected with layers of bags of sand.

There are still several years of evaluation and study of artefacts to be carried out, but a full archaeological report will eventually be published. Meanwhile, there is a gradual trickle of conserved artefacts from various laboratories back into the major display at the Poole Waterfront Museum at the Quay end of Poole High Street. Because of the protected status, diving is illegal within 75m of the wreck buoy. There is a possibility that undiscovered parts of the ship, together with artefacts may lay well outside the designated area. Any diver finding such an object should, if possible, record the position and without disturbing the item report the find to the Poole Waterfront Museum.

**274 Elizabeth Robertson** 50 29.20N; 01 54.30W. This wooden motor fishing vessel of 69 gross tons was lost at this approximate position on 24 April, 1975, the victim of a fire. Her crew of two were rescued by helicopter from Portland helicopter base but the wreck has not been found. *Boats: Poole 12 miles, Swanage 8 miles.*

**275 Middle Poole Patch** 50 41.08N; 01 53.58W. This small reef is the most south-westerly of several groups of rocks known collectively as Poole Rocks. The rock patches rise like islands out of a plain, sandy bottom. Although a satisfying dive can be had on any of these rocks, Middle Poole Patch is the highest and most scenic. As in other Poole Bay rock patches, there are what appear to be fossilised trees, but nowhere else can these strange shapes in the vertical rock faces be so clearly seen. In one place they stand upright like organ pipes in a cathedral. Depths vary from 4m at the highest point of the rock to 13m on the level sands. Currents are weak. Visibility in settled periods can be up to 10m, but is usually around 3 to 5m. Besides crabs and lobsters, the rocks are inhabited by fish of many varieties. In common with most Poole Bay sites, only a single, short variety of weed grows here.

An archaeological mystery is centred around this patch of rocks. Over a period of many years, divers have discovered a number of what appear to be stone anchors. In the early 1980s, Alan Owen, a Bournemouth diver, delivered five of the "anchors" to the Institute of Geological Sciences (now the British Geological Survey) for identification. Intensive study revealed that three were of local Purbeck stone and one was of Isle of Wight stone. But the fifth was not local; the only comparable rock is to be found in the Mediterranean area. This obviously clearly opened up the possibility of an exciting Roman connection.

*The ancient stone anchor, weighing 83kg, recovered from Chapman's Pool by Chris Franklin and now on display in the County Museum at Dorchester. Archaeologists are still researching the mystery symbol that appears on both faces.* Photo: Mike Markey

In 1992, the saga of the stone anchors came to the notice of a Southampton diver, Mike Markey, who had been in charge during most of the work on the nearby Studland Bay wreck. He had earlier formed the Poole Bay Archaeological Research Group and now set to work to solve this mystery. First he managed to trace no less than 26 stone anchors that had been recovered from the sea bed. The majority of these had been found in Poole Bay, mainly around the Middle Poole patch. Mike managed to borrow all these artefacts and they were subjected to an intensive study at Southampton University. They appear to be of local origin – the majority being of Purbeck limestone – and are assumed to be medieval fishing weights, though without conclusive proof.

One anomaly turned up by the study was an "anchor" recovered from Chapman's Pool, by Wimborne diver Jackie Elston. This had a second hole running transversely across it. The real excitement came when Christopher Franklin, from Emsworth, announced the recovery of a ship's stone anchor, obviously genuine and weighing 83.5kg, also from just outside Chapman's Pool (near the shore line, out towards St Aldhelm's Head). This prompted a thorough search of the area – but nothing was found on the hard, flat sea bed. Some anchors are still to be seen around the Middle Poole Patch. *Launching: Shore Road 1½ miles.*

**276 Bournemouth Rocks** 50 42.30N; 01 53.25W. This small reef, surrounded by a sandy desert, makes an interesting dive. The rocks rise to within 5m of the surface at one point, forming an almost vertical rock face some 5m in height. The depth to the surrounding sand is 11m. Crabs, lobsters and many fish are to be seen and parts of fossilised trees are visible in the rock. The higher slopes are covered in short weed. Currents are weak. The visibility is usually about 5m, and can, exceptionally, rise to 10m. Winds from the southern half bringing surf on to nearby sandy beaches will, however, reduce it to nil. The rocks lie almost 600yds offshore from Alum Chine.

A large yellow buoy approximately 120yds to the west marks the position of the outer end of a long-defunct outfall pipe. *Launching: Durley Chine ½ mile – see Site **254**.*

**277 Durley Rocks** 50 42.50N; 01 53.00W. This large patch of rocks (clearly marked on the chart) makes an ideal first boat dive for beginners, but with lots of crabs, lobsters, and many varieties of fish it is an interesting site for any grade of diver. The rocks lie just over ¼ mile out from the mouth of Durley Chine. Especially at the eastern end of the area, they largely form shapes of the stubs and roots of trees. There are tree trunks of up to 3ft diameter and standing up to 5ft high. The explanation of these shapes is that millions of years ago a forest had become engulfed in deep sand and gravel beds, probably caused by a river changing its course. The wood of the trees slowly rotted away and was replaced by iron pyrites, which faithfully took up their shape. The resultant rock is today extremely rich in iron pyrites.

Iron pyrites deposits are present in the nearby cliffs and were mined commercially in the past, to be used in the production of alum. The next chine west from Durley Chine is named Alum Chine, because of this activity. The fact that Durley Rocks are completely surrounded by featureless sand makes underwater navigation very easy. Stay on the rocks and you are never far from your waiting boat. The depth to the sand is 9m, but the rocks rise a good 3m above this in places. Tidal currents are weak. Visibility in quiet periods can be up to 10m but less than half this is more normal. Winds blowing strongly from the southern half can reduce it to nil. *Launching: Durley Chine Beach, ¼ mile – see Site **254**.*

WARNING Divers should not try to swim to these rocks from the shore. This is definitely a boat dive.

**278 Unidentified wreck** 50 37.76N; 01 52.80W. Exactly 2 miles south-east of Handfast Point, the Admiralty chart shows, in the above position, an area of spoil ground, but divers from Poole Charter boat *James Alexander* found the remains of a very old wooden wreck, partially buried in the sandy sea bed. Exploring and poking about in the remains, they discovered a ship's bell – unluckily, it had no name on it. This site could be worth archaeological exploration. Depth 18m. *Boats: Poole 7 miles, Swanage 3 miles.*

**279 Leny** 50 38.79N; 01 52.51W. Lying some 1½ miles east of Handfast Point, the remains of this wreck are low in the sand, but at least its propeller, its shaft and plates can be found. She was a Dutch motor vessel of 343 tons gross with a length of 136ft and was carrying a cargo of coal from Swansea to Poole when she struck a mine on 23 June, 1942. The divers who occasionally visit her say she is still an interesting dive with an excellent chance of encountering large lobsters around her plates. Depths are about 17m. Currents can be fairly strong at times, particularly during the flood tide. *Launching: Studland, 3 miles.*

**280 Fluent** 50 28.83N; 01 51.43W. Only one thing is certain about the wreck at this position: it is not the *Hazelwood* (though many have dived her in the belief that they were diving the 3,120 gross ton collier of that name, which has yet to be located). The wreck is upright and has sunk to the level of the main deck into a soft shingle sea bed but, being a very large ship, still stands at least 5m high in 40m. Her three boilers, consisting of two main and one donkey, together with the engine, which is laid over to the port side, are all situated amidships. Her propeller is still in place. Apart from the gravel that has entered her holds, all but No. 2 hold seem to be empty. No. 2 hold is two thirds full of what appear to be many large 16in solid shot shell heads, similar to those seen in the old range area of Lulworth Banks. The wreck is almost certainly the *Fluent*, a 3,660 gross ton British merchantman sunk by a torpedo fired by the German submarine *UC-65* on 20 July, 1917.

The *Fluent* was sailing from New York to London with a cargo listed as oats and "steel ingots" for the Ministry of Munitions. The ship measured 350ft long with a beam of 50ft and had a steel screw driven by machinery situated in a midships position, consisting of a triple-expansion engine developing 325hp. The design of her hull included a total of six bulkheads. Built by J. Priestman at their Sunderland yard for original owner J. Westhall, she was later purchased as a wreck by the now defunct Southampton salvage company Rizdon Beazley. Controversy erupted over ownership of the wreck in the 1980s, prompting a visit by the Devon and Dorset Police diving team who surveyed the wreck in an attempt to identify it for required evidence for a pending prosecution. The police divers failed to identify the wreck positively; it is certainly a puzzle awaiting some diving detective work. *Boats: Poole 15 miles.*

*The wreck of the 3,120 ton collier Hazelwood (see Site 280) has yet to be located.*
Photo: Steve Shovlar collection

**281 Start** 50 28.27N; 01 49.57W. This small Norwegian steamer of 728 tons gross had her holds full of coal when torpedoed on 22 December, 1917 – only 2 of her crew of 14 survived. She measured 204ft in length with a beam of 29ft. She was built on the Clyde by Scott and Sons of Glasgow in 1896 and was of steel construction, with a steel propeller. Her position on the sea bed was always thought to be just over 7 miles south of St Aldhelm's Head, but in 1985 Dave Saywell in his charter boat *James Alexander* decided to drop a shot 10 miles farther to the east, at a point on the sea bed where something showed on his echo sounder. Aboard were a group of very keen wreck divers who, within minutes, were quickly swarming down the shot line to find a sea bed of gravel and hard mud at 39m. There, sitting on the gravel in front of them, was what Dave had seen on the echo sounder – the remains of the *Start*, covered in detached brass fittings, with an identifying ship's bell that had lain there for almost 70 years.

The easiest part to locate is the boiler and engine at her stern end. The midships small bridge and accommodation form a mound with a residue of artefacts at her centre. The wreck tends to fade to nothing at the forward end, but the stem of the bow is still in place. The stern is partially collapsed and twisted over to port, but the aft steering position with the steering wheel intact is still in position, almost upright. *Boats: Poole 16 miles.*

*The Start (Site 281) was identified when her bell was recovered.* Photo: Dave Saywell

197

**282 Betsy Anna** 50 37 00N; 01 48 86W. Discovered in the early 1980s, this wreck was thought to be – and figures in hundreds of diver's log books as – the *Dagmar* until a local diver recovered a maker's label from the boiler and, with a deft bit of detective work, proved the ship to be the *Betsy Anna* (known earlier in her career as the *Ashington*). Built in 1892 on the Tyne, she foundered in Poole Bay in October, 1926 having had originally come to grief and torn her plates at Prawle Point in Devon. After temporary repairs at Salcombe, she was being towed to Cowes, but took on a lot of water, broke her tow, drifted and sank.

Today, she makes a very interesting dive. The bow of the ship has collapsed backwards, so now stands 4m high, pointing upwards. Moving aft, the hold is easy to see. Next, there are two boilers, both in position and upright. The propeller is missing. Depth 24m. *Boats: Poole 10 miles, Swanage 5 miles.*

**283 Galia** 50 26.41N; 01 48.10W. The large, previously unidentified wreck at the above position, lying so well over that she is almost upside down, is now believed to be this Italian steamer (formerly the *Olive Branch*). She was torpedoed on 24 October, 1917 by the German submarine *UB-40*. When her end came, she was sailing from the Tyne to Sevona with her holds full to the top with a cargo of coal. This cargo is plain to see, still spilling out from her holds, and mixes into the stone and pebble sea bed.

The wreck lies north–south, across the tide. A feature amidships is one of her boilers, which has partially fallen out of the hull and now has what looks like a large unexploded bomb lying alongside it on the sea bed. Built in 1887 with a gross tonnage of 2,728, the *Galia* measures 300ft long with a beam of 39ft. The hull still stands up a full 7m from the sea bed depth of 37m. *Boats: Poole 18 miles.*

*The Betsy Anna (Site 282), hard on the rocks at Prawle Point in Devon. After being towed off and undergoing emergency repairs at Salcombe she eventually sank south of Bournemouth.* Photo: Richard Larn collection

**284 Everleigh** 50 29.30N; 01 47.10W. The *Everleigh* is a large British steamship and became one of the last casualties of World War Two, sunk by a German torpedo fired by *U-1017* on 6 February, 1945, when bound from London to New York. She measured 406ft with a beam of 56ft and was a massive 5,222 gross tons. She was built in 1930 and still has plenty of her brass fittings. The wreck is owned by a Swanage man who purchased her in about 1970 from her original owners. Although for a long period she was regularly worked for scrap, and before that was partly dispersed by the Navy, she is still a big wreck and an excellent dive. The sea bed depth is 43m, but the wreck stands up, at her highest, 11m off the sea bed. One reason why she remains so high is the solid rock bed.

When built, the ship was fitted out with a very large three-cylinder triple-expansion engine capable of an output of 527hp. It is the area of her engine and boiler plant, situated just aft of midships, that has borne the brunt of the salvage operations, other sections of the ship remaining virtually intact. A 4in gun had been fitted, so somewhere are some nice 4in brass shell cases. She lies east–west on her port side, the bows facing east. *Boats: Poole 14 miles, Swanage 14 miles.*

**285 Aircraft** 50 36.70N; 01 46.79W. Discovered by members of Poole and Bournemouth BSAC in 1975, this is the wreck of a World War Two bomber, almost certainly a Halifax. It lies just over a mile east of the wreck of the *Betsy Anna*. No one seems to have done any serious research, so there is a reasonably easy task of detection just waiting for a keen group to undertake – and no doubt discover an interesting story. Depth to the sandy sea bed is 25m. *Boats: Poole 10 miles, Swanage 6 miles.*

*The British steamship Everleigh (Site 284) now rests on a rocky sea bed, having been torpedoed in February 1945 when on her way from London to New York.*

Photo: Steve Shovlar collection

**286 Clan Macvey** 50 39.69N; 01 46.71W. In the eastern part of Poole Bay, a good three miles offshore and plainly marked on the chart just north of the Dolphin Sand Bank, lie the substantial remains of a large ship. This is the wreck of the armed British merchant steamship of 5,815 gross tons, the *Clan Macvey*. Her Scottish owners Cayzer Irvine & Company took delivery of her in 1918 and christened her *Clan Macvey*. She measured 400ft long with a beam of 53ft. She was sent straight to Newcastle to collect a Government cargo of coal, with orders to deliver it to Port Said.

Fully loaded, she left Newcastle and made her way safely down the North Sea and entered the English Channel. Her brand new large triple-expansion engine delivered constant, unfailing power to a huge bronze propeller, ensuring steady progress on her maiden voyage. However, her Captain did not know about the German submarine *UB-57*, which lay in wait for such a vessel as this. Just past the Needles, the submarine managed to manoeuvre into a suitable position and fired a torpedo that almost blew the steamship in half and killed seven of her crew. Amazingly, despite the inrush of water and the weight of her cargo, she remained afloat. Help was soon at hand, and an attempt was made to tow her towards Poole, but after 4 hours she finally broke in half and sank. The date was 8 August, 1918.

She now lies virtually upright but has sunk into soft sand right up to the level of her deck. Sea bed depth is 18m. Her superstructure, which came to within 6m of the surface, has been cleared long ago by the Navy, so she now only rises up a maximum of 4m. A scour has developed around her and this seems to stop the surrounding sands from completely engulfing her. There is still a big ship there to be explored, even though much is below the sea bed. The wreck was purchased in March 1980 by Dave Saywell. Divers are welcome to enjoy diving and exploring his wreck, but he will prosecute anyone attempting commercial salvage.

One unsolved mystery is whether her bronze propeller is attached deep down under the sand or whether the stern half is elsewhere. A rather puzzling Admiralty report, dated 18 September, 1918, states that a mast was showing in position 50 39.66N; 01 48.00W – and a danger to shipping. This is considerably farther west than the known wreck site. Another strange fact is that in the 1970s there was a strong rumour in the Bournemouth area that a diver, drifting in the general area of this wreck, came upon the tip of a blade of a large bronze propeller sticking up out of the sand. A subsequent expedition is said to have failed to relocate this object. Could it have been part of the *Clan Macvey*? Boats: Poole 7 miles.

**287 Baron Gariock** 50 31.34N; 01 45.80W. After a 10-year search, this wreck was located in 1993 but was not positively identified until late in the autumn of 1994, when divers from the charter boat *Doraydo* discovered the ship's bell lying on the sea bed 10yds from the bow. For skipper Jim Scott this was a day of celebration – not only had his divers had a brilliantly exciting dive but he had at last found his property, for he had purchased the *Baron Gariock* many years earlier.

The ship was sunk on 28 October, 1917, by a torpedo fired by the German submarine *UC-63*. The torpedo slammed into her No. 3 hold, devastating her stern. Two of the ship's crew died, and the rest were lucky to escape in the lifeboats, for she sank within 6 minutes. The *Baron Gariock* (the former *Kirkstall*) was one of fourteen ships lost by the Baron Line during World War One. Built in

1895, she was 265ft long with a beam of 37ft and displaced 1,831 gross tons. Requisitioned by the Government and armed with a 13lb gun, she was about her war duties and sailing from Calais to Liverpool in ballast when the disaster overwhelmed her.

Lying at a depth of 38m, the wreck has sunk three-quarters of her height into a sea bed of fairly loose sandy gravel. The bow section, despite a 45° list to starboard, rises up 4m from the bottom and is the highest point of the wreck. Amidships, forward and aft of the engine room, gravel has entered her spaces and only the top of the hull, forming an outline of the ship, is visible. The stern end is badly broken, probably due to the torpedo strike. Amidships are two boilers and an engine block, partially obscured with collapsed plating. The 13 pounder gun is easily seen in the stern area, as is a copious amount of ammunition. Lots of brass fittings are still being found and the compass binnacle is still missing! Particularly around the stern area are quantities of pottery with the Baron Line logo. *Boats: Poole 16 miles, Swanage 8 miles.*

**288 Albert C Field** 50 28.25N; 01 45.34W. The wreck at this position has always been thought to be that of the Canadian steamship *Albert C Field*, but perhaps this is not correct. The account of her loss states that the ship was hit by a torpedo dropped by a German aircraft on 18 June, 1944. She was a ship of 1,764 gross tons, measuring 252ft long with a broad beam of 43ft and specially built on Teesside in 1923 for her owners the Upper Lakes and St Lawrence Transportation Company Ltd for service on the Canadian Great Lakes – her type being known as a Great Lakes Steamer. She resembled a huge, oblong motorised barge with her accommodation and bridge right up on the bow, leaving lots of clear space for cargo to be carried in her copious holds. She had been requisitioned by the British Government and pressed into service helping with the war effort.

On her last journey she was on her way to the Normandy beaches, carrying 2,500 tons of ammunition and bags of mail. Reports of her sinking state that after the torpedo hit she caught fire and then started to break in two by rising amidships, with her bow and stern starting to sink. Several members of her crew were already swimming in the water and others were trying to lower boats when the ammunition apparently went up in one big bang. Certainly the wreck on the sea bed here is surrounded by a carpet of twisted brass shell cases and bits and pieces of ship. The only recognisable features of the wreck are her boilers.

But if this is the *Albert C Field*, how did all but 4 of the crew survive a colossal explosion? Perhaps the *Albert C Field* only partially blew up and is elsewhere, and this wreck – obviously having suffered a catastrophic explosion – is a different ship. This wreck is on a stony sea bed at 36m and rises up to 4m. *Boats: Poole 17 miles, Swanage 11 miles.*

**289 Braedale** 50 33.38N; 01 45.34W. This wreck was discovered by Dave Saywell in 1986 while lobster potting in the area. For a long period it was thought to be the wreck of the *Sargasso*, but Dave has closely studied the wreck and is now sure it cannot be, being much larger and with a completely different layout. She sits in a wide and deep scoured hollow in loose shingle, complete with propeller. The wreck is well over on its starboard side with the port side intact. The boiler and triple expansion engine are aft, within 10 to 15ft of her stern. Dave Saywell identifies her as the steamship *Braedale* (her previous name was the

*The Braedale (Site 289) sank off Bournemouth, but is here seen in the Clifton Gorge on the River Avon.* Photo: Steve Shovlar collection

*Bessie Bar)* as this was the only ship with engines aft that was reported sunk anywhere in the area.

The *Braedale* was lost on 16 October, 1932 in a reported position 8 miles south-west of the Needles. She was sailing from Dieppe to Bristol with a cargo of apples. Owned by the Eltham Shipping Company and built in 1894, she measured 142ft long with a beam of 25ft, was 406 gross tons and fitted out with an aft mounted triple-expansion engine. Depth to the sea bed is 33m; the wreck rises 7m. The *Sargasso* has still not been found. *Boats: Poole 13 miles, Swanage 8 miles.*

**290 Excelsior** 50 40.41N; 01 44.80W. In this position, 2 miles west of the offshore end of Christchurch Ledge, lie the very broken remains of a British vessel, described as a steel built fishing drifter. She sprang a leak and foundered on 5 September, 1924 when on a journey from Portsmouth to Newport with a cargo of metal scrap. Part of her cargo which can still be seen, consists of pipes and, accordingly, for a long while, she was known as "the pipe wreck". The sea bed depth is 19m and the highest part of the wreck, her boiler, stands up 1.5m. *Launching: Mudeford 5 miles. Boats: Poole 10 miles.*

**291 Unidentified wreck** 50 28.30N; 01 44.75W. Less than ½ mile due east of the shattered wreck of the *Albert C Field* lie the remains of a small steam-driven coaster. Divers from the Poole charter boat *James Alexander* have explored the wreck at this position, but so far have failed to identify it. This wreck lies half buried in shingle. Her main features are a boiler, plates and larger sections of a steel hull. Depth to sea bed is 36m with the wreck standing up 2m. A name suggested for this little-dived wreck is the *Britannia*, but evidence to support this is obscure. *Boats: Poole 17 miles, Swanage 11 miles.*

**292 German Submarine** 50 22.08N; 01 44.17W. Lying in deep water, with all hatches sealed, and 22 miles almost due south of Hengistbury Head is an exceptionally interesting, almost undamaged, and probably unflooded wreck of a U-boat. She has been little dived, but the range finder from the top of her conning tower, plainly inscribed with a swastika, can be seen in the Blue Boar Inn at Poole. She was discovered by John, Steve and Mike Ballett, who found the wreck in 1994 while potting an area of steep banks and gullies.

When the original dive took place, they found the submarine lying with a deep scour in the shingle sea bed, around both the bows and the stern; depth at the scour was 59m. She was upright and level on the bottom with her decks at 56m and the top of the conning tower at 53m. The shroud from around the conning tower was off and lying alongside, her deck gun was missing and there was slight damage to the stern where one of the rudders was off, otherwise she was, and still is, a complete submarine – in mint condition. An interesting feature was the thick rubber matting covering her decks. This was fitted by the Germans to their submarine fleet after 1943 in an effort to deaden the ASDIC reflection, and evade searching or attacking surface ships.

On a more recent dive, the Balletts were taken aback to find that the submarine had changed her attitude on the sea bed. The stern, with its twin propellers, had rocked backwards into its deep scour and the bows were 6m clear of the sea bed! This buoyancy is fairly convincing evidence that she is unflooded. Further dives have been carried out and a rippled distortion has been noticed in the steel of her forward end, which suggests she was very closely depth charged or crashed into the sea bed at high speed. It seems that other people are interested in this wreck, for on another day a French Telecom ship was seen hanging around and eventually to launch a submersible. *Boats: Poole 32 miles.*

**293 Christchurch Ledge** 50 42.00N; 01 44.10W. This ledge stretches out from the shore at Hengistbury Head for almost 3 miles, giving good diving all along its length between the shore and the navigation buoy on its southern tip. First of all, at the landward end, in the shallow Beer Pan Rocks area, lie the remains of a World War Two Spitfire. Along the outer third of the ledges, which is also the best area for plaice, there is a geological aberration – the top of the ledge is as shallow as 8m, but diving instructor Darren Sargeant has discovered a number of holes extending down to 23m! Visibility on Christchurch Ledge can, exceptionally, be as high as 10m, but it is more normally in the 1 to 3m range. Currents can be fairly strong over the ledge. Unless a drift dive is contemplated, outings should be planned for slack water – a good ½ hour before low water at Christchurch or 6 hours later. *Launching: Mudeford Quay or any Southbourne launch site, 2 miles.*

**294 Venezuela** 50 36.60N; 01 43.60W. Divers from Bournemouth & Poole BSAC were probably the first to visit this wreck, on 1 June, 1975. Ted Bishop, a Lymington fisherman, had discovered the wreck while potting and took the divers out to the wreck, re-finding it with landmarks and a pair of field glasses – electronic navigational equipment was rare in those days. The highlight of the day's diving was the recovery by Tony Hales of a silver hunter watch. In the early 1980s, divers from Swindon BSAC removed a gun and, later still, a diver from the same branch noticed odd shapes under concretion on the vertical hull. He scraped off the growth and discovered two rows of brass letters reading "Venezuela Buenos

*The 90mm French breech-loading gun from the deck of the*
*Venezuela (Site 294).*

Aires". Up until then, local divers had thought she was the *Empire Crusader*, but at last the wreck's correct identity was established.

The Argentinean-owned ship had called at Falmouth and was sailing to Rouen as part of a convoy attacked on 14 March, 1918 by the German submarine *UB-59*. Two torpedoes were fired, one of which hit and quickly sank the *Venezuela*. The ship of 730 gross tons measured 190ft in length. She now sits perfectly upright, but has sunk well into the sandy gravel sea bed. She lies north–south at a sea bed depth of 27m, with the wreck rising up 4m. There should still be some brass portholes about. The *Empire Crusader* remains unfound. *Boats: Poole 12 miles.*

**295 Trial Oil Well** 50 37.68N; 01 42.78W. The oil drilling jack-up platform *Menrod 85* established an exploratory oil well at this position, approximately 5 miles south of Hengistbury Head, during the last quarter of 1993. It is now capped off. Sea bed depth 26m.

**296 Unidentified wreck** 50 25.52N; 01 42.16W. In this position, well offshore, and coinciding with a wreck symbol on the Admiralty Chart, is the wreck of a fairly small steamship, lying at a depth of 38m and rising up, at its highest point, to 4m. Not much is known about this wreck, but it might be the 897 gross ton French vessel *Azemmour* (formerly the *Wistaria*). Built in 1909 and torpedoed on 20 March, 1918, she measured 205ft long with a beam of 33ft. She was fitted out with a three-cylinder triple-expansion engine. *Boats: Poole 21 miles, Swanage 15 miles.*

**297 Borgny** 50 35.44N; 01 41.64W. For many years, the wreck in the above position was thought to be the *Asborg*, but a positive identification came when members of Hurn SAC recovered brass letters from the wreck's stern. The *Borgny* was sunk on 22 February, 1918 by a German submarine. She was a Norwegian steam-driven merchantman of 1,149 gross tons, built in 1909 and measuring

228ft long with a beam of 36ft. The wreck lies twisted and broken in sandy gravel at a sea bed depth of 27m. Despite having sunk into the gravel, the wreck still rises up 5m in parts. Her stern is completely upside down with the rudder and propeller easy to recognise, completely clear of the sea bed. *Boats: Poole 13 miles, Swanage 10 miles.*

**298 Eleanor** 50 30.11N; 01 40.35W. For many years, this little dived site was thought to contain the wrecks of the small Dutch steamer *Ajax* and the 1,597 gross ton British steamer *Coquetdale*, which were supposed to be lying almost touching each other. But there is only one large ship on this site – and it is neither of the above. It is the World War One wreck of the 1,980 gross ton British steamship *Eleanor*, torpedoed on 12 February, 1918 by the German submarine *UB-57* while sailing from Immingham to Falmouth. She carried a very sinister cargo: her manifest included 270 depth charges and 1,494 anti-shipping mines of various types. The wreck sits more or less upright and her large cargo of mines is still intact in her holds. Recently, a diver gave a report of looking into a hold and seeing nothing but a mass of horns sticking up everywhere.

The ship was built on the Tyne by Edwards in 1888, and was fitted out with a three cylinder expansion engine. She measured 270ft long with a beam of 36ft. At the time of her sinking, 34 men including the captain were lost. The wreck has sunk well into the soft gravel bottom, but still rises up 5m from the sea bed depth of 39m. What of the *Ajax* and *Coquetdale*? They lie undiscovered elsewhere. *Boats: Poole 16 miles, Swanage 12 miles.*

**299 Unidentified wreck** 50 38.40N; 01 40.22W. At a sea bed depth of 21m, just one mile west of the Needles Channel fairway marker, is a small wreck, thought to be that of a 20ft motor fishing vessel. There is a lack of diving information about this wreck. It is just possible that this site is the *Caroline Susan* – listed in the companion volume *Dive Wight and Hampshire* – a 23 ton British motor yacht, which either foundered or hit a mine in the area, on 13 June, 1940. *Launching: Mudeford, 6 miles. Boats: Poole 13 miles.*

*The Coquetdale (see Site 298) was a victim of the Luftwaffe's onslaught against shipping off Bournemouth on 8 August, 1944. Photo: Adrian Ponchaud collection*

*Chesil Beach provides exceptional shore diving opportunities.*
Photo: Roy Smallpage

# APPENDIX 1:

# Dive Services

## Boats for hire

**Lyme Regis** *Miss Pattie* (10m Cygnus 32) with large deck space. All usual electronics, toilet and oxygen. John Walker, Bols Hayne Farm, South Leigh Road, Colyton, Devon (tel. 01297 552160).

*Predator* (Offshore 10.5m 105) has all necessary electronics for wreck finding. Harry May, Quilleys, Cob Road, Lyme Regis (tel. 01297 442397).

*Blue Turtle* (Offshore 10.5m 105) has a DoT licence for 60 miles and all necessary wreck location electronics. Diving and bed and breakfast package available. Douglas Lanfear, The Lodge, Lyme Road, Aximinster (tel. 01297 34892).

**West Bay** *Channel Warrior* (10.5m Offshore 105) Chris Reeks, 33 Stapleton Close, Martock, Somerset (tel. 01935 822011).

*Lindy Lou* (Lockin 33), all electronics, oxygen and toilet. Ian Cornwell, Afante, West Cliff, West Bay (tel. 01308 423706).

**Weymouth** *Tiger Lily* (10.5m) all usual electronic navigation, oxygen. Chris Caines, 22 Killicks Hill, Portland (tel./fax 01305 821177).

*Dive Time II* (Offshore 125) with huge 16ft wide deck. Fully equipped with latest navigational aids. Paul Pike, 33 St Leonards Road, Weymouth (tel. 01305 773032).

*Skin Deep* (10.8 metre, fast twin screw purpose-built diving boat) with all usual electronic navigation, compressor (tel. 01305 782556).

*Channel Chieftain* (10.5m Offshore 105) with all necessary electronics for wreck location. Pat Carlin, 23 South Down Road, Rodwell, Weymouth (tel. 01305 787155).

*Our W* (12.5m Offshore) with a large wheelhouse, all usual electronic navigation including colour sounder, oxygen. Richard (Woody) Wood. Richard's address is 8 Throop Road, Templecombe, Somerset (tel. 01963 370268).

*JBC* (10.2m Aqua Star) all usual electronic navigation, oxygen. Brian Charles, 15 Old Coastguard Cottages, Portland Bill (tel. 01305 822846).

*White Horse* (18m 12 berth live-aboard luxury diving boat with spacious saloons, hot showers and bar) all usual electronic navigation plus compressor. John and Barbara Ayling, The Barbican, 3 Lower St Edmund Street, Weymouth (tel. 01305 789492).

*Top Cat* (10.2m fast catamaran, spacious wheelhouse) all usual electronic navigation, plus magnetometer. DoT licence for 60 miles. Ivan Wellington, Pound Piece, Portland (tel. 01305 823443).

*Our Phyliss* (10m) with all the usual electronic navigation equipment. Richard Swain and Clive McCraw, 8 Norwich Road, Rodwell (tel. 01305 760009).

*Autumn Dream* (11.5m Offshore 105) with full electronics for fast wreck location, oxygen, toilet. Len Hurdiss, 8 Knightsdale Road, Weymouth (tel. 01305 786723).

*Kyarratoo* (10.5mm Offshore 105), large deck area, all usual electronics including GPS differential positioning, oxygen (tel. 01305 821261).

*Wey Chieftain II* (700hp Offshore 125) with 16ft wide deck. All electronics including side scan; toilet, oxygen. Grahame Knott, 38 Grove Avenue, Weymouth (tel. 01305 771371).

*Hurricane* (10.5m Offshore 105) with full electronic navigation equipment and fitted with a mermaid engine which gives a speed of 25 knots, oxygen. Mike O'Shea, 30 Grove Avenue, Lodmoor, Weymouth (tel. 01305 781732).

*Catharine* (10.5m Offshore 105) with all necessary electronics for navigation onto wrecks, oxygen. Bob Acton, 20 Roundhayes Close, Weymouth (tel. 01305 775690).

*Protector* (11m RIB) with cabin and twin 212hp inboard diesels. All electronics; equipped for Trimix; DOT licence for 60 miles. Dive shuttle and charter service. Portland Dive Centre, 6 Albion Crescent, Fortuneswell, Portland (tel./fax 01305 820870).

**Castletown, Portland** *Top Gun* (10m Portland 10) extremely fast planing hard boat Cabin with all necessary electronics for wreck pinpointing. Also *Saracen* (8.5m RIB, takes 12 divers) and three smaller RIBs (all kitted out with necessary electronics). Eric Burgess, The Breakwater Dive Centre, Castletown, Portland (tel. 01305 860269).

*Gold Palm* (6.85m Ribcraft) with twin 90hp engines. Equipped for 12 divers to full DoT and MSA Code 4 specification. Also three other fully kitted RIBs. Fathom & Blues, Portland Port Business Centre, Castletown (tel. 01305 826789).

*Ptarmigan* (25ft boat), specialising in shuttle trips to wrecks in Portland Harbour. Individuals or small groups charged per head. Skipper Reg Studley. All bookings through Parry's Dive Centre (tel. 01305 821261, fax 01305 861511).

*Tideflow* (fast Offshore 27m), specialising in shuttle trips to local sites and covering the area off Lulworth. All bookings through Parry's Dive Centre (tel. 01305 821261, fax 01305 861511).

**Swanage** *Sidewinder* (10m Berry Boat) all necessary electronics fitted for wreck location, oxygen. Richard Titchener, 10 Gordon Road, Swanage (tel. 01929 427064).

*Okeanos* (7m RIB) available for charter from the Divers Down Diving School on the Pier at Swanage. Contact the owner, Mike Kent (tel. 01929 423565).

**Poole Harbour** *James Alexander* (10m Lochin 33) fitted with Decca, GPS, radar and a magnetometer, oxygen. Dave Saywell, 12, Waterford Close, Parkstone, Poole (tel. 01202 749122).

*Nat West II* (10m catamaran fitted with a 420hp engine) seating for 10 inside cabin. All usual electronic navigation with both Decca and GPS, oxygen. Frank Elston, 97 Cutlers Place, Wimborne (tel. 01202 884077).

*Sea Ranger* (10m Senior Marine Fisherman) all modern electronic aids including Decca and a magnetometer, oxygen. Gordon McGrail, Grailsden, 21 Rectory Road, Oakdale, Poole (tel. 01202 686454).

*Poole Angler* (11m twin screwed catamaran) extremely stable boat especially in a beam on sea. Well equipped with Decca/GPS, oxygen. Dave Fairclough, 58 Muscliffe Road, Winton, Bournemouth (tel. 01202 518673).

*Doraydo* (10m Mitchell 32) affords a large sheltered area for divers. Well equipped with all usual navigational aids, oxygen. Jim Scott, 8 Seabank Close, Upton, Poole (tel. 01202 621868).

*Muircu* (11m Star Fish 10 with 300hp turbo charged engine) fitted out with all usual wreck finding and navigation electronics, oxygen. Jeff Way, 141 Symes Road, Hamworthy, Poole (tel. 01202 684301).

*Nancy Ann* (10m purpose-built dive boat) lots of electronic navigation equipment, including magnetometer, oxygen. Mike Cooper, 70 Bradpole Road, Bournemouth (tel. 01202 527336).

*Beowulf* (12m Deep Sea 38) fast and spacious vessel with all usual electronics, oxygen. Peter Gough, 47 Blythe Road, Corfe Mullen (tel. 01202 697844).

*Dawn Louise* (live aboard 18m converted Danish wooden motor fishing vessel sleeping 12) all usual electronic navigation instruments. On board compressor. Provided is a Sea Rider RIB with 90hp outboard motor. Oxygen carried. Gary Snook (tel. 0976 252248) or Dave Coles (tel./fax 0181 777 0328).

# Launching

Below is a complete list of launching sites. Asterisks denote sites where direct launching from a trailer is possible.

### Area 1

Monmouth Beach (Site **1**)

The Cobb, Lyme Regis (Site **2**) *

Charmouth (Site **3**) *

Seatown (Site **4**)

Eypemouth (Site **5**)

Table Rock (Site **6**)

West Bay Harbour (Site **7**) *

East Beach Car Park (Site **8**)

Burton Bradstock (Site **10**)

West Bexington (Site **12**)

Abbotsbury Beach (Site **14**)

## Area 2

It is possible to launch across the Fleet at Langton Herring, the Moonfleet Hotel and Chickerell (*see* page 70) and also at the following sites:

East Fleet (Site **91**)

Chesil Cove (Site **77**)

Portland Bill (Site **82**)

Castletown (Site **88**) *

Oil Tanks Beach (Site **89**)

Ferrybridge (Site **90**) *

Sandsfoot Castle Beach (Site **92**) *

Weymouth Harbour (Site **94**) *

Overcombe Corner (Site **95**)

Bowleaze Cove (Site **96**) *

Ringstead Bay (Site **99**)

## Area 3

Lulworth Cove (Site **167**)

Kimmeridge Bay (Site **169**) *

Swanage Boat Park (Site **176**) *

Swanage Pier and Monkey Beach (Site **178**)

Swanage Quay (Site **179**)

Swanage Parish Slip (Site **180**) *

Swanage Ocean Bay Beach (Site **181**) *

## Area 4

Studland Bay (Site **231**) *

Shell Bay (Site **232**)

Shell Bay Marine and Watersports Centre (Site **233**) *

Redcliffe Farm (Site **235**) *

Wareham Bridge (Site **236**) *

Rockley Point (Site **237**) *

Rockley Pier (Site **239**)

Lake Road (Site **240**) *

Branksea Avenue (Site **241**)

Hamworthy Park (Site **242**)

Slip Way (Site **243**)

Wilkins Way Slip (Site **244**) *

Fishermans Dock (Site **246**) *

Baiter (Site **247**) *

North Haven Lake (Site **248**)

Davis's Boatyard (Site **249**)

Sandbanks Yacht Company (Site **250**) *

Shore Road (Site **251**)

Branksome Chine (Site **252**)

Branksome Dene Chine (Site **253**)

Durley Chine (Site **254**)

Boscombe Pier (Site **256**)

Southborne Warren Edge Car Park (Site **257**)

Southborne Point House Café (Site **258**)

Southborne Solent Beach Car Park (Site **259**)

Christchurch Harbour (four slipways) (Site **261**) *

Mudeford Quay (Site **262**) *

Avon Beach to Highcliffe (three locations) (Site **263**)

# Anchoring and mooring

**Area 1**  Only at West Bay are facilities provided for anchoring or mooring, and the harbour may become full during the peak season. The harbourmaster must be contacted. The harbour gives good shelter, but can be very tricky to enter or leave if a swell is running.

**Area 2**  Mooring for visiting vessels of any size is provided in Weymouth Harbour, boats up to 10m are accommodated mainly in the area called The Cove, on the southern side of the harbour, near The Old Rooms Inn. All visiting craft must report to the Harbour Office at 13 Customs House Quay, which is on the town side of the harbour; try to contact them in advance (tel. 01305 206363 or 206423). The radio at the harbour office calls on Channel 16 and works on Channel 12.

Warning  Do not anchor in this harbour. There are many unmarked cables crossing the harbour bed, and anchoring is prohibited.

In Portland Harbour there is an area near the northern shore allocated to yachting clubs. Here there are many permanent moorings and some anchoring areas. To anchor or moor here contact, in advance if possible, The Castle Cove Sailing

Club (tel. 01305 783708), or Royal Dorset Yacht Club (tel. 01305 786258). There are no public quays or shore facilities. On a short-term basis, boats may anchor near the Ferrybridge area but visiting boats entering the harbour should call the Harbourmaster on Channel 13 to obtain permission. Generally, anchoring is not encouraged and visitors are mainly advised to go into Weymouth Harbour.

At Ringstead (Site **99**) it is possible, in the summer months, to anchor or put your own temporary mooring down in a shallow area near the shore which is protected from offshore swell by the reefs.

**Area 3** Lulworth Cove has good anchorage in calm weather, but a heavy swell can enter the cove at times of strong winds from the southern half. Light anchors will then drag shorewards through the mainly loose gravel sea bed. At Swanage, except when an easterly wind blows, there is a good, sheltered anchorage in the southern part of the bay between pier and town. Small moorings available for visitors. Details from Divers Down Diving Shop on the pier (tel. 01929 423565).

**Area 4** Studland Bay, as long as the wind remains between south and north-west (particularly near the shoreline), is a safe anchorage. It is, however, completely open to all other winds. These can quickly drive a boat ashore. During the summer months, visiting diving boats may moor against the quay in Poole Harbour but are requested to use the top end, near the bridge. Report on arrival to the Moorings Inspectors office (portacabin on the quay). Contact can be made in advance on Channel 14. A safe anchorage out in the harbour is available off Pottery Pier, at the western end of Brownsea Island. Elsewhere in the harbour anchoring is not recommended owing to heavy traffic, strong currents and the fact that large areas dry out.

In Christchurch Harbour, boats may moor for short periods on the seaward side of Mudeford Quay; but owing to strong currents and several other factors, this is not an overnight mooring. Suitable anchoring areas are in the lower half of the harbour. Particularly good are the Hengistbury Head corner of the harbour (very sheltered from south-west winds), and the area at the rear of Mudeford Quay. Anchoring is not allowed in the navigable channels. There is a speed limit of four knots within the harbour. Overnight anchoring is free in the lower parts of the harbour near the Mudeford Quay, but in the western and upper half a fee is charged.

# Harbour offices

**Lyme Regis** The Cobb, Lyme Regis (tel. 01297 442137).

**West Bay** West Bay Harbour (tel. 01308 423222).

**Weymouth** 13 Customs House Quay, Weymouth (tel. 01305 206363 or 206423).

**Portland** Portland Port, Castletown, Portland (tel. 01305 824044).

**Poole Harbour** New Quay Road (tel. 01202 440220).

**Christchurch Harbour and Mudeford Quay** Christchurch Civic Centre (tel. 01202 486321).

# Coastguard stations

Portland Marine Rescue sub centre (tel. 01305 760439). In an emergency dial 999 and ask for the Coastguard.

There is a RNLI lifeboat stationed at Weymouth.

There are "look out" stations at Portland Bill, St Aldhelm's Head and also at Peveril Point at Swanage (tel. 01929 422596), staffed at weekends and during summer holiday periods by volunteers of the National Coast Watch Institution. A visual and radio listening watch is kept (a flag is flown when these posts are staffed). The Institute works closely with the local Coastguard Marine Rescue centres.

There is an RNLI Lifeboat station at Swanage.

Inshore and offshore RNLI lifeboats are stationed in Poole Harbour, and there is an inshore rescue boat at Mudeford Quay.

# Air stations, dive shops and diving schools

**Area 1** Seaton/Axmouth: Seaton Scuba School, Unit 4, The Harbour, Axmouth, Devon (tel. 01297 24332).

West Bay Watersports: 10a Westbay, Bridport (tel./fax 01308 421800)

**Area 2** Parry's Dive Centre, Shop & School, which is also known as Subaquatics Diving Supplies, Victoria Square, Portland (tel. 01305 821261, fax 01305 861511).

Weymouth Scuba Centre 43 Walpole Street, Weymouth (tel. 01305 774652).

Old Harbour Dive Centre, 11 Nothe Parade, Weymouth (tel. 01305 760888).

Old Harbour Divers, 8a Castletown, Portland (tel./fax 01305 861000).

The Breakwater Diving Centre Ltd is based within the Aquasport Hotel at Castletown, Portland (tel. 01305 860269 or 860670).

Portland Oceaneering dive shop and school, 15 Castletown, Portland (tel. 01305 860402).

O'Three Custom Wet Suits, 15 Cambridge Road, Granby Industrial Estate, Weymouth (tel. 01305 776754).

Fathoms & Blues Ltd, Unit 545, Portland Port Business Centre, Castletown, Portland (tel. 01305 826789).

Portland Dive Centre (school), 6 Albion Crescent, Fortuneswell, Portland (tel./fax 01305 820870).

Dive Dorset Adventure Sports, The Green, Stoford, Yeovil, Somerset (tel. 01935 77585).

Sea-Jules Scuba Shack and diving school, run by Bob Elliot within the area of the Weymouth Sailing Centre, Old Castle Road, Weymouth (tel. 01305 788832).

**Area 3** Situated on the pier at Swanage is Divers Down shop and school (tel. 01929 423565).

Ocean and Action 11 The Square, and is run by experienced diver Russell Lockwood (tel. 01929 427600).

Dorset Diving Services operate a BSAC registered school from New House, East Stoke, Wareham (tel. 01929 463732) and their shop near Poole (tel. 01202 580065).

**Area 4** Dorset Diving Services, Units 6 and 7, Elliot Road, West Howe Industrial Estate, Bournemouth (tel. 01202 580065).
Diving Leisure Unlimited, Rockley Park Holiday Estate, Hamworthy, Poole (tel. 01202 680898).
Forward Diving Services, Unit M, Arthur Brays Yard, West Quay Road, Poole (tel. 01202 677128).
Seatek Dive Centre, Walkford Farm Offices, Walkford Lane, New Milton (tel. 01425 616062).

# Fuel

**Area 1** Although petrol can easily be obtained at garages in the area (except at Lyme Regis, where there is no petrol outlet), there is no retail outlet for RED diesel. In emergency, approach local fishing-boat owners who usually have their own onshore storage tanks and buy in bulk.

**Area 2** There are good supplies of red diesel in Weymouth Harbour at the old harbour side (south) on a pontoon (tel. 01305 787039), but *no petrol*. The nearest petrol to the harbour is at Broadway Motors (tel. 01305 779797) near the Asda supermarket and the Fire Station.

**Area 3** There is no fuel available at Lulworth Cove. The nearest garage is East Lulworth Garage, situated in the village of East Lulworth, almost four miles from the Cove: In emergency the garage will, for an extra charge, bring petrol or diesel to you (tel. 01929 400238). In Swanage, a good 15-minute walk away from the pier and nearby beaches, at the rear of the town, is Triangle Garage, 106 Victoria Avenue. Petrol and diesel. There are no marine diesel suppliers in the area.

**Area 4** Poole Bay Fuels operate from a large barge moored in Poole Harbour, near the Aunt Betty Buoy at Admiralty Chart Ref. Lat 50° 41.82N Long, 01° 57.32W. A watch is kept on VHF Marine Channel 37, call sign Poole Bay Fuels (when closed tel. 01202 842877). Marine diesel is also supplied by Corralls Fuel Distributors at Corrall's Quay, adjacent to Poole Bridge (tel. 01202 674551). For diesel in Christchurch Harbour, Rossiter Yachts (Christchurch Marine Ltd), supply marine diesel but not petrol (tel. 01202 483250).

# Engine maintenance and chandlers

Rob Perry, Cobb Garage, Lyme Regis (tel. 01297 445816).
Dennis Ackerman, Old Railway Station, West Bay.
Fathom Marine Chandlers, The Boat Store, St Andrews Industrial Estate, Bridport (tel. 01308 420988).
W.C. Bussel & Company, 30 Hope Street, Weymouth (tel. 01305 785633).
Ron Davis Marine, Castletown, Portland (tel. 01305 821175).
Ferrybridge Marine Services, Ferrybridge (tel. 01305 781518).
Ocean and Action, 11 The Square, Swanage (tel. 01929 427600).
Dorset Marine Services (tel. 01929 421280 or contact through Ocean and Action).

Divers requiring engine or boat servicing should be able to find a suitable shop or workshop within the complex of Cobbs Quay on the shore of Holes Bay at Hamworthy (open 7 days a week). Some other specialists are:

Shell Bay Marine and Watersports Centre, North Haven Point (tel. 01929 450340).
Sandbanks Yacht Company Panorama Road, Sandbanks (tel. 01202 707500).
Mitchell & Sons, Turks Lane, off Sandbanks Road, Parkstone (tel. 01202 747857).
Select Marine Engineering. Also within Mitchell's Boatyard (tel. 01202 742474).
Piplers, Poole Quay (tel. 01202 673056).
Rossiter Yachts (Christchurch Marine Ltd), Bridge Street, Christchurch (tel. 01202 483250).

# Accommodation

Virtually the whole of the Dorset coastline is popular with tourists. Consequently, there are a great number of premises offering accommodation. Usually there is plenty of spare capacity for the visiting diver, whether he seeks simple bed and breakfast accommodation or a grand hotel. The only exception is during the school holiday period of July and August, when booking well in advance is recommended. Away from the coast there is a surprisingly large amount of accommodation offered in the villages. For the diver who intends travelling to different sites on different days this can be just as convenient as being based on the coast.

A short list of recommended accommodation is given below.

**Area 1** There are a number of bed and breakfast, guest houses and Hotels at West Bay that welcome divers. Details of these can be obtained from West Bay Water Sports (tel. 01308 421800). There are also a number of caravan and camping sites, the following situated almost on the shoreline:

West Bay Holiday Park, Haven Holidays, West Bay (tel. 01308 422424).
Golden Cap Caravan Park, Seatown, Chideock (tel. 01297 489341).
Eype House Caravan Park, Eype (tel. 01308 424903).
Eype's Mouth Hotel (tel. 01308 423300).
Freshwater Caravan and Camping Park, Burton Bradstock (tel. 01308 897317).
Further information on accommodation is available from the Lyme Regis Tourist Information Office, Guild Hall Cottage, Church Street, Lyme Regis (tel. 01297 442138).

**Area 2** The Royal Breakwater Hotel, Castletown, Portland (tel. 01305 820476). Caters especially for divers.

Bagwell Farm Caravan and Camp Site, Chickerell, Weymouth (tel. 01305 782575). Ideal for, and extensively used by, divers visiting the Portland and Weymouth area.

East Fleet Farm, Fleet Lane, Chickerell, Weymouth, has a small site for visitors touring caravans (tel. 01305 785768).

The Creek, Ringstead, Dorchester (tel. 01305 852251). Freda and Michael Fisher provide bed and breakfast, let flats and have caravans for hire on their caravan park (by the beach).

There are a number of private guest houses for divers and their families in Weymouth. Advice on these can be obtained from Weymouth Scuba Centre (tel. 01305 774652).

Excellent bunkhouse accommodation in Victoria Square, Portland (tel. 01305 782556).

The Aquasport Hotel, Breakwater Diving Centre, Castletown, Portland (tel. 01305 860269 or 860670). Bunks to en-suite rooms.

Fathom & Blues Ltd, Unit 545 and 232, Portland Port Business Centre, Castletown, Portland (tel. 01305 826789). Simple accommodation for divers.

Portland Dive Centre, 6 Albion Crescent, Fortuneswell, Portland. Accommodation specially for divers (tel. 01305 820870).

**Area 3** Durdle Door Caravan and Camping Park (tel. 01929 400352). Adjacent to cliff top.

There are Youth Hostels at School Lane, West Lulworth (tel. 01929 400564) and at Cluny Crescent, Swanage (tel. 01929 422113). Persons of any age welcome; members only, but you can join on arrival.

Around Swanage there are many large and small camping and caravan sites – details from the Tourist Information Office, Shore Road, Swanage (tel. 01929 422885).

Sandyholm Holiday Park at Owermoigne is popular with divers (tel. 01305 852677).

**Area 4** The following cater for divers:
Gordon McGrail, 21 Rectory Road, Oakdale, Poole (tel. 01202 686454).
Canute House Study Centre, Strand Street, Off Hennings Wharfe, The Quay, Poole (tel. 01202 669498).

# Special pubs

The Sailor's Return, on the quay side of the harbour in Weymouth near the Town Bridge, has become established as an evening venue for divers.

The Blue Boar Inn is situated in the Old Town area of Poole at 29 Market Close. It is not to be missed. Diving landlord Jim Kellaway provides a wide variety of good food and excellent beer but the great attraction is the hundreds of shipwreck artefacts he has collected, which are exhibited throughout the building.

# Local diving clubs

**Area 1** Lyme Bay Divers (tel. 01404 42416).
Port Bredy Divers (tel. 01308 421800).
Dive Dorset Adventure Sports Diving Club (tel. 01935 77585).
Westlands Helicopter BSAC Special Branch (tel. 01935 703810).

**Area 2** Dorset SAC (tel. 01305 821261).
Portland Plungers (tel. 01305 771371).
Smugglers Sub-aqua Club (tel. 01305 760888).

Weymouth and Portland BSAC meet in The Angling Club, Commercial Road, Weymouth.
Parrys Bubblers (tel. 01305 821261).
Osprey SAC (tel. 01305 820311 ext 3610).
Portland SAC (tel. 01305 860670).

**Area 3** Winfrith SAC dive from Lulworth Cove on Tuesday and Thursday evenings.
North Dorset BSAC train at Clayesmore School pool at Iwerne Minster on Thursdays.
Isle of Purbeck Sub-Aqua Club (tel. 01929 422463).

**Area 4** Bournemouth and Poole BSAC (tel. 01202 580065).
Ringwood Sub-Aqua Club (tel. 01425 478813).
Dorset Diving Sub-Aqua Club (tel. 01202 580065).
The Brewers Sub-Aqua Club (tel. 01202 682247).
Hamworthy Sub-Aqua Club (tel. 01202 666211).
East Dorset Sub-Aqua Club (tel. 01202 877468).
Arnewood Divers (tel. 01202 485123).
Hurn Sub-Aqua Club (tel. 01202 580065).
707 Divers (in the bar of Littledown Sports Centre, Bournemouth, first Friday each month)
Plessey Dorset Sub-Aqua Club (tel. 01202 486344).
Dorset Divers (tel. 01202 518673).
Poole Dam Divers (tel. 01202 672911).
Chase Manhattan Sub-Aqua Club (tel. 01202 342000).

*A diver swims over the wreckage of the United States Tank Landing Craft off Chesil Beach (Site 76).*
Photo: Peter Glanvill

# The Diver's Code of Conduct

Divers must at all times adhere to the BSAC code of conduct. It is reproduced here with the kind permission of the British Sub-Aqua Club, and has been extracted from the BSAC *Safe Diving Practices* booklet, available from BSAC Headquarters.

## THE DIVER'S CODE OF CONDUCT

More and more people are taking to the water. Some for recreation; some to earn their living. This code is designed to ensure that divers do not come into conflict with other water users. It is vital that you observe it at all times.

## Before leaving home

Contact the nearest British Sub-Aqua Club Branch or the dive operator local to the dive site for their advice. Seek advice from them about the local conditions and regulations.

## On the beach, river bank or lakeside

1. Obtain permission, before diving in a harbour or estuary or in private water. Thank those responsible before you leave. Pay harbour dues.

2. Try to avoid overcrowding one site, consider other people on the beach.

3. Park sensibly. Avoid obstructing narrow approach roads. Keep off verges. Pay parking fees and use proper car parks.

4. Don't spread yourselves and your equipment since you may upset other people. Keep launching ramps and slipways clear.
5. Please keep the peace. Don't operate a compressor within earshot of other people – or late at night.

6. Pick up litter. Close gates. Be careful about fires. Avoid any damage to land or crops.

7. Obey special instructions such as National Trust rules, local bye-laws and regulations about camping and caravanning.

8. Remember divers in wetsuits are conspicuous and bad behaviour could ban us from beaches.

## In and on the water

1. Mark your dive boats so that your Club can be identified easily. Unmarked boats may become suspect.

2. Ask the harbour-master or local officials where to launch your boat – and do as they say. Tell the Coastguard, or responsible person, where you are going and tell them when you are back.

3. Stay away from buoys, pots, and pot markers. Ask local fishermen where not to dive. Offer to help them recover lost gear.

4. Remember ships have not got brakes, so avoid diving in fairways or areas of heavy surface traffic and observe the "International Regulations for the Prevention of Collisions at Sea".

5. Always fly the diving flag when diving, but not when on the way to, or from, the dive site. Never leave a boat unattended.

6. Do not come in to bathing beaches under power. Use any special approach lanes. Do not disturb any seal or bird colonies with your boats. Watch your wash in crowded anchorages.

7. Whenever possible, divers should use a surface marker buoy.

## On conservation

1. Never use a speargun with an aqualung. Never use a speargun in fresh water.

2. Shellfish, such as crabs and lobsters, take several years to grow to maturity; over-collecting in an area soon depletes stocks. Only take mature fish or shellfish and then only what you need for yourself. Never sell your catch or clean it in public or on the beach. Don't display your trophies.

3. Be conservation conscious. Avoid damage to weeds and the sea bed. Do not bring up sea-fans, corals, starfish or sea urchins – in one moment you can destroy years of growth.

4. Take photographs and notes – not specimens. Shoot with a camera not a speargun – spearfishing makes fish shy of divers. Never spearfish wrasse or other inshore species since once an area is depleted of such fish, it may take a long time for them to re-colonise.

# On wrecks

1. Do not dive on a designated wreck site. These are indicated on Admiralty Charts and marked by buoys or warning notices on the shore nearby.

2. Do not lift anything which appears to be of historical importance.

3. If you do discover a wreck, do not talk about it. Pinpoint the site, do a rough survey and report it to the BSAC Archaeology Adviser and the Council for Nautical Archaeology who will advise you.

4. If you do not lift anything from the wreck, it is not necessary to report your discovery to the Receiver of Wreck. If you do lift, you must report.

5. If your find is important, you may apply for it to be designated a protected site. Then you can build up a well qualified team with the right credentials and proceed with a systematic survey or excavation under licence without outside interference.

*Don't Let Divers Down – Keep To The Diver's Code*

*The Tilly Whim Caves, above Site 173 near Anvil Point, are a well known local feature.*
*Photo: Roy Smallpage*

# APPENDIX 3:

# Further Reading

*A Circumstantial Narrative of the Loss of the Halsewell (East Indiaman).* Meriton, H and Rogers, J. 1796. Captain Richard Pierce.

*Amazon to Ivanhoe.* John English. 1993. World Ship Society. ISBN 0 90561 764 9.

*British Merchant Ships Sunk by U Boats in the 1914–1918 War.* Tennent, A. J. 1990. The Starling Press Ltd, Newport. ISBN 0 95163 140 3.

*British Vessels Lost at Sea 1914–18.* (HMSO, reprint). 1977. Patrick Stephens Ltd, Cambridge. ISBN 0 85059 291 7.

*British Vessels Lost at Sea 1939-45.* (HMSO, reprint). 1983. Patrick Stephens Ltd, Cambridge. ISBN 0 85059 659 9.

*Channel Firing.* Nigel Lewis. 1994. Harbour Books, Dartmouth. ISBN 0 90790 612 5.

*Dictionary of Disasters at Sea During the Age of Steam 1824–1962.* Hocking, C. A. 1990. London Stamp Exchange Ltd. ISBN 0 94813 068 7.

*Discover Dorset: Shipwrecks.* Attwooll, M. 1998. Dovecote Press Ltd, Wimborne. ISBN 1 874336 59 8.

*Dorset Shipwrecks.* Shovlar, S. 1996. Freestyle Publications Ltd, Poole. ISBN 0 95265 760 0.

*Dorset Shipwrecks.* Burnett, D. 1982. Dovecote Press Ltd, Wimborne. ISBN 0 94615 904 1.

*Dorset Shipwrecks.* Maureen Boddy. 1975/76. A three part series in numbers 48, 49, 50 of Dorset – The County Magazine. Dorset Publishing Company.

*Great British Wrecks Vols I, II, III.* McDonald, K. 1986–87. Underwater World Publications Ltd, Teddington. ISBN 0 94602 007 8, 0 94602 008 6 and 0 94602 012 4.

*Inshore Along the Dorset Coast.* Bruce, P. 1996. Boldre Marine, Lymington. ISBN 1 87168 006 9.

*Lloyd War Losses, The First World War.* 1989. Lloyd's of London Press Ltd. ISBN 1 85044 314 9.

*Lloyd War Losses, The Second World War.* 1989. Lloyd's of London Press Ltd. ISBN 1 85044 217 7.

*Shipwrecks Around Britain, A Diver's Guide.* Zanelli, L. 1970. Kay & Ward Ltd, London. ISBN 0 7182 0866 8.

*Shipwreck Index of the British Isles Vol I.* Larn, B. and R. 1995. Lloyd's Register of Shipping. ISBN 0 90052 888 5.

*The Royal Navy at Portland Since 1845.* Carter, G. 1987. Maritime Books, Liskeard. ISBN 0 90777 129 7.

*Unknown Shipwrecks Around Britain.* Zanelli, L. 1974. Kay & Ward Ltd, London. ISBN 0 7182 0963 X.

*Wreck and Rescue on the Dorset Coast.* Farr, G. 1971. D. Bradford Barton Ltd, Truro.

*Tidal Streams Between Portland Bill and St Alban's Head.* Bruce, P. and Watson, G. 1998. Boldre Marine. ISBN 1 87168 016 6.

# Index

The bold numbers in parentheses are dive site numbers

*A velvet swimming crab, at 35m depth, is caught by the photographer's flash. Its bright, bead-like eyes compromise its excellent camouflage. Photo: Janine Gould*